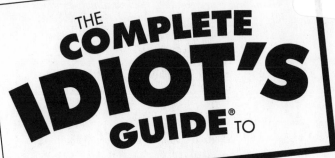

THE COMPLETE **IDIOT'S** GUIDE® TO

Slow Cooker Cooking

Second Edition

by Ellen Brown

ALPHA

A member of Penguin Group (USA) Inc.

This book is dedicated to David Krimm and Peter Bradley, the best almost-brothers a woman could have.

ALPHA BOOKS

Published by the Penguin Group

Penguin Group (USA) Inc., 375 Hudson Street, New York, New York 10014, USA

Penguin Group (Canada), 90 Eglinton Avenue East, Suite 700, Toronto, Ontario M4P 2Y3, Canada (a division of Pearson Penguin Canada Inc.)

Penguin Books Ltd., 80 Strand, London WC2R 0RL, England

Penguin Ireland, 25 St. Stephen's Green, Dublin 2, Ireland (a division of Penguin Books Ltd.)

Penguin Group (Australia), 250 Camberwell Road, Camberwell, Victoria 3124, Australia (a division of Pearson Australia Group Pty. Ltd.)

Penguin Books India Pvt. Ltd., 11 Community Centre, Panchsheel Park, New Delhi—110 017, India

Penguin Group (NZ), 67 Apollo Drive, Rosedale, North Shore, Auckland 1311, New Zealand (a division of Pearson New Zealand Ltd.)

Penguin Books (South Africa) (Pty.) Ltd., 24 Sturdee Avenue, Rosebank, Johannesburg 2196, South Africa

Penguin Books Ltd., Registered Offices: 80 Strand, London WC2R 0RL, England

International Standard Book Number: 978-1-59257-623-4
Library of Congress Catalog Card Number: 2007926848

09 08 07   8 7 6 5 4 3 2 1

Interpretation of the printing code: The rightmost number of the first series of numbers is the year of the book's printing; the rightmost number of the second series of numbers is the number of the book's printing. For example, a printing code of 07-1 shows that the first printing occurred in 2007.

Printed in the United States of America

Note: This publication contains the opinions and ideas of its author. It is intended to provide helpful and informative material on the subject matter covered. It is sold with the understanding that the author and publisher are not engaged in rendering professional services in the book. If the reader requires personal assistance or advice, a competent professional should be consulted.

The author and publisher specifically disclaim any responsibility for any liability, loss, or risk, personal or otherwise, which is incurred as a consequence, directly or indirectly, of the use and application of any of the contents of this book.

Most Alpha books are available at special quantity discounts for bulk purchases for sales promotions, premiums, fundraising, or educational use. Special books, or book excerpts, can also be created to fit specific needs.

For details, write: Special Markets, Alpha Books, 375 Hudson Street, New York, NY 10014.

Publisher: *Marie Butler-Knight*
Editorial Director: *Mike Sanders*
Managing Editor: *Billy Fields*
Acquisitions Editor: *Michele Wells*
Senior Development Editor: *Christy Wagner*
Production Editor: *Megan Douglass*
Copy Editor: *Ross Patty*

Cartoonist: *Richard King*
Cover Designer: *Kurt Owens*
Book Designer: *Trina Wurst*
Indexer: *Heather McNeill*
Layout: *Ayanna Lacey*
Proofreader: *Mary Hunt*

Contents at a Glance

Contents

What the recipe symbols mean:
▲ Chilled dish
● Healthy
■ Make-ahead
+ Vegan

Introduction

It's really easy to make great food in a slow cooker. You fill it up, plug it in, turn it on, and walk away. Then voilà! You walk back into the kitchen or the house hours later to be greeted by the luxurious aroma of the delicious, homemade dinner that awaits you. It's not magic, but it sure seems like it if you're harried and stressed—and hungry—at the end of a busy workday. Or for those times when you have an enjoyable day of leisure, now you don't have to feel tied to the stove or feel guilty that your pleasure precluded a home-cooked meal for your family. With the slow cooker, neither work nor play requires sacrificing a nutritious dinner.

There's no question about it: slow cooking has a role in our fast-paced lives. As time has become such a precious commodity, our dinner tables are increasingly filled with cardboard boxes from nutritionally bankrupt fast-food chains. Slow cooking provides the alternative. It does take some advance planning, but that becomes almost second nature once you've started using this simple electric appliance.

The recipes in this book are "real food." They're not made with convenience products that list more chemicals on their labels than words recognizable as foods. A slow cooker doesn't need modern magic. The principles of slow cooking go back centuries.

Economy is another benefit of slow cooking. It's the less-tender and less-expensive cuts of meat that are best suited to a slow cooker's low heat. They become incredibly tender after a few hours in the slow cooker. And foods like dried beans, the basis for a treasure-trove of dishes, are just pennies per serving.

Slow cooking is also easy, and this book assumes only the most basic cooking skills. Many of the recipes take no more than 15 minutes of "hands-on" preparation time, and I've included many tips for how to accomplish most, if not all, of the work the night before you cook the food. Because few cooking skills are required, readying food for the slow cooker can even be a job parceled out to young family members—and why not make meal prep family time?

The slow cooker solves another of the societal quandaries we face today. On nights the family can't eat together, dinner can become a catch-as-catch-can feeding frenzy rather than a well-balanced meal. Problem solved with the slow cooker. When the slow cooker has completed its work, it can keep dinner hot for a few hours. That means one member of the family can eat before a sports practice and another can enjoy the same quality of food after a movie.

The slow cooker is not a miracle machine. It can't do everything. It will never produce a crispy french fry or a fluffy angel food cake. But when you know what it can do—and learn that what it does, it does very well—the slow cooker will become part of your cooking regimen.

How This Book Is Organized

The book is divided into seven parts:

Part 1, "A Fast Course in Slow Cooking," teaches you all you need to know before turning on a slow cooker for the first time. Sections explain how slow cooking works, giving facts about food safety, tips for using the slow cooker, and how to modify your favorite recipes for slow cooking. I also include slow cooker versions of basic recipes for stocks, rice, beans, and more.

Part 2, "Stellar Starters," showcases one of the slow cooker's many strengths—making delicious hot dips for parties. You also learn the range of other appetizers the slow cooker can create, from satiny, rich spreads to toppings for pizza.

Part 3, "The Bountiful Bowl: Soups as Supper," will convince you that soup is food for the soul. The recipes in this part run the gamut from a wide range of vegetarian and bean soups to meals in a bowl made with seafood, poultry, and meats.

The title of **Part 4, "Stews to Savor,"** says it all. But the only common denominator of the recipes in these four chapters are that all the foods are cut into bite-size pieces. There are vegetarian stews and ones made with fish and seafood. On the meat side, there's a chapter devoted to poultry stews and another starring all sorts of grazing greats.

Part 5, "Main Dishes for All Times of Day," demonstrates the slow cooker's versatility in creating delicious main dishes. The recipes in this part are for large fish steaks and fillets, whole poultry pieces, and meat roasts cooked whole or as chops. Completing the section are dishes appropriate for breakfasts and brunches.

Part 6, "The Side Show," focuses attention away from the center of the plate. In this part, you find recipes for those all-important supporting players. There's a chapter on vegetables and another on beans—both hot and as bean salads. Carbohydrates—potatoes, rice, and other grains—are stars of another chapter, and there's a group of little touches—the sauces and jams that can make meals special.

Part 7, "Grand Finales," includes dozens of homey desserts that are as delicious as they are easy to make. Included are recipes for healthful fruit dishes that glorify the best of the produce department, and also decadent chocolate and other rich concoctions that satisfy even the most demanding sweet tooth.

After the dessert chapters come some useful appendixes. There's a glossary to add to your knowledge of cooking lingo, and tables to aid in converting measurements to the metric system.

Extras

In every chapter, many boxes give you extra information that's either helpful or just interesting. Here's what to look for:

Crock Tales

Check out these boxes for tidbits of food history and amusing quotes about food. They're fun to read and share with friends, and they'll make you sound like a real gourmet.

Cooker Caveats

It's always a good idea to be alerted to potential problems in advance. Cooker Caveats provide just such a warning, either about cooking in general or the recipe in particular.

Slow Speak

Cooking has a language all its own, and some of the terms and ingredients can be intimidating if you don't know what they mean. Look to these boxes for technique and ingredient definitions if you don't want to flip to the glossary.

Slow Savvy

Slow Savvy boxes are full of cooking tips. Some are specific to the recipe they accompany; others boost your general cooking skills or give you ideas for food presentation. These tips are meant to make your life easier and your time in the kitchen more pleasurable.

Acknowledgments

Writing a book is a solitary endeavor, but its publication is always a team effort. My thanks go to ...

Michele Wells of Alpha Books for seeing the need for an updated volume.

Ed Claflin, my agent, for his constant support and great humor.

Gene Brissie, who led me masterfully through the book's first edition.

Christy Wagner, Ross Patty, and Megan Douglass for their eagle-eyed editing.

My many friends whose palates aided me in recipe development, including Suzanne Cavedon, Janet Morell, Grace Lefrancois, Vicki Veh, Nick Brown, Heidi Howard, Dan Potter, Constance Brown, Kenn Speiser, Edye DeMarco, and Tom Byrne.

Trademarks

Part 1

A Fast Course in Slow Cooking

Dishes made in a slow cooker deliver the same great taste as those cooked on top of the stove or in the oven. But there are fundamental differences in how those dishes get from mere ingredients to finished dish. In Part 1, you learn about slow cookers and how to use them to become a slow cooking connoisseur.

After you become familiar with your slow cooker and its potential, you'll probably want to adapt your favorite recipes to cook in "slow mode." There's a section in Part 1 to help you accomplish just that.

When you've made a permanent place for your slow cooker on the kitchen counter, you'll use it frequently for some of the basics of cooking, like rice and stocks. There's a chapter on those foods, too.

"This time, we'll see who can make the better meal."

Gearing Up for Great Food

In This Chapter

◆ Slow cookers and how they work

◆ Choosing the slow cooker that's right for you

◆ Slow cooker food safety

◆ Adapting recipes for slow cooking

The mouthwatering aroma that greets you when you walk into your home at the end of the day is the first benefit of a slow cooker. Although the food is barely simmering, it's been cooking for long enough that the innate flavors of all the ingredients have blended together and filled the air. By the time a dish is ready, it's been simmering for some time. Like a puff of smoke coming up from a genie's bottle, it lures you right to the kitchen.

With some advance preparation, busy people like you can enjoy a delicious, homemade meal that cooked without you needing to stand around to watch it, thanks to the slow cooker! In this chapter, you learn everything you need to know to choose and use a slow cooker so you, too, can get your dinner wish.

A Quick Look at Slow Cookers

Turning a piece of meat over an open flame was prehistoric man's first culinary technique. This incendiary school of cookery was the only act in town for more than a millennium before it was complemented by slow cooking. The first slow cooking was done in pottery, as it is still today. By the fifth century B.C.E., iron pots holding simmering food were left to cook all day and night in the fire's embers.

> **Crock Tales**
>
> Rival introduced the first slow cooker, the Crock-Pot, in 1971, and the introductory slogan remains true more than 35 years later: it "cooks all day while the cook's away." Crock-Pots were originally produced in colors popular for appliances at the time—avocado and harvest gold.

Although slow cooking was a necessity in the past, today it's a choice—and growing in popularity. In 2001, *Appliance* magazine's annual survey of households showed 65 percent of American homes contained a slow cooker. By 2006, surveys place that figure at about 80 percent; Rival, manufacturer of the Crock-Pot, estimates it at 79 percent while a Betty Crocker study found that 82 percent of moms between the ages of 25 and 45 owned slow cookers. *Gourmet Retailer* magazine reports that more than 9 million slow cookers were sold in 2004, and that's up 2.8 percent from the year before. And cooks are also realizing the benefits of using a slow cooker as a serving device to keep foods hot for guests, too.

Success Is the Sum of Its Parts

Part of the popularity of slow cookers is their simplicity. They are by no means rocket science; they are uncomplicated electric devices—energy efficient, too. A slow cooker uses about as much power as a 60-watt bulb. And it only contains a few parts.

A glass or plastic cover sits on top so you can see if the food is simmering without raising the lid—and lowering the temperature inside. A crockery insert holds the food and insulates it from contact with the heating elements. Once the food has cooked, the pottery holds the heat and keeps the food warm. A wrap-around heating element sits encased between the slow cooker's outer and inner metal layers that never directly touches the crockery insert. As the element heats, it gently warms the air between the two layers of metal. The hot air heats the inner metal casing that touches the crockery. This construction eliminates the need for stirring because no part of the pot gets hotter than any other.

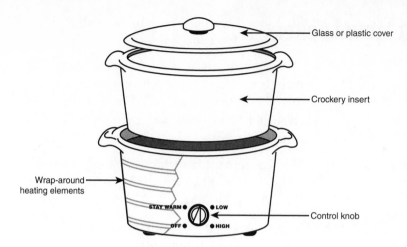

Glass or plastic cover

Crockery insert

Wrap-around heating elements

STAY WARM ● ● LOW

OFF ● ● HIGH

Control knob

Each part of the slow cooker has a purpose that, when combined with the others, helps produce the low, even heat needed for long cooking times.

Slow Savvy

Slow cookers cook food using indirect heat at a low temperature for an extended period of time. Direct heat is the power of a stove burner underneath a pot; indirect heat is the overall heat that surrounds food in the oven. Think of it this way: if you're standing on a hot sidewalk, you're feeling direct heat, but the heat you feel when you're lounging on the beach under the sun and your whole body is warm is indirect heat.

And last but not least, there's the control knob. All slow cookers have low and high settings. Some also have a "stay warm" position. Some new machines are programmable, letting you start food on high and then the slow cooker automatically reduces the heat to low after a programmed time. The low setting for most appliances is about 180°F, and high is about 300°F.

Reasons to Believe

One obvious reason to use a slow cooker is the flexibility it provides, especially for people who work outside the home during the day. Slowly cooked dinners can replace the nutrient-poor fast-food option, and most often are healthier for you, too. Here are some other slow cooker advantages:

◆ The slow cooker's long cooking time tenderizes less-expensive cuts of meat, stretching your food budget.

♦ Foods such as thick stews and bean dishes that tend to stick to the bottom of a pan placed over direct heat don't stick in a slow cooker.

Cooker Caveats

Some appliances on the market now are called slow cookers, but they're really not. These machines have a different assembly structure not consistent with the way true slow cookers operate: a metal insert sits on a base and cooks by *direct* heat. Unless food is stirred frequently, it will burn on the bottom.

♦ Slow cookers provide a third hand for party prep. Use a slow cooker to free up the oven for food that needs higher heat. Plus, a slow cooker can be left alone while you're tending to food in pans on the stove.

♦ Slow cookers are forgiving. A dish can cook for an extra hour or two, especially on low, without the risk of it burning.

♦ Slow cookers don't heat up the kitchen so they're perfect for summer cooking.

♦ Slow cookers keep food warm so family members can still eat a hot meal at different times, if necessary.

Picking Your Pot

Shape and size are the two criteria to consider when buying a slow cooker. The tiny 1-quart models are a great party pal and hold dips warm for hours, but they're not very versatile. If you're going to have only one slow cooker, it should have a 3½- or 4-quart capacity. These sizes hold enough food for 4 to 6 servings. This is the size I term "medium" for the recipes in this book.

Slow Savvy

Cookers come in round and oval shapes, and both work equally well. I prefer the oval shape for general cooking because it accommodates larger pieces of meat better. However, round slow cookers are better for desserts because the regular shape ensures even cooking of the center of puddings or cakes.

The 6-quart models are good for larger families or for cooks who like to make large batches of food and freeze some for future meals. Also, some dishes such as lamb shanks take up so much space that a 6-quart model is needed just to hold all the food. This is the size I call "large" in the recipes.

I was initially reluctant to try one of the relatively new programmable slow cookers because I have never successfully programmed a VCR (it inevitably flashes 12:00 until I cover the clock with duct tape). However, these new pots are easier than a VCR and solve a number of slow cooking dilemmas.

None of the pots currently on the market are tied to a clock—that is, you can't program them to start at noon when you leave the house at 8 A.M. That's a good thing, though, in terms of food safety because you don't have to think about the food spoiling in the intervening hours (as you'll read in the next section). These slow cookers do cook the food once programmed and then either turn off or turn to the stay warm setting.

There's variation among brands, but most allow you to program a number of hours either on low or high, or a combination thereof. So if you're out for a 10-hour day and you're cooking a dish that even on low completes in 8 hours, the slow cooker will automatically turn down to stay warm until your arrival. A few models specify only a certain amount of time such as a maximum of 10 hours on low or 7 hours on high. These are not as convenient, especially if you're cooking on low.

Safety First

Cooking with a slow cooker is not only easy, it's also safe. The Food Safety and Inspection Service of the U.S. Department of Agriculture approves slow cooking as a method of safe food preparation. The lengthy cooking and the steam created within the tightly covered pot combine to destroy any bacteria that might be present in the food. Although slow cooking is innately safe, it's up to you as the cook to be sure this translates to the food in your pot. A slow cooker should always be at least half full so it can generate the necessary steam. A smaller quantity of food won't produce the steam needed to kill bacteria.

Cooker Caveats

Never leave a slow cooker plugged in when not in use. It's all too easy to accidentally turn it on and not notice until the crockery insert cracks from overheating with nothing in it.

Banishing Bacteria

Fruits and vegetables can contain some bacteria, but it's far more likely that the culprits will grow on meat, poultry, and seafood. Store these foods on the bottom shelves of your refrigerator so their juices cannot accidentally fall on other foods. And keep these foods refrigerated until just before they go into the slow cooker, as bacteria multiply at room temperature.

It's not wise to cook whole chickens or cuts of meat larger than those specified in the recipes in this book because during slow cooking, these large items stay too long in the bacterial "danger zone"—between 40°F and 140°F. It's important that food reaches the higher temperature in less than 2 hours and remains at more than 140°F for at least 30 minutes.

Cooker Caveats

If you're dusting off a slow cooker that's been in the basement for years, it's a good idea to test it to be sure it still has the power to heat food sufficiently. Leave 2 quarts water at room temperature overnight and then pour the water into the slow cooker in the morning. Heat it on low for 8 hours. Use an instant read thermometer to measure the water temperature. It should be 185°F after 8 hours. If it's lower, any food you cook in this cooker might not pass through the danger zone rapidly enough.

If you want to cook large roasts, brown them in a skillet on top of the stove over direct heat before you place them into the slow cooker. This helps the chilled meat heat up faster as well as produces a dish that's more visually appealing.

Slow Savvy

If there's condensation on the lid, rather than lifting it to see inside, jiggle it and the condensation will dribble into the food so you can see what's going on without affecting the temperature inside.

Don't Peek!

It's always tempting to pick up that lid and see what's happening in the pot. But resist the temptation. Every time you peek, you let out some heat and steam, so you need to add some cooking time to the total. If cooking on low, add 15 minutes for each peek. If cooking on high, add 10 minutes. That's why slow cookers all have transparent lids, so you can see what's going on without lifting the lid.

A Safe Head Start

Because mornings can be frantic times in a household, you might want to prepare the dish you're cooking for the next day the night before. If you cut meat or vegetables in advance, store them separately in the refrigerator and layer them in the slow cooker in the morning. Always defrost meats and poultry before placing them in the slow cooker. Frozen foods cool the contents of the slow cooker and prolong the time period spent in the danger zone.

Do not store the cooker insert in the refrigerator because that also increases the amount of time it takes to heat the food to a temperature that kills bacteria. Also, do not preheat the empty insert while you're preparing the food because the insert could crack when you add the cold food.

Cooker Caveats _____

Even though slow cookers don't require a lot of power to operate, they are electrical appliances, and the same safety rules apply as with any electrical appliance. Be careful that the cord is not frayed in any way, and plug the slow cooker into an outlet that is not near the sink. Never immerse the metal housing into water, even if the slow cooker is not plugged in, and never puncture the metal casing. Clean the metal casing with a soapy sponge only when the slow cooker is disconnected from the outlet.

Worst-Case Worries

A slow cooker needs electricity to cook, so the lack thereof is about the biggest food safety worry you have with a slow cooker. If you've been cooking in your slow cooker and can tell from your electric clocks that the power has been off, throw away the food in the slow cooker, even if it looks done. You have no idea if the power outage occurred before the food passed through the danger zone.

If you're home when the electricity goes off, finish cooking the food by another method. If you have a gas stove, transfer the dish to a pot and finish it that way. You can also place it in a metal pot on a charcoal or gas grill. Or call a friend who might have power and rush your slow cooker right over.

Speeding Up Slow Cooking

If at all possible, start the slow cooker on high for the first hour of cooking time to boost it through the bacterial danger zone. If you're running out of the house and won't be home to turn the heat to low after an hour, don't worry. Remember that 1 hour of cooking on high is equal to 2 hours of cooking on low, so calculate accordingly.

> **Cooker Caveats** _____
>
> Appliance manufacturers say slow cookers can be left on either high or low unattended, but use your own judgment. If you're going to be out of the house all day, it's advisable to cook food on low. If, on the other hand, you're going to be gone for just a few hours, the food will be safe on high.

To trim hours off a slow cooked meal, add boiling liquid rather than room temperature or chilled liquid. To test how much time can be trimmed, place the amount of liquid in the slow cooker and see how long it takes to come to a boil on high. Don't subtract that time, because when cooking, there will be other ingredients, too. Instead, subtract _half_ the time.

Slow Cooking High Up

All cooking is different at high altitudes because the air is thinner so water boils at a lower temperature and comes to a boil more quickly. Slow cooking also changes above 3,000 feet. The rule is to always cook on high when above 3,000 feet; use the low setting as a keep warm setting.

Other compensations include reducing the liquid in a recipe by a few tablespoons and adding about 5 to 10 percent more cooking time. The liquid may be bubbling, but it's not 212°F at first.

Slowing Down Family Favorites

Once you feel comfortable with your slow cooker, you'll probably want to use it to prepare your favorite recipes you now cook on the stove or in the oven. The best recipes to convert are "wet" ones with a lot of liquid, like stews, soups, chilies, and other braised foods.

The easiest way to convert your recipes is to find a similar one in this book and use its cooking time for guidance. When looking for a similar recipe, take into account the amount of liquid specified as well as the quantity of food. The liquid transfers the heat from the walls of the insert into the food itself, and the liquid heats in direct proportion to its measure. Also, be sure the food fills the slow cooker at least half-way to ensure food safety. If it's a smaller quantity, you might want to increase the size of the batch.

Here are some more guidelines to keep in mind:

◆ Most any stew or roast takes 8 to 12 hours on low and 4 to 6 hours on high.

◆ Chicken dishes cook more rapidly. Count on 6 to 8 hours on low and 3 or 4 hours on high.

◆ Quadruple the time from conventional cooking to cooking on low, and at least double it for cooking on high.

Retooling the Recipe

The quantity of ingredients and when to add them also change when converting recipes to the slow cooker. First, cut back on the amount of liquid used in stews and other braised dishes by about half. Unlike cooking on the stove or in the oven, there's little to no evaporation in the slow cooker. If the food isn't totally covered with liquid when you start to cook, don't worry. Ingredients like meat, chicken, and many vegetables give off their own juices as they cook.

For soups, cut back on the liquid by one third if the soup is supposed to simmer uncovered, and cut back by one fourth if the soup is simmered covered. Even when covered, a soup that's simmering on the stove has more evaporation than one cooked in the slow cooker.

Put the vegetables in the slow cooker first, at the bottom. They take longer to cook than meat.

> **Cooker Caveats**
>
> Not all dishes can be easily converted to slow cooked dishes. Even if a dish calls for liquid, if it's supposed to be cooked or baked uncovered, chances are it won't successfully transform to a slow cooker recipe because the food won't brown and the liquid won't evaporate.

Use leaf versions of herbs such as thyme and rosemary rather than ground versions. Ground herbs tend to lose potency during many hours in the slow cooker. And season the dishes with pepper at the end of cooking because it can become harsh.

Remember, this dish is cooking in your slow cooker, so don't peek at or stir it!

Other Adaptations

You might find that even though you cut back on liquid, a dish still doesn't have the intense flavor it did when it was cooked on the stove. Don't fret. After the dish has finished cooking, remove as much liquid as possible from the slow cooker with a bulb baster or strain the liquid from the solids in a colander. *Reduce* the liquid in a saucepan on the stove until it has the right flavor and consistency. Then return it to the slow cooker before serving.

Slow Speak

To **reduce** in cooking terms means to cut down on the volume of a liquid by applying heat, which speeds evaporation. Simmering a gravy or sauce evaporates some of the water, which concentrates the flavor of the resulting liquid. Many recipes call for liquid to be reduced by half, but it can be a greater or smaller amount.

If rice or small pasta is part of a recipe, add it only during the last 2 hours of cooking on low or 1 hour on high. The same rules apply to tender vegetables and dairy products.

The Least You Need to Know

◆ Slow cookers are simple electrical devices that cook food for long periods of time at low temperatures by indirect heat.

◆ A slow cooker's low setting is 180°F to 200°F; the high setting is 280°F to 300°F.

◆ When food safety precautions are followed, slow cookers kill any bacteria that might be present in the uncooked food.

◆ Many conventional recipes can be adapted to slow cooking by changing the quantity of liquid and the cooking time, and the best dishes for adaptation are soups, stews, and other "wet" foods.

2

Building Blocks

In This Chapter

◆ Slow cooking beans and rice

◆ Stocks to use for soups and stews

◆ Foolproof ways to cook onions and garlic

Any food that cooks for a long time over low heat (like beans) and has a propensity to burn (like rice) is a natural candidate for the slow cooker. So in this chapter, you'll find information that helps you transform your slow cooker into a rice cooker or a bean pot. And while burning isn't a problem when cooking stocks, the slow cooker relieves you of the worry about a pot simmering when you're out of the house. You'll find great stock recipes in this chapter, too.

If you've ever been chained to the stove stirring onions to achieve that caramelized glow, you'll love the freedom of cooking them perfectly in the slow cooker. Not to mention how many ways you'll find to use sweet and mellow roasted garlic once you have it in the kitchen.

The recipes in this chapter aren't intended to be showstoppers, but they will give you easy and indispensable ways to create foods you use all the time in myriad ways.

Raves for Rice

Go into almost any Asian home, and you'll find an electric rice cooker. No electric rice cooker in your cupboard? No problem, because your slow cooker can double as a rice cooker for not only white rice but for whole-grain brown rice, too. The main difference when cooking rice in the slow cooker is that you can use less water because it doesn't evaporate as quickly as when cooking rice conventionally. (Brown rice takes longer to cook so you'll use a bit more water to compensate for eventual evaporation.)

In the following table, I list some cook times, temperature, and rice and water measurements to help you get started slow cooking rice.

Rice	Water	Butter	Serves	Cook Time (on High)
White rice:				
1 cup	1¾ cups	1 TB.	4	1½ hours
2 cups	3⅓ cups	2 TB.	8	2 hours
3 cups	4¼ cups	3 TB.	12	2¼ hours
Brown rice:				
1 cup	2 cups	1 TB.	4	2½ hours
2 cups	3⅔ cups	2 TB.	8	3 hours
3 cups	4¾ cups	3 TB.	12	3¾ hours

I usually season rice with salt and pepper after it's cooked, but I add butter at the beginning of the cooking process. The butter lubricates the rice grains so they don't become gummy and stick together.

Bean Basics

When working with dried beans, the first step is to rinse the beans in a sieve or colander and look them over carefully to discard any broken beans or the occasional pebble that sneaks into the bag. Also, keep in mind when you're cooking beans to not fill the slow cooker more than one third full with beans because they more than double in volume when they're cooked.

Although I include guidelines for how long each bean recipe takes to cook, variables can influence this time. If beans are a few years old, they'll take longer to cook. Also, the minerals in your tap water can retard the softening and require a longer cooking time.

The Soaking Step

With the exception of lentils and split peas, all beans should be soaked before cooking. For many years, it was believed that soaking was beneficial because the enzymes that make beans difficult for some people to digest leach out into the soaking water, which is then discarded. Lately, researchers have questioned whether the amount of enzyme removed in this way is significant. Many cooks agree, however, that soaking does soften the beans and save cooking time.

You can soak beans using one of two methods:

Cover the beans with water and let them sit on the counter at least 6 hours or overnight. This method is consistent with slow cooking because you might have already decided to cook a recipe the next morning.

The "quick soak": in a medium saucepan, cover the beans with water and bring to a boil over high heat. Boil the beans for 1 minute, cover the pan, and turn off the heat. Let the beans soak for 1 hour.

Whichever method you use, drain the beans and discard the soaking liquid.

Cooker Caveats

Even if you've soaked beans in cold water, they should be refrigerated if not cooked immediately. Dried beans are only marginally perishable (which is why dehydration is such an important form of food preservation), but once even partially hydrated, they become very perishable.

Time Talk

After you've soaked the beans (using either soaking method), place them in the slow cooker and cover them with hot water by at least 3 inches. Here's a table to help you figure out how long it will take to make your beans tender (based on 2 cups dried beans, which yields 6 cups cooked beans):

Bean Type	Cook Time
Black beans	3 hours
Black-eyed peas	3¼ hours
Fava beans	2¾ hours
Garbanzo beans	3½ hours
Great Northern beans	2¾ hours

continues

continued

Bean Type	Cook Time
Kidney beans	3 hours
Lentils	2 hours (no presoaking)
Lima beans	2½ for baby, 3½ for large
Navy beans	2½ hours
Split peas	2½ hours (no presoaking)
White beans	3 hours

Beans should always be covered with liquid at all times while they're cooking, so toward the end of the cooking process, take a look through the glass lid and add boiling water if the water seems almost evaporated.

Bean Cuisine

It's best to soften the beans before adding other ingredients to the slow cooker because certain foods can actually harden beans while they're cooking—exactly what you *don't* want! Two families of ingredients can retard bean softening as they cook: sweeteners and acids.

Sweeteners include honey, any type of sugar, molasses, and maple syrup. Acids include tomatoes, any sort of vinegar, red and white wine, and lemon and lime juice. If you use any of these ingredients in your bean dishes, be sure you fully soften the beans beforehand.

Cooker Caveats

Although many dried beans can be substituted for one another, don't substitute with canned beans in the slow cooker. Canned beans are already fully cooked, and they'll fall apart before they absorb the flavoring from the slow cooked dish.

Stocking Up

In a pinch, it's great to have a can of stock to open, but nothing compares with the rich flavor homemade stocks add to soups, stews, and braised dishes. Making stock is about as difficult as boiling water, and stock is great made in the slow cooker. You'll notice that none of these stocks is salted so you can add just the right amount of salt to a dish.

Chicken Stock

Chicken stock is the most versatile food you can have in your house. You can cook rice in it for additional flavor or add vegetables for a quick soup.

2 qt. water

2 lb. chicken pieces (bones, skin, wing tips, etc.)

1 carrot, scrubbed, trimmed, and cut into ½-in. chunks

1 medium onion, peeled and sliced

1 celery rib, rinsed, trimmed, and sliced

12 black peppercorns

3 parsley sprigs, rinsed

3 thyme sprigs, rinsed, or 1 tsp. dried

2 garlic cloves, peeled

1 bay leaf

Yield: 2 quarts
Prep time: 10 minutes
Cook time: 5 hours in a medium slow cooker

1. Pour water into the slow cooker. Add chicken pieces, carrot, onion, celery, peppercorns, parsley, thyme, garlic, and bay leaf. Cook on low for 10 to 12 hours or on high for 5 or 6 hours.

2. Strain stock through a sieve into a mixing bowl. Press down on solids with the back of a spoon to extract as much liquid as possible. Discard solids.

3. Chill stock. Remove and discard fat layer from top. Ladle stock into containers, and either use refrigerated within 4 days or freeze for up to 6 months.

Variation: If you want stock that's a dark color, start by browning the chicken bones under a preheated broiler until browned.

Slow Savvy

Saving meat and poultry scraps in plastic bags in the freezer is the most economical way to make stocks. Cut your own stew meat from a chuck roast and freeze the bones. And keep the tips from chicken wings and the necks and gizzards from whole chickens (but not the livers).

Beef Stock

This hearty stock adds richness to meat stews and soups.

Yield: 2 quarts
Prep time: 15 minutes
Cook time: 5 hours in a medium slow cooker

2 lb. beef shank, or 1 lb. beef stew meat or chuck roast

2 qt. water

1 carrot, scrubbed, trimmed, and cut into ½-in. chunks

1 medium onion, peeled and sliced

1 celery rib, rinsed, trimmed, and sliced

12 black peppercorns

3 parsley sprigs, rinsed

3 thyme sprigs, rinsed, or 1 tsp. dried

2 garlic cloves, peeled

1 bay leaf

1. Preheat the oven broiler, and line a broiler pan with heavy-duty aluminum foil. Broil beef for 3 minutes per side or until browned.

2. Transfer beef to the slow cooker along with any pan juices, and add water, carrot, onion, celery, peppercorns, parsley, thyme, garlic, and bay leaf. Cook on low for 10 to 12 hours or on high for 5 or 6 hours.

3. Strain stock through a sieve into a mixing bowl. Press down on solids with the back of a spoon to extract as much liquid as possible. Discard solids.

4. Chill stock. Remove and discard fat layer from top. Ladle stock into containers, and either use refrigerated within 4 days or freeze for up to 6 months.

Variation: If you want a more delicate stock, use veal bones and meat instead of beef. Veal breast is an inexpensive cut that's great for stock.

Slow Savvy

Measure the capacity of your ice cube trays with a measuring spoon and then freeze stock in the trays. Transfer the cubes to a heavy plastic bag when they're frozen and then just grab as many as you need from the freezer when a recipe calls for just a few tablespoons of stock.

Vegetable Stock

You can always use vegetable stock either as a substitute for or in addition to protein-based stocks to enhance the flavor of foods.

2 qt. water

2 carrots, scrubbed, trimmed, and thinly sliced

2 celery ribs, rinsed, trimmed, and sliced

2 leeks, white part only, trimmed, rinsed, and thinly sliced

1 small onion, peeled and thinly sliced

12 black peppercorns

3 parsley sprigs, rinsed

3 thyme sprigs, rinsed, or 1 tsp. dried

2 garlic cloves, peeled

1 bay leaf

Yield: 2 quarts
Prep time: 10 minutes
Cook time: 3 hours in a medium slow cooker

1. Pour water into the slow cooker, and add carrots, celery, leeks, onion, peppercorns, parsley, thyme, garlic, and bay leaf. Cook on low for 6 to 8 hours or on high for 3 or 4 hours or until vegetables are soft.

2. Strain stock through a sieve into a mixing bowl. Press down on solids with the back of a spoon to extract as much liquid as possible. Discard solids.

3. Ladle stock into containers, and either use refrigerated within 4 days or freeze for up to 6 months.

Variation: If you're using the stock for Asian cooking, feel free to add a few slices of ginger and replace the leeks with 4 scallions. If you're making Latin American food, substitute cilantro for parsley, and add a halved jalapeño pepper.

Cooker Caveats

You can add the water in which mildly flavored vegetables such as green beans or carrots cook to vegetable stocks. Don't add the cooking water from members of the cabbage family like broccoli or cauliflower; the flavors will become too assertive.

Seafood Stock

White wine and herbs add flavor nuances to this stock that makes any soup or stew elegant.

Yield: *3 quarts*
Prep time: 10 minutes
Cook time: 4 hours in a medium slow cooker

3 lobster bodies (whole lobsters from which the tail and claw meat has been removed) or 2 lobster bodies and the shells from 2 lb. raw shrimp

2 qt. water

1 cup dry white wine

1 carrot, scrubbed, trimmed, and cut into ½-in. chunks

1 medium onion, peeled and sliced

1 celery rib, rinsed, trimmed, and sliced

12 black peppercorns

3 parsley sprigs, rinsed

3 thyme sprigs, rinsed, or 1 tsp. dried

3 tarragon sprigs, rinsed, or 1 tsp. dried

2 garlic cloves, peeled

1 bay leaf

Slow Savvy

Seafood stock is perhaps the hardest to make if you don't live near the coast. Here's a good substitute: bottled clam juice. Use it in place of the water, and simmer it with vegetables and wine, as in the Chicken Stock recipe, to intensify its flavor.

1. Pull top shell off lobster body. Scrape off and discard feathery gills, and break body into small pieces. Place pieces into the slow cooker, and repeat with remaining lobster bodies. Add shrimp shells, if using.

2. Pour water and wine into the slow cooker, and add carrot, onion, celery, peppercorns, parsley, thyme, tarragon, garlic, and bay leaf. Cook on low for 8 to 10 hours or on high for 4 or 5 hours or until vegetables are soft.

3. Strain stock through a sieve into a mixing bowl. Press down on solids with the back of a spoon to extract as much liquid as possible. Discard solids.

4. Ladle stock into containers, and either use refrigerated within 4 days or freeze for up to 6 months.

Variation: Use the same recipe with 1½ pounds fish trimmings like skin, bones, or heads to make a finfish stock. Or you can combine finfish and shell fish in the same stock.

Caramelized Onions

There's no end to the ways you can use caramelized onions. In addition to the recipes in other chapters of this book, try them in mashed potatoes or as an addition to omelets.

4 TB. unsalted butter, cut into small pieces

3 TB. olive oil

3 lb. sweet onions, such as Vidalia or Bermuda, peeled and thinly sliced

1 TB. granulated sugar

Salt and freshly ground black pepper

Yield: 3 cups
Prep time: 15 minutes
Minimum cook time: 4 hours in a medium slow cooker

1. Set the slow cooker on high and add butter and olive oil. Add onions after butter melts, followed by sugar, salt, and pepper. Toss well to coat onions.

2. Cook for 1 hour, remove the cover, and stir onions. Cook for an additional 3 or 4 hours or until onions are golden brown. Season with salt and pepper.

3. Transfer onions to a storage container or heavy resealable plastic bag. Refrigerate for up to 5 days or freeze for up to 3 months.

 Slow Savvy

Adding salt to onions aids in softening them because the salt draws out the natural moisture. Adding sugar helps in the browning process.

Roasted Garlic

In the past decade, roasted garlic, with its sweet and nutty flavor, has become a staple in many kitchens. Serve it instead of butter with bread, or present whole heads with bread as an appetizer.

Yield: 1 cup
Prep time: 10 minutes
Minimum cook time: 3 hours in a medium slow cooker

8 heads garlic

1 cup olive oil

1 TB. fresh thyme or 1 tsp. dried

Salt and freshly ground black pepper

1. Cut off top ½ inch of each garlic head to expose cloves. Place heads in the slow cooker, and pour olive oil over them. Sprinkle with thyme, salt, and pepper.

2. Cook on high for 3 or 4 hours or until garlic is very tender when pierced with the tip of a paring knife. Turn off the slow cooker, remove the cover, and allow garlic to cool in oil.

3. Remove garlic from oil with a slotted spoon. Pop cloves out of heads, and discard skins. Transfer garlic to a storage container or heavy resealable plastic bag. Refrigerate for up to 5 days or freeze for up to 3 months.

Variation: Try oregano or sage instead of thyme; each herb adds its distinctive flavor to the mellow garlic.

Cooker Caveats

As garlic ages, bitter green shoots emerge from the individual cloves. Never buy a head if the shoots are visible, and for a recipe like this one, don't use heads if you see green shoots after cutting off the top of the head. You don't have to discard the heads; break them into individual cloves and remove the green centers before chopping or mincing.

Part 2

Stellar Starters

When you're planning a party, you often think you need an extra set of hands—or two—because you usually have many more dishes to prepare than for your average meal. Enter your kitchen pal, your slow cooker. Now you can go about your party-prepping, confident that the slow cooker's low heat is producing delicious hot dips that you don't have to think twice about burning. And when it's time, you can whisk the slow cooker out to the table and use it as a serving dish that will keep the dips hot.

The slow cooker proves its versatility for first courses beyond just dips, though. And Part 2 ends with a chapter on appetizers, many of which can also be served as hors d'oeuvres.

"I see a delectable nacho dip in your future."

In the Beginning: Dips

In This Chapter

- ◆ Traditional cheese dips from around the globe
- ◆ Hearty meaty and beany dips
- ◆ Delicate vegetable and seafood dips

If you haven't guessed by now, the slow cooker can be used to make every part of your meal—including dips to serve as appetizers or that precede the main event. Those are the recipes you'll find in this chapter, everything from gooey and rich cheese fondue to bean dips with Southwestern flair. In addition to dips served hot from the slow cooker, you'll also find some cold dips that are slow cooked and then chilled.

There are many advantages to using a slow cooker for dips. Hot dips made in the slow cooker stay hot and don't burn. And if you like to serve hot dips as an hors d'oeuvre, it's worth the small expense of buying a small, 1-quart slow cooker. Dips can be cooked in a larger cooker in greater quantities, but a small cooker doubles as a serving dish. Plus, you'll have one less dish to clean up!

What to Dip With

All the dips in this chapter are thick dips and would break delicate potato chips or other fragile dippers. You'll find that sturdy corn chips work best for dipping with all the Mexican and Southwestern dips. Bread cubes on bamboo skewers or slices of bread and crackers are better choices for the subtle flavors of cheese and vegetable dips.

Pita toasts are great dippers, too, and really easy to make. Separate pita breads into their two natural layers and spread each layer with melted butter. Sprinkle the pieces with salt, pepper, and any herbs you like—from oregano to chili powder. Bake the bread at 375°F for 10 to 15 minutes or until browned and crisp. Then break into dipping-size pieces.

Cooker Caveats

Remember, for the sake of hygiene, double dipping is never acceptable!

Tuscan White Bean Dip

Flecks of roasted red pepper and parsley enliven this garlicky dip that also makes a great bread spread.

1 cup dried navy beans, cooked (see Chapter 2) and drained

⅓ cup extra-virgin olive oil

¼ cup freshly squeezed lemon juice

3 garlic cloves, peeled

½ cup chopped fresh parsley

1 TB. fresh thyme or 1 tsp. dried

2 jarred roasted red bell peppers, seeds removed and cut into 1-in. pieces

Salt and freshly ground black pepper

Serves: 8 to 10
Prep time: 15 minutes
Minimum cook time: 2½ hours in a medium slow cooker

1. Combine beans, olive oil, lemon juice, and garlic in a food processor fitted with a steel blade. *Purée* until smooth.

2. Add parsley, thyme, and roasted red bell peppers. Chop finely, using on-and-off pulsing. Season with salt and pepper.

3. Serve immediately or refrigerate for up to 2 days, tightly covered. Serve with crostini, pita crisps, bagel chips, or crudités.

Slow Speak

Purée is a French term that means to process until you have a thick and totally smooth liquid, instead of a thinner liquid containing solid pieces of foods. This can be done in a food processor fitted with a steel blade, in a blender, or by pushing foods through a food mill.

Roasted Garlic Hummus

The mellow flavor of sweet roasted garlic blends well with the nutty garbanzo beans and sesame flavor in this classic Middle Eastern dip.

Serves: 8 to 10

Prep time: 15 minutes

Minimum cook time: 3 hours in a medium slow cooker

1½ cups dried garbanzo beans, cooked (see Chapter 2) and drained, or 2 (15-oz.) cans garbanzo beans, drained and rinsed

2 TB. roasted garlic, cooked (see Chapter 2)

⅔ cup well-stirred *tahini*

⅓ cup freshly squeezed lemon juice

⅓ cup olive oil

¼ cup water

Salt and freshly ground black pepper

¼ cup chopped fresh parsley

1. Combine garbanzo beans, garlic, tahini, lemon juice, olive oil, and water in a food processor fitted with a steel blade or in a blender. Purée until smooth.

2. Scrape mixture into a mixing bowl, season with salt and pepper, and stir in parsley. Refrigerate until chilled or serve at room temperature. Serve with crostini, pita crisps, bagel chips, or crudités.

Variation: Want hummus that's a bit spicier? Add 1 tablespoon puréed chipotle chiles in adobo sauce.

Slow Speak _____

Tahini (*tah-HEE-knee*) is a Middle Eastern paste made from sesame seeds. It's what gives hummus its characteristic sesame flavor. The oil always rises to the top, so it's important to stir it well before measuring it.

Artichoke and Parmesan Dip

Herbs and mayonnaise add to the flavor and creaminess of this easy dip.

1 cup freshly grated Parmesan cheese

⅔ cup mayonnaise

½ cup crème fraîche

2 TB. freshly squeezed lemon juice

2 TB. chopped fresh parsley

1 TB. fresh thyme or 1 tsp. dried

1 garlic clove, peeled and minced

3 scallions, white part only, rinsed, trimmed, and cut into ½-in. pieces

2 (10-oz.) pkg. frozen artichoke hearts, thawed and drained

Salt and freshly ground black pepper

Serves: 8 to 10
Prep time: 15 minutes
Minimum cook time: 1 hour in a small slow cooker

1. Combine Parmesan cheese, mayonnaise, crème fraîche, lemon juice, parsley, thyme, and garlic in the slow cooker. Stir well.

2. Place scallions and artichoke hearts in the bowl of a food processor fitted with a steel blade. Chop finely using an on-and-off pulsing action. Scrape mixture into the slow cooker, stir well, and season with salt and pepper.

3. Cook on low for 2 or 3 hours or on high for 1 to 1½ hours or until mixture is bubbly and hot. Serve with crostini, pita crisps, bagel chips, or crudités.

Variation: Asparagus is just as delicious as artichokes in this dip, but don't try to mix the two.

Crock Tales

Artichokes do not pair well with wine because they contain cynarin, a bioactive substance that reacts with food eaten immediately afterward, causing it to take on a sweet taste. The cheese in this recipe mitigates that effect.

Spinach Dip with Feta and Dill

This dip is right out of the Greek islands with tangy cheese, aromatic dill, and lemon flavors.

Serves: 8 to 10	
Prep time: 15 minutes	
Minimum cook time: 1½ hours in a medium slow cooker	

2 (10-oz.) pkg. frozen chopped spinach, thawed

2 TB. unsalted butter

1 medium onion, peeled and chopped

1 garlic clove, peeled and minced

½ lb. (2 cups) crumbled *feta cheese*

1 (3-oz.) pkg. cream cheese, softened

¼ cup chopped fresh dill or 3 TB. dried

2 TB. chopped fresh oregano or 2 tsp. dried

3 TB. freshly squeezed lemon juice

Salt and freshly ground black pepper

1. Place spinach in a colander or strainer, and press with the back of a spoon to extract as much liquid as possible. Set aside.

2. Heat butter in a small skillet over medium heat. Add onion and garlic, and cook, stirring frequently, 3 minutes or until onion is translucent. Scrape mixture into the slow cooker.

3. Stir spinach, feta cheese, cream cheese, dill, oregano, and lemon juice into the slow cooker.

4. Cook on low for 3 or 4 hours or on high for 1½ to 2 hours or until bubbly. Season with salt and pepper. Serve with crostini, pita crisps, cooked tortellini, cooked gnocchi, or crudités.

Slow Speak

Feta cheese is a classic Greek cheese traditionally made from sheep's or goat's milk, although today it's often made with cow's milk. White, crumbly, and rind-less, feta is usually pressed into square cakes. It has a rich, tangy flavor and can range in texture from soft to semidry.

Cheese Fondue

There's nothing like the creamy richness of a classic Swiss fondue, complete with a pair of tasty cheeses.

1 garlic clove, peeled and halved

¾ cup dry white wine

½ lb. grated Gruyère cheese

½ lb. grated Swiss cheese

2 TB. cornstarch

3 TB. *kirsch*

Serves: 6 to 8
Prep time: 15 minutes
Minimum cook time: 1½ hours in a small slow cooker

1. Rub inside of the slow cooker with cut side of garlic. Discard garlic.

2. Pour wine into the slow cooker, and stir in Gruyère and Swiss cheeses. Cook on high for 1 or 2 hours or until cheeses are melted and bubbly.

3. Stir cornstarch into kirsch, and stir mixture into cheese. Cook for an additional 15 to 20 minutes or until bubbly and cheese thickens. Serve with bread cubes, cooked tortellini, cooked potatoes, or crudités.

Slow Speak

Kirsch, also called **kirschwasser,** is a clear, tart cherry-flavored liqueur. There's really no substitute for its taste. It's excellent sprinkled on fresh berries and enhances their fruity taste. It can also be added to sweetened whipped cream to give it a more complex flavor.

Crab Dip

The "secret ingredient" to this creamy dip is an herb and spice blend called Old Bay.

Serves: 8 to 10
Prep time: 15 minutes
Minimum cook time: 1½ hours in a small slow cooker

½ lb. crabmeat

2 TB. unsalted butter

1 small onion, peeled and finely chopped

1 (8-oz.) pkg. cream cheese, softened

¾ cup mayonnaise

½ to 1 tsp. *Old Bay* seasoning

1. Place crabmeat on a dark-colored plate, and pick it over gently with your fingertips to discard all shell and cartilage fragments. Place picked-over crabmeat in the slow cooker.

2. Melt butter in a small skillet over medium heat. Add onion and cook, stirring frequently, for 3 minutes or until onion is translucent. Scrape onion into the slow cooker, and stir in cream cheese and mayonnaise.

3. Cook on low for 1½ to 2 hours or until cheese is bubbly. Stir in Old Bay seasoning. Serve with crostini, pita crisps, cooked tortellini, cooked gnocchi, or crudités.

Variation: This dip is just as delicious when made with small shrimp, cooked salmon, or finely chopped cooked chicken.

Slow Speak

Old Bay is a seasoning mix developed for the Chesapeake Bay's prized steamed crabs. It contains celery salt, mustard, cayenne, bay leaves, cloves, allspice, ginger, and paprika.

Crab Rangoon Dip

Creamy coconut milk and subtle Asian seasonings add nuances of flavor to this elegant cream cheese–based dip.

½ lb. crabmeat

3 scallions

1 (8-oz.) pkg. cream cheese, softened

½ cup coconut milk

2 garlic cloves, peeled and minced

2 TB. soy sauce

2 TB. grated fresh ginger

1 TB. Worcestershire sauce

2 TB. chopped fresh cilantro

Salt and freshly ground black pepper

Serves: 8 to 10

Prep time: 15 minutes

Minimum cook time: 1½ hours in a small slow cooker

---

1. Place crabmeat on a dark-colored plate, and pick it over gently with your fingertips to discard all shell and cartilage fragments.

2. Rinse and trim scallions. Discard all but 2 inches of green tops, and chop scallions.

3. Combine cream cheese, coconut milk, scallions, garlic, soy sauce, ginger, and Worcestershire sauce in the slow cooker. Cook on low for 3 or 4 hours or on high for 1½ to 2 hours or until mixture is hot and bubbly.

4. Stir in crabmeat and cilantro. Season with salt and pepper. Serve with wonton crisps, crostini, pita crisps, bagel chips, or crudités.

Variation: Cooked fish or poultry (½ pound) can be used instead of crab, or substitute finely chopped firm tofu to make this a vegetarian dip.

Crock Tales

Crab Rangoon was popularized in the 1950s at the Trader Vic's chain of Polynesian restaurants that sprang up across the country. Capitalizing on the popularity of movies such as *South Pacific* as well as thousands of soldiers returning from serving in the region, the restaurants featured exotic rum drinks and appetizers dubbed Pu-Pu.

Thai Shrimp and Coconut Dip

Cream cheese is enlivened with some hot peppers and other Thai flavors for this easy dip.

Serves: 8 to 10

Prep time: 15 minutes

Minimum cook time: 1½ hours in a small slow cooker

---

3 scallions

1 (8-oz.) pkg. cream cheese, softened

½ cup coconut milk

2 garlic cloves, peeled and minced

¼ cup chopped fresh cilantro

1 jalapeño chile, seeds and ribs removed, and finely chopped

3 TB. *fish sauce (nam pla)*

½ lb. small (45 or more per lb.) cooked shrimp, peeled

Salt and freshly ground black pepper

1. Rinse and trim scallions. Discard all but 2 inches of green tops, and chop scallions.

2. Combine cream cheese, coconut milk, scallions, garlic, cilantro, jalapeño, and fish sauce in the slow cooker. Cook on low for 2 or 3 hours or on high for 1 or 2 hours or until mixture is hot and bubbly.

3. Stir in shrimp, and season with salt and pepper. Serve with plantain chips, wonton crisps, crostini, pita crisps, or crudités.

Variation: Don't feel like seafood? Substitute an equal amount of anything from chopped cooked poultry or pork to tofu or chopped cooked zucchini.

Slow Speak

Fish sauce (*nam pla*), a salty sauce with an extremely pungent odor, is made from fermented fish. It's used as a dipping sauce/condiment and seasoning ingredient throughout Southeast Asia. *Nam pla* is the Thai term; it's known as *nuoc nam* in Vietnam and *shottsuru* in Japan.

Welsh Rarebit Dip

Beer is the liquid in this fonduelike dip, with crunchy bacon and colorful tomatoes dotting the creamy cheddar base.

¾ cup lager beer

4 cups (1 lb.) grated sharp cheddar cheese

1 TB. prepared mustard

¼ lb. bacon, cooked until crisp and crumbled (optional)

2 tomatoes, cored, seeded, and finely chopped

1 TB. cornstarch

1 TB. cold water

Salt and cayenne

Serves: 6 to 8
Prep time: 15 minutes
Minimum cook time: 1¼ hours in a small slow cooker

1. Combine beer, cheese, mustard, bacon (if using), and tomatoes in the slow cooker. Cook on low for 2 or 3 hours or on high for 1 or 2 hours or until cheese is melted and mixture is bubbly.

2. If cooking on low, raise the heat to high. Stir cornstarch into cold water, and stir mixture into the slow cooker. Cook for an additional 10 to 20 minutes or until dip is bubbly and thickens. Season with salt and cayenne. Serve with crostini, pita crisps, cooked tortellini, cooked gnocchi, or crudités.

Variation: Try smoked cheddar cheese or smoked Gouda in this dip, and to make it vegetarian, omit the bacon but add some chopped sun-dried tomatoes to complement the fresh ones.

Crock Tales

Welsh Rarebit, sometimes called Welsh Rabbit, is a classic dish served for high tea in English pubs. Unlike afternoon tea, which was for the gentry, high tea was the supper of the working class because their main meal of the day was at noontime.

Mexican Beef and Chili Dip
(Chili con Queso)

For a different way to serve this hearty dip made with two cheeses, mound it on corn chips and broil it as nachos.

Serves: 8 to 10

Prep time: 15 minutes
Minimum cook time: 2 hours in a medium slow cooker

---

2 TB. olive oil

1 onion, peeled and diced

3 garlic cloves, peeled and minced

1 lb. lean ground beef

1 (15-oz.) can petite cut diced tomatoes, drained

1 (4-oz.) can chopped mild green chiles, drained

½ cup heavy cream

½ lb. (2 cups) Monterey Jack cheese, coarsely grated

½ lb. (2 cups) cheddar cheese, coarsely grated

1 TB. cold water

1 TB. cornstarch

Salt and freshly ground black pepper

 Slow Savvy

Petite cut tomatoes are a relative newcomer to the market, and they're great for dips. Regular diced tomatoes should really be cut into smaller pieces or someone's dip into the bowl could yield nothing but a tomato. The petite cut ones are preferable and save prep time.

1. Heat olive oil in a large, heavy skillet over medium-high heat. Add onion, garlic, and ground beef. Cook, breaking up lumps with a fork, for 3 to 5 minutes or until beef is brown and no pink remains. Add tomatoes and green chiles, and cook for an additional 3 minutes. Remove the contents of the skillet with a slotted spoon, and transfer it to the slow cooker.

2. Add cream, Monterey Jack cheese, and cheddar cheese, and stir well. Cook on low for 3 or 4 hours or on high for 1½ to 2 hours or until cheese is bubbly.

3. If cooking on low, raise the heat to high. Combine water and cornstarch in a small bowl, and stir to dissolve cornstarch. Stir mixture into the slow cooker. Cook for an additional 15 to 20 minutes or until bubbly and cheese thickens. Season with salt and pepper. Serve with tortilla chips, plantain chips, crostini, pita crisps, or crudités.

Variation: Want this dip to have zestier flavor? Use chorizo or linguiça sausage instead of ground beef. Or you can use ground turkey to cut back on saturated fat.

4

Appealing Appetizers

In This Chapter

◆ Asian-flavor appetizers

◆ Vegetables-as-wrappers snackers

◆ Cold dishes for noshing

Appetizers are so popular that some restaurants have adopted appetizer-size portions—a.k.a. "little plates"—for their entire menu. These dishes are intended to be served at the table, but many of them can do double duty as hors d'oeuvres for a cocktail party.

Shrinking the Size

When turning an appetizer into an hors d'oeuvre, the key rule to follow is to make the food bite size and easy to eat. For example, cut the French Onion Pizza into 1-inch squares rather than larger slices, or make the Southwest Black Bean Cakes into 1-inch cakes.

Also the dishes really have to become finger food. All of the roll-ups made with lettuce leaves qualify, as do the steamed dumplings and chicken wings. For dishes like the Chinese Chicken Liver Pâté, offer it with crackers or toast points and a knife for spreading. Dishes like the Garlic-Steamed Clams should only be served at the table, while the Spanish Shrimp can be served with toothpicks.

Southwest Black Bean Cakes

These sautéed cakes are flavored with herbs and spices, and they double as a side dish for Mexican or Southwestern meals.

Serves: 6
Prep time: 30 minutes
Minimum cook time: 3 hours in a medium slow cooker

6 TB. olive oil

1 medium onion, peeled and coarsely chopped

3 garlic cloves, peeled and minced

2 serrano chiles, seeds and ribs removed, and diced

2 TB. chili powder

1½ TB. ground cumin

2 cups dried black beans

½ cup chopped fresh cilantro

6 cups water

Salt and freshly ground black pepper

1 cup sour cream

1 cup good-quality refrigerated tomato salsa

> **Cooker Caveats**
>
> You might think it's not necessary to dice and chop ingredients that are destined to become a purée, but it really is important. If the pieces are too large, they won't cook properly and your finished dish will taste like your raw ingredients.

1. Heat 2 tablespoons olive oil in a large, heavy skillet over medium-high heat. Add onion, garlic, and serrano chiles, and cook, stirring frequently, for 3 minutes or until onion is translucent. Add chili powder and cumin, and cook, stirring constantly, for 1 minute. Scrape mixture into the slow cooker.

2. Add beans, cilantro, and water to the slow cooker, and stir well. Cook on low for 6 to 8 hours or on high for 3 or 4 hours or until beans are tender.

3. Drain beans, and transfer mixture to a food processor fitted with a steel blade and purée. Scrape mixture into a mixing bowl, and season with salt and pepper.

4. Roll enough mixture into a ball the size of a golf ball. Flatten between two sheets of plastic wrap until patty is ¼-inch thick. Repeat with remaining mixture.

5. Heat remaining 4 tablespoons olive oil in a large, heavy skillet over high heat. Add bean cakes, and cook for 1 or 2 minutes per side or until crisp, turning gently with a slotted spatula. Drain cakes on paper towels, and continue until all cakes are cooked.

6. To serve, place 1 or 2 cakes on a plate and top each with 1 tablespoon sour cream and 1 tablespoon salsa. Serve immediately. (Bean mixture can be made up to 1 day in advance and refrigerated, tightly covered. Fry cakes just prior to serving.)

Variation: Want a lighter look? Use garbanzo beans; you'll have to cook them for 3½ hours.

French Onion Pizza (*Pissaladière*)

Sweet caramelized onions are spread on top of an herb base and dotted with black olives in this classic snack food from Provence.

½ cup olive oil

½ cup firmly packed fresh parsley leaves, rinsed

3 TB. anchovy paste

3 garlic cloves, peeled

2 TB. balsamic vinegar

1 large egg yolk

2 tsp. fresh thyme or ½ tsp. dried

Freshly ground black pepper

½ cup plain breadcrumbs

1 unbaked pizza crust, home-made or purchased

2 cups Caramelized Onions (recipe in Chapter 2)

½ cup Niçoise or other black oil-cured olives, chopped

Serves: 4 to 6
Prep time: 20 minutes
Minimum cook time: 4 hours in a medium slow cooker plus 45 minutes for baking

1. Combine olive oil, parsley, anchovy paste, garlic, vinegar, egg yolk, thyme, and pepper in a food processor fitted with a steel blade or in a blender. Purée until smooth. Add breadcrumbs, and purée again. Scrape mixture into a mixing bowl.

2. Preheat the oven to 375°F and sprinkle a baking sheet with cornmeal. Arrange pizza crust on the baking sheet and spread with herb mixture. Top mixture with onions, and sprinkle olives over all.

3. Bake for 45 to 50 minutes or until crust is brown and topping is bubbly. Allow to sit for 10 minutes and then cut into servings and serve.

Variation: Not crazy about anchovy paste? No problem! Omit it and use salt in the herb mixture instead.

Crock Tales

Pissaladière vendors are the hot dog stands all along the French Riviera, and the aroma of sweet caramelized onions blends with the salty smell of the sea. The authentic version frequently has whole anchovies as part of the topping, but I've modified it to just add their salty flavor to the mixture covering the crust.

Garlic-Steamed Clams

This is a very easy dish to make because the clams open themselves during the cooking process and their juice creates the flavorful broth.

Serves: 4 to 6
Prep time: 15 minutes
Minimum cook time: 1½ hours in a medium slow cooker

3 dozen littleneck or small cherrystone clams

3 TB. olive oil

6 garlic cloves, peeled and minced

¼ cup water

¼ cup white wine

¼ cup chopped fresh parsley

Salt and freshly ground black pepper

1. Scrub clams well under cold running water with a stiff brush. Discard any that do not shut tight while being scrubbed.

2. Heat olive oil in a small skillet over medium heat. Add garlic and cook, stirring frequently, for 2 minutes. Scrape mixture into the slow cooker. Add water, wine, and clams. Cook on high for 1½ to 2 hours or until clams open. Shake the slow cooker a few times—without opening it—to redistribute clams.

3. Remove clams from the slow cooker with a slotted spoon, discarding any that did not open. Stir in parsley, salt, and pepper. To serve, place clams in shallow bowls and ladle broth on top. Serve with soup spoons as well as seafood forks.

Variation: If you prefer, you can use the same amount of fresh mussels instead of clams.

 Slow Savvy

Leftover broth from a steamed mollusk recipe is a treasure trove of flavor for saucing future fish dishes. Freeze it, and be sure to note what dish it's from so you know what flavors you're adding.

Spanish Shrimp

This dish is part of the range of *tapas* served in Spanish bars; the shrimp are cooked with lots of garlic and paprika and then served over rice.

½ cup olive oil

6 garlic cloves, peeled and crushed

1 TB. paprika

2 lb. extra-large (16 to 20 per lb.) shrimp, peeled and deveined

3 TB. chopped fresh parsley

2 (5-oz.) pkg. yellow rice mix, preferably Carolina brand

Salt

Red pepper flakes

Serves: 6 to 8
Prep time: 15 minutes
Minimum cook time: 1½ hours in a medium slow cooker

1. Combine olive oil, garlic, paprika, shrimp, and parsley in the slow cooker. Cook on low for 3 or 4 hours or on high for 1½ to 2 hours or until shrimp are pink and cooked through.

2. While shrimp are cooking, cook rice according to package directions. Season shrimp with salt and red pepper flakes.

3. Divide rice onto serving plates and top with shrimp. Serve immediately.

Variation: You can make this dish with 2 pounds of 1-inch cubes of cod or any firm-fleshed whitefish or with bay scallops. The cooking time will be the same.

 Slow Savvy _____

When you buy shrimp that are still in their shells, they need to be peeled. That's step one. Step two is to devein them. See Chapter 10 for the procedure on deveining.

Spicy Asian Chicken Wings

After trying these, you'll never want a buffalo wing again! When they're slow cooked to tender and flavorful, they're browned under the broiler to crisp them.

Serves: 6
Prep time: 15 minutes
Minimum cook time: 2 hours in a medium slow cooker

18 chicken wings (about 3 lb.)

2 scallions, rinsed, trimmed, and finely chopped

2 garlic cloves, peeled and minced

2 TB. grated fresh ginger

¾ cup chicken stock

¼ cup soy sauce

¼ cup dry sherry

2 TB. rice wine vinegar

¼ cup hoisin sauce

¼ to ½ tsp. red pepper flakes

1. Cut off tips from chicken wings, and save them for making stock. Cut wings into 2 sections at the joint, and arrange wings in the slow cooker.

2. Combine scallions, garlic, ginger, chicken stock, soy sauce, sherry, vinegar, hoisin sauce, and red pepper flakes in a mixing bowl. Stir well and pour mixture over chicken wings. Cook on low for 4 to 6 hours or on high for 2 or 3 hours or until wings are tender.

3. Preheat the oven broiler, and line a broiler pan with heavy-duty aluminum foil. Arrange wings in the broiler pan, and broil for 3 or 4 minutes per side or until they're lightly browned. Serve hot, at room temperature, or chilled.

Variation: Don't want the mess of eating wings? You can cook 1½ pounds 2-inch cubes of boneless, skinless chicken breast or 1-inch cubes of boneless, skinless chicken thighs the same way.

Slow Savvy

You'll sometimes find the lower part of roaster wings in the poultry case. They're called "chicken drumettes." These are larger than fryer wings, so you'll need to add about 1 hour to the cooking time on low or 30 minutes on high.

Chinese Chicken in Lettuce Cups

Crunchy water chestnuts add textural interest to the sweet and sour chicken filling in these healthful roll-ups.

2 TB. Asian sesame oil

6 scallions, rinsed, trimmed, and thinly sliced

3 garlic cloves, peeled and minced

1 TB. grated fresh ginger

1 lb. ground chicken or ground turkey

1 (8-oz.) can water chestnuts, drained and chopped

2 TB. soy sauce

2 TB. *hoisin sauce*

1 TB. cider vinegar

1 TB. cornstarch

1 TB. cold water

Salt and freshly ground black pepper

18 Boston or iceberg lettuce cups

Serves: 6	
Prep time: 20 minutes	
Minimum cook time: 2 hours in a small slow cooker	

1. Heat sesame oil in a medium saucepan over medium-high heat. Add scallions, garlic, and ginger. Cook, stirring constantly, for 1 minute or until mixture is fragrant. Scrape mixture into the slow cooker.

2. Add chicken and water chestnuts to the slow cooker. Combine soy sauce, hoisin sauce, and vinegar in a small bowl, and stir well. Add mixture to the slow cooker, and stir well again. Cook on low for 4 or 5 hours or on high for 2 or 3 hours or until chicken is cooked through and no longer pink.

3. If cooking on low, raise the heat to high. Mix cornstarch and cold water in a small bowl. Stir cornstarch mixture into the slow cooker, and cook for an additional 5 to 15 minutes or until mixture is bubbling and thickened. Season with salt and pepper.

4. Place 1 tablespoon chicken mixture at the stem end of each lettuce cup. Tuck the sides over the filling, and roll up the cup like an egg roll. Serve immediately.

 Slow Speak

Hoisin (*HOY-zan*) **sauce** is like a great Asian ketchup. It's a mixture of soybeans, garlic, chiles, and Chinese five-spice powder. It's a thick, reddish-brown sauce that's simultaneously sweet and spicy.

Chinese Chicken Liver Pâté

Aromatic sesame oil, ginger, and crunchy water chestnuts add Asian flair to this rich dish.

1 lb. chicken livers, rinsed	2 TB. Chinese *oyster sauce*
2 TB. Asian sesame oil	2 TB. soy sauce
6 scallions, rinsed, trimmed, and finely chopped	½ cup finely chopped fresh water chestnuts
3 garlic cloves, peeled and minced	Salt and freshly ground black pepper
1 TB. grated fresh ginger	Crackers or toast points
2 TB. rice wine or dry sherry	

Serves: 6 to 8

Prep time: 15 minutes

Minimum cook time: 1½ hours in a small slow cooker, plus at least 2 hours for chilling

---

Slow Speak

Oyster sauce is a traditional Chinese condiment and cooking sauce, and although it does contain oysters, it's not "fishy" in flavor. The oysters and their liquor are cooked with soy sauce and some subtle seasonings until thick, which gives dishes a richness.

---

1. Trim chicken livers of all fat, and discard veins connecting the 2 lobes. Cut livers into ½-inch pieces, and set aside.

2. Heat sesame oil in a small skillet over medium-high heat. Add scallions, garlic, and ginger, and cook, stirring constantly, for 1 minute or until fragrant. Scrape mixture into the slow cooker.

3. Arrange chicken livers on top of vegetables in slow cooker. Combine rice wine, Chinese oyster sauce, and soy sauce in a small bowl, and pour mixture over livers. Cook on low for 3 or 4 hours or on high for 1½ to 2 hours or until livers are cooked through.

4. Scrape mixture into a food processor fitted with a steel blade or a blender, and purée until smooth. Scrape mixture into a mixing bowl, and stir in water chestnuts. Season with salt and pepper.

5. Line a loaf pan with plastic wrap, and pack pâté into the container. Cover with plastic wrap, and refrigerate for at least 2 hours or until well chilled. (You can do this up to 2 days in advance.)

6. To serve, invert the pan onto a platter, and discard the plastic wrap. Cut pâté into serving pieces, and serve with crackers or toast points.

Duck Confit Turnovers

These are incredibly luscious, with sweet onions and tender duck
flavored with herbs and tart dried cranberries in flaky puff pastry.

3 cups diced Duck Confit (recipe in Chapter 15)	**1 TB. fresh thyme or 1 tsp. dried**
1 cup Caramelized Onions (recipe in Chapter 2)	**Salt and freshly ground black pepper**
½ cup dried cranberries	**½ lb. puff pastry, thawed**
2 TB. chopped fresh parsley	**1 large egg, whisked well**

1. Preheat the oven to 400°F, and liberally grease a baking sheet
   with vegetable oil spray.

2. Combine confit, onions, cranberries, parsley, and thyme in a
   mixing bowl. Season with salt and pepper.

3. Roll puff pastry to ¼ inch thick, and cut into 4 to 6 squares.
   Place a portion of filling in the center of 1 square, and fold it
   into a triangle. Seal the edges by pressing down with the tines
   of a fork. Repeat with remaining filling.

4. Arrange triangles on the prepared baking sheet, and brush tops
   with beaten egg. Cut 3 (1-inch) slits in tops to allow steam to
   escape. Bake turnovers for 15 to 18 minutes or until browned
   and puffed. Serve immediately.

> *Serves: 4 to 6*
>
> **Prep time:** 20 minutes
> **Minimum cook time:** 7 hours in a medium slow cooker

 Slow Savvy

Don't own a rolling pin? Or it's propping open the kitchen window? No problem. Use any glass bottle, dusting it with flour first so the dough doesn't stick.

Asian Beef and Barley Lettuce Cups

Toothsome barley and hearty beef are flavored with Asian seasonings and then rolled up in crispy lettuce leaves.

Serves: 6 to 8
Prep time: 20 minutes
Minimum cook time: 2¼ hours in a small slow cooker

2 TB. Asian sesame oil

4 scallions, rinsed, trimmed, and thinly sliced

2 garlic cloves, peeled and minced

1 TB. grated fresh ginger

½ lb. lean ground beef

¼ cup pearl barley, rinsed

¾ cup water

2 TB. soy sauce

1 TB. cornstarch

1 TB. cold water

⅔ cup fresh bean sprouts, rinsed and cut into 1-in. pieces

Salt and freshly ground black pepper

18 Boston or iceberg lettuce leaves

Slow Savvy

Some cookbooks tell you to pinch the ends off the bean sprouts. This takes a lot of time and really isn't necessary. Once the bean sprouts are stirred into a dish, no one will ever notice the ends.

1. Heat sesame oil in a medium skillet over medium-high heat. Add scallions, garlic, and ginger, and cook, stirring frequently, for 3 minutes or until scallions are translucent. Scrape mixture into the slow cooker.

2. Add ground beef to the skillet, break up any lumps with a fork, and cook until beef is browned. Remove beef from the skillet with a slotted spoon, and place it in the slow cooker. Add barley, water, and soy sauce to the slow cooker. Cook on low for 3 or 4 hours or on high for 2 or 3 hours or until barley is tender.

3. If cooking on low, raise the heat to high. Combine cornstarch and cold water in a small cup, and stir mixture into the slow cooker. Cook for an additional 15 to 20 minutes or until juices are bubbling and thickened. Turn off the slow cooker, stir in bean sprouts, and season with salt and pepper.

4. Place 1 tablespoon mixture at the stem end of each lettuce leaf. Tuck the sides over the filling, and roll up the cup like an egg roll. Serve immediately.

Variation: Want to make these lighter? Use ground pork or ground turkey instead of beef.

Lamb and Garbanzo Bean Pizza

Tart goat cheese is a foil to rosy rich lamb and seasoned beans in this Middle Eastern pizza.

2 cups dried garbanzo beans	**1 TB. dried cumin**
¼ cup olive oil	**½ lb. lean ground lamb**
1 large onion, peeled and chopped	**Salt and freshly ground black pepper**
4 garlic cloves, peeled and minced	**6 oz. goat cheese**
2 TB. dried oregano	**¼ cup chopped fresh parsley**
	1 unbaked pizza crust

> *Serves: 4 to 6*
>
> **Prep time:** 25 minutes
>
> **Minimum cook time:** 3½ hours in a medium slow cooker plus 15 minutes for baking

1. Rinse beans in a colander, place them in a mixing bowl, and cover with cold water. Allow beans to soak overnight. Or place beans into a saucepan and bring to a boil over high heat. Boil 1 minute. Turn off the heat, cover the pan, and soak beans for 1 hour. Drain, and discard soaking water. Place beans in the slow cooker.

2. Heat 2 tablespoons olive oil in a small skillet over medium-high heat. Add onion and garlic, and cook, stirring frequently, for 3 minutes or until onion is translucent. Stir in 1 tablespoon oregano and cumin, and cook, stirring constantly, for 1 minute. Scrape mixture into the slow cooker.

3. Add enough hot water to the slow cooker to cover beans by 3 inches. Cook on low for 7 to 9 hours or on high for 3½ to 4 hours or until beans are tender.

4. While beans are cooking, heat remaining olive oil in a medium skillet over medium-high heat. Add lamb and break up any lumps with a fork, and cook until lamb is browned. Remove lamb from the skillet with a slotted spoon. Add remaining 1 tablespoon oregano to lamb, and season with salt and pepper.

5. Preheat the oven to 400°F, and sprinkle a baking sheet with cornmeal. Drain beans, and purée them with ⅓ goat cheese in a food processor fitted with a steel blade. Scrape beans into a mixing bowl, stir in parsley, and season with salt and pepper.

6. Spread beans on crust, and top with lamb. Top with remaining goat cheese. Bake pizza for 15 minutes or until crust is browned and cheese melts.

Slow Speak

Goat cheese, or *chevre*, is a white cheese with a tart flavor that sets it apart from other cheeses. Goat cheese comes in a variety of shapes and is sometimes coated with edible ash, herbs, or pepper.

Stuffed Grape Leaves (*Dolmas*)

The grape leaves hold a filling of herbed lamb and rice and then they're cooked with lots of lemon in this Mediterranean appetizer.

Serves: 6 to 8

Prep time: 25 minutes

Minimum cook time: 3 hours in a medium slow cooker

2 (8-oz.) jars grape leaves packed in brine

1 lb. lean ground lamb

1 small onion, peeled and grated

2 garlic cloves, peeled and minced

½ cup uncooked white rice

3 TB. chopped fresh parsley

1 TB. chopped fresh oregano or ½ tsp. dried

½ tsp. dried thyme

Salt and freshly ground black pepper

3 TB. olive oil

3 TB. fresh lemon juice

1 cup chicken stock

Slow Savvy

If you live near a grape vine, feel free to use fresh grape leaves for this recipe. They must be simmered for at least 10 minutes to make them pliable enough to use and to cook them sufficiently.

1. Separate grape leaves and rinse under cold running water. Place grape leaves in a mixing bowl, and cover with boiling water. Soak for 1 hour, drain, and run under cold water again.

2. While leaves are soaking, combine ground lamb, onion, garlic, rice, parsley, oregano, thyme, salt, and pepper in a mixing bowl. Stir well to combine.

3. Place a grape leaf vein side up on a plate. Place 1 heaping tablespoon stuffing on the stem end, and pat mixture into an oval. Fold the sides of leaf over filling, and roll leaf like an egg roll. Place stuffed leaf in the slow cooker, and continue with remaining leaves, placing them tightly together in the slow cooker.

4. Combine olive oil, lemon juice, and chicken stock in a small bowl, and pour over stuffed grape leaves. Cook on low for 6 to 8 hours or on high for 3 or 4 hours or until meat is cooked through and rice is soft. Serve at room temperature or cold.

Variation: To make this a vegetarian dish, substitute 1 pound zucchini for the lamb, and chop it finely for the filling. Use vegetable stock instead of chicken stock, too.

Part 3

The Bountiful Bowl: Soups as Supper

Soups are the quintessential comfort food. Lewis Carroll of *Alice in Wonderland* fame wrote "Beautiful soup! Who cares for fish, game, or any other dish? Who would not give all else for two pennyworth only of beautiful soup?"

In Part 3, you'll find a range of recipes for satisfying soups to fill the soul with joy as they fill the stomach with delicious tastes. There's a whole chapter on vegetable soups, ranging from light and thin to hearty and thick. And the same holds true for the chapter on soups made with fish and seafood. In Chapter 7, you'll find that cooks all over the world have ways with chicken (and turkey) soups. And when it comes to meat soups, your slow cooker will make you a star! Recipes for beef, lamb, and pork are included here as well.

"Let's get out of here. I've got a bad feeling."

5

Vibrant Vegetable Soups

In This Chapter

◆ Chunky soups

◆ Creamy soups

◆ Beany soups

A steaming bowl of French onion soup or a hearty mug of black bean soup is a great way to start a dinner—and can be dinner itself if served in a larger portion. Those and other great soups are the recipes you'll find in this chapter.

Vegetable soups are a great way to keep up the number of servings of fresh vegetables in your diet. And many children will gobble down their vegetables when presented as soups while the same vegetables presented on a dish might not be a welcome sight.

In addition, you'll find many recipes for hearty bean soups here. The great advantage to simmering bean soups in the slow cooker is the low heat. You'll never find burned beans stuck to the bottom of the pot.

In recipes for creamed soups, it's the stock that actually cooks the vegetables. The cream itself is added at the end of the cooking cycle because cream and other dairy products tend to curdle and separate if cooked for long hours, even at low heat.

Classic French Onion Soup

Sweet onions floating in a broth enriched with red wine are the hallmarks of a great onion soup like this one.

Serves: 6

Prep time: 15 minutes

Minimum cook time:
3 hours in a medium slow cooker

---

3 cups Caramelized Onions (recipe in Chapter 2)

3 TB. all-purpose flour

6 cups beef stock or vegetable stock

¾ cup dry red wine

1 bay leaf

1 TB. fresh thyme or 1 tsp. dried

2 TB. chopped fresh parsley

Salt and freshly ground black pepper

6 slices French or Italian bread, cut ½ in. thick

⅓ cup freshly grated Parmesan cheese

1½ cups grated Gruyère or Swiss cheese

Slow Savvy

The purpose of cooking the onions and flour before adding the liquid is to cook the flour to remove a "pasty" taste. Because the onions are already cooked, it's fine to lift up the lid and stir them a few times; the heat to cook the flour won't change.

1. Combine Caramelized Onions and flour in the slow cooker, and stir well. Cook on high for 20 minutes, stirring occasionally. Add stock, wine, bay leaf, thyme, and parsley. Cook on high for 2½ hours. Season with salt and pepper.

2. While soup is cooking, preheat the oven to 450°F and cover a baking sheet with heavy-duty aluminum foil. Sprinkle bread with Parmesan cheese, and bake slices for 5 to 8 minutes or until browned. Remove from the oven and set aside. (You can do this up to 3 days in advance. Reheat soup over low heat, stirring occasionally, and keep toasts at room temperature, covered with plastic wrap.)

3. Preheat the broiler. Ladle hot soup into ovenproof soup bowls and top each with 1 toast slice. Divide Gruyère on top of toast, and broil 6 inches from the heating element for 1 or 2 minutes or until cheese melts and browns. Serve immediately.

Potato Leek Soup

Leeks are the mildest member of the onion family, and their delicate flavor is showcased when potatoes are the foil.

6 leeks, white part only

2 TB. unsalted butter

**2 large boiling potatoes
(about 1½ lb.), peeled and cut
into ½-in. dice**

**4 cups chicken stock or veg-
etable stock**

½ cup half-and-half (optional)

**Salt and freshly ground black
pepper**

Serves: 4 to 6
Prep time: 20 minutes
Minimum cook time: 3¼ hours in a medium slow cooker

1. Trim leeks, split lengthwise, and slice thinly. Place leek slices in a
   colander and rinse well under cold running water, rubbing with
   your fingers to dislodge all dirt. Shake leeks in the colander.

2. Melt butter in a medium saucepan over medium heat. Add
   leeks, and toss with butter. Cover the pan, reduce the heat
   to low, and cook for 10 minutes. Scrape leeks into the slow
   cooker.

3. Add potatoes and stock to the slow cooker, and cook on low
   for 6 to 8 hours or on high for 3 or 4 hours or until potatoes
   are tender.

4. If cooking on low, raise the heat to high. Add half-and-half
   (if using), and season with salt and pepper. Cook for 15 to 20
   minutes or until simmering.

5. Use a potato masher to crush some of potatoes in the slow
   cooker before serving. (You can do this up to 3 days in advance
   and refrigerate soup tightly covered. Reheat over low heat, stirring occasionally.)

 Slow Savvy

If you're serv-
ing a soup
cold rather than hot,
always check the sea-
soning before serv-
ing it. Chilled foods
tend to need more
salt than hot foods
because the cold tem-
perature numbs the
taste buds.

Variation: This soup is incredibly versatile. You can purée it in
a food processor fitted with a steel blade or in a blender until it
becomes smooth and then chill it. Voilà! You've got *Vichyssoise!*
And if you can't find leeks, you can always use 1 pound onions,
although the flavor won't be as delicate.

Sweet-and-Sour Red Cabbage Soup

Red cabbage is the mild cousin in the cabbage family. Here, its inherent sweetness is amplified by hints of heady balsamic vinegar contrasted with brown sugar.

Serves: 4 to 6
Prep time: 20 minutes
Minimum cook time: 4 hours in a medium slow cooker

1 (1½-lb.) red cabbage

2 TB. olive oil

1 large red onion, peeled and diced

2 garlic cloves, peeled and minced

3 cups chicken stock or vegetable stock

1 (14.5-oz.) can crushed tomatoes

¼ cup balsamic vinegar

¼ cup firmly packed dark brown sugar

1 TB. fresh thyme or 1 tsp. dried

1 bay leaf

Salt and freshly ground black pepper

¼ cup minced fresh chives

4 to 6 TB. sour cream or crème fraîche (optional)

Slow Savvy

The vinegar in this soup serves a second function by keeping the cabbage's bright red color rather than turning it purple. If you're cooking cabbage as a side dish, add 2 tablespoons vinegar or lemon juice to the water to keep the color bright.

1. Discard outer leaves from red cabbage, cut cabbage in half, and discard core. Shred cabbage finely, and place it into the slow cooker.

2. Heat olive oil in a medium skillet over medium-high heat. Add onion and garlic, and cook, stirring frequently, for 3 minutes or until onion is translucent. Scrape mixture into the slow cooker, and add stock, tomatoes, balsamic vinegar, brown sugar, thyme, and bay leaf.

3. Cook on low for 8 to 10 hours or on high for 4 or 5 hours or until cabbage is tender. Remove and discard bay leaf, season soup with salt and pepper, and stir in chives. (You can do this up to 3 days in advance and refrigerate soup tightly covered. Reheat over low heat, stirring occasionally.) Serve immediately, garnished with sour cream (if using).

Butternut Squash Bisque

Sweet molasses, heady bourbon, and spices enliven the flavor of this sweet and creamy soup.

3½ lb. butternut squash, peeled and cut into 1-in. chunks

3 cups chicken stock or vegetable stock

⅓ cup molasses

⅓ cup bourbon

2 TB. chopped fresh parsley

½ tsp. ground cinnamon

1 pinch ground nutmeg

1 cup half-and-half

Salt and freshly ground black pepper

Serves: 4 to 6
Prep time: 20 minutes
Minimum cook time: 3½ hours in a medium slow cooker

1. Place squash, stock, molasses, bourbon, parsley, cinnamon, and nutmeg in the slow cooker. Cook on low for 6 to 8 hours or on high for 3 or 4 hours or until squash is tender.

2. If cooking on low, raise the heat to high. Add half-and-half, and cook for an additional 20 to 30 minutes or until bubbly.

3. Drain soup into a colander placed over a mixing bowl, and purée squash in a food processor fitted with a steel blade or in a blender. Stir purée back into soup, and season with salt and pepper. (You can do this up to 3 days in advance and refrigerate soup tightly covered. Reheat over low heat, stirring occasionally.)

Variation: For any squash dish, you can use acorn squash interchangeably with butternut. Feel free to jazz up this soup: instead of bourbon, try rum or a fruit-flavored liqueur, and use Chinese five-spice powder instead of cinnamon for a more complex flavor.

 Slow Savvy

Many supermarkets now have peeled butternut squash, at least during the winter months—a huge time-saver when making a soup such as this one. Cut back to 3 pounds squash to compensate for the peels.

Provençal Tomato Soup

This soup with rice added for additional texture has all the sunny flavors of Provence, including a hint of orange zest.

Serves: 4 to 6
Prep time: 25 minutes
Minimum cook time: 3½ hours in a medium slow cooker

2 lb. ripe tomatoes

1 large onion, peeled and diced

1 carrot, peeled and cut into 1-in. pieces

1 celery rib, rinsed, trimmed, and cut into 1-in. pieces

2 garlic cloves, peeled

2 TB. olive oil

4 cups chicken stock or vegetable stock

3 TB. tomato paste

1 TB. grated orange zest

1 TB. fresh thyme or 1 tsp. dried

2 tsp. granulated sugar

1 bay leaf

1 pinch crumbled saffron threads

⅓ cup long-grain white rice

¼ cup chopped fresh parsley or 1 TB. dried

Salt and freshly ground black pepper

1. Bring a large pot of salted water to a boil. Cut a shallow X on the stem of each tomato. Blanch tomatoes for 30 seconds, remove them from the pot with a slotted spoon, and plunge them into ice water to stop the cooking action. Peel tomatoes and halve them crosswise. Squeeze tomatoes over a sieve placed over a mixing bowl. Discard seeds and reserve juice. Finely chop tomatoes, and place them in the slow cooker along with reserved tomato juice.

2. Combine onion, carrot, celery, and garlic in a food processor fitted with a steel blade. Chop finely using on-and-off pulsing action. Set aside.

3. Heat olive oil in a medium skillet over medium-high heat. Add vegetable mixture and cook, stirring frequently, for 3 minutes or until onion is translucent. Scrape mixture into the slow cooker, and add stock, tomato paste, orange zest, thyme, sugar, bay leaf, and saffron. Stir well to dissolve tomato paste.

4. Cook on low for 5 to 7 hours or on high for 2½ to 3 hours or until vegetables are almost tender.

5. If cooking on low, raise the heat to high. Stir in rice and parsley, and cook for an additional 30 to 45 minutes or until rice is soft. Remove and discard bay leaf, and season with salt and pepper. (You can do this up to 3 days in advance and refrigerate soup tightly covered. Reheat over low heat, stirring occasionally.)

Variation: You can use the same basic recipe but give it more Italian influence: omit the orange zest and saffron and add ¼ cup chopped fresh oregano instead.

Slow Savvy

The most time-consuming part of this recipe is peeling the tomatoes. If a little tomato skin doesn't bother you, skip this step and save time. You can add the tomato seeds, too, for a more rustic look.

Curried Carrot Soup

Apple accentuates the inherently sweet flavor of carrots in this vividly colored soup.

Serves: 4 to 6
Prep time: 20 minutes
Minimum cook time: 3½ hours in a medium slow cooker

2 TB. unsalted butter

1 medium onion, peeled and diced

2 TB. all-purpose flour

1½ to 2 tsp. curry powder or to taste

6 carrots, peeled and thinly sliced

1 apple, peeled, cored, and sliced

5 cups chicken stock or vegetable stock

½ cup heavy cream

Salt and freshly ground black pepper

1. Melt butter in a medium saucepan over medium heat. Add onion, and cook, stirring frequently, for 3 minutes or until onion is translucent. Reduce the heat to low, and stir in flour and curry powder. Cook for 2 minutes, stirring constantly. Scrape mixture into the slow cooker.

2. Add carrots, apple, and stock to the slow cooker. Cook on low for 6 to 8 hours or on high for 3 or 4 hours or until carrots are tender.

3. If cooking on low, raise the heat to high. Add cream and cook for an additional 20 to 30 minutes or until bubbly. Drain soup into a colander placed over a mixing bowl, and purée solids in a food processor fitted with a steel blade or in a blender. Stir purée back into soup, and season with salt and pepper. (You can do this up to 3 days in advance and refrigerate soup tightly covered. Reheat over low heat, stirring occasionally.)

Variation: Try subtle and sweet parsnips in this soup for a delicate beige color. Use the same 6 as the carrots.

Cooker Caveats

One small step that makes a big difference in your final results is properly stirring and cooking the flour used as a thickener for a good 2 minutes, until the flour is thoroughly incorporated into the liquid and fully cooked. These few minutes of stirring ensures that your soup won't have the underlying library paste flavor.

Southwest Corn and Sweet Potato Chowder

Bits of bright red bell pepper and the smoky nuances of chipotle chiles add interest to this creamy soup.

3 TB. unsalted butter

1 red bell pepper, seeds and ribs removed, and chopped

1 large onion, peeled and diced

2 garlic cloves, peeled and minced

2 large sweet potatoes, peeled and cut into ½-in. dice

2 (14.5-oz.) cans chicken stock or vegetable stock

3 canned *chipotle chiles* in adobo sauce, finely chopped

1 TB. adobo sauce

1 (15-oz.) can creamed corn

1 cup frozen corn, thawed

2 cups half-and-half

Salt and freshly ground black pepper

Serves: 6 to 8
Prep time: 15 minutes
Minimum cook time: 3½ hours in a medium slow cooker

1. Heat butter in a heavy skillet over medium-high heat. Add red bell pepper, onion, and garlic. Cook, stirring frequently, for 3 minutes or until onion is translucent. Scrape mixture into the slow cooker.

2. Add sweet potatoes, stock, chipotle chiles, and adobo sauce to the slow cooker. Cook on low for 6 to 8 hours or on high for 3 or 4 hours or until potatoes are almost tender.

3. If cooking on low, raise the heat to high. Stir in creamed corn, corn, and half-and-half. Cook for an additional 30 to 40 minutes or until corn is cooked and soup is bubbly. Season with salt and pepper, and serve immediately. (You can do this up to 3 days in advance and refrigerate soup, tightly covered. Reheat over low heat, stirring occasionally, until it comes to a simmer.)

 Slow Speak

Chipotle (*chee-POHT-lay*) are dried jalapeño chiles that have then been smoked. They are canned in a spicy sauce similar to a hot red pepper sauce made from chiles, vinegar, and salt.

Cuban Black Bean Soup

Garlic and aromatic spices like cumin and coriander add sparkle to this thick and hearty soup.

Serves: 4 to 6
Prep time: 15 minutes
Minimum cook time: 4 hours in a medium slow cooker

1 lb. dried black beans

¼ cup olive oil

1 large onion, peeled and diced

1 green bell pepper, seeds and ribs removed, and finely chopped

6 garlic cloves, peeled and minced

1 or 2 jalapeño chiles, seeds removed, and finely diced

1 TB. ground cumin

2 tsp. ground coriander

5 cups chicken stock or vegetable stock

Salt

¼ cup chopped fresh cilantro

Freshly ground black pepper

4 to 6 TB. sour cream (optional)

4 to 6 lime wedges

Cooker Caveats

Some cookbooks tell you to wear rubber gloves when handling hot chiles. That's not really necessary (unless you have sensitive skin), but you do need to take care. I cut the chiles on a glass plate rather than on my cutting board so the volatile oils do not penetrate. What's most important is that you wash your hands thoroughly after handling chiles.

1. Soak beans (see Chapter 2). Drain beans, and discard soaking water.

2. Heat olive oil in a medium skillet over medium heat. Add onion, green bell pepper, garlic, and jalapeño. Cook, stirring frequently, for 3 minutes or until onion is translucent. Reduce the heat to low, and stir in cumin and coriander. Cook, stirring constantly, for 1 minute. Scrape mixture into the slow cooker.

3. Place beans in the slow cooker, and stir in stock. Cook soup on low for 8 to 10 hours or on high for 4 or 5 hours or until beans are soft. Season with salt during the last hour of cooking.

4. Purée soup in a food processor fitted with a steel blade or in a blender. (You can do this up to 3 days in advance and refrigerate soup tightly covered. Reheat over low heat, stirring occasionally.) Stir in cilantro, and season with salt and pepper. Top with a dollop of sour cream, if desired, and serve with lime wedges.

Red Lentil and Carrot Soup

Lentils have an almost meaty texture, and the Indian spices used to flavor them make this a most hearty soup with a vivid orange color.

3 TB. olive oil

2 carrots, peeled and finely chopped

2 garlic cloves, peeled and minced

1 large onion, peeled and finely chopped

1 tsp. ground cumin

1 tsp. ground coriander

1 tsp. turmeric

2 cups red lentils, rinsed

6 cups chicken stock or vegetable stock

1 TB. grated orange *zest*

Salt and freshly ground black pepper

Serves: 6
Prep time: 15 minutes
Minimum cook time: 3 hours in a medium slow cooker

1. Heat olive oil in a medium skillet over medium-high heat. Add carrots, garlic, and onion. Cook, stirring frequently, for 3 minutes or until onion is translucent. Add cumin, coriander, and turmeric. Cook, stirring constantly, for 1 minute. Scrape mixture into the slow cooker.

2. Add lentils, and stir in stock and orange zest. Cook on low for 7 to 9 hours or on high for 3 to 5 hours or until lentils are very soft. Remove 2 cups solids from soup with a slotted spoon. Purée until smooth in a food processor fitted with a steel blade or in a blender.

3. Return purée to the soup, and season soup with salt and pepper. (You can do this up to 3 days in advance and refrigerate soup tightly covered. Reheat over low heat, stirring occasionally.)

Slow Speak

Zest is the very thin, colored coating on citrus fruits that contains the aromatic oils. You can buy a gizmo called a zester that strips off the zest in neat little strips, or you can use the fine side of a box grater to remove it. Just be sure you stay out of the white pith, which can be bitter.

Italian Garbanzo Bean Soup

Zesty tomato and aromatic rosemary add their vibrant flavors to this subtle soup.

Serves: 6
Prep time: 15 minutes
Minimum cook time: 3 hours in a medium slow cooker

3 TB. olive oil

1 large onion, peeled and diced

1 celery rib, rinsed, trimmed, and chopped

3 garlic cloves, peeled and minced

3 cups chicken stock or vegetable stock

1 (14.5-oz.) can petite diced tomatoes, undrained

1½ cups dried garbanzo beans (see Chapter 2) or 2 (15-oz.) cans garbanzo beans, drained and rinsed

2 TB. chopped fresh rosemary or 2 tsp. dried

Salt and crushed red pepper flakes

¾ cup freshly grated Parmesan cheese

1. Heat olive oil in a medium skillet over medium-high heat. Add onion, celery, and garlic, and cook, stirring frequently, for 3 minutes or until onion is translucent. Scrape mixture into the slow cooker.

2. Add stock, tomatoes, garbanzo beans, and rosemary to the slow cooker, and stir well. Cook on low for 6 to 8 hours or on high for 3 or 4 hours or until vegetables are tender. Season with salt and red pepper flakes. (You can do this up to 3 days in advance and refrigerate soup tightly covered. Reheat over low heat, stirring occasionally.)

3. Serve immediately, passing Parmesan cheese separately.

 Slow Savvy

> For a soup like this one, in which the beans are added already cooked, you can always substitute canned beans. In general 1 (15-ounce) can beans contains 2 cups, drained.

Chapter 6

Soups from the Seas

In This Chapter

- ◆ Marvelous mollusks
- ◆ Creative crustaceans
- ◆ Fabulous finfish

From the sun-drenched shores of the Mediterranean coast of France to the rocky coastline of New England, wherever you find water, you'll find great fish soups. Every culture with a coastline has a fish soup that's a national favorite and often a meal in itself. Those are the dishes you'll find in this chapter. All you need to complete dinner is a tossed green salad and perhaps some crusty bread from the same region.

Cooking fish soups in the slow cooker is most often a two-step process because the vegetables and soup base require a much longer cooking time than the seafood. But the majority of the cooking can be done unattended.

Mad for Mollusks

Mollusks, along with crustaceans, are a large family of seafood that ranges from tiny cockles to massive abalone. What they all have in common is that they protect their soft bodies with hard shells.

When selecting mollusks, the most critical consideration is whether they are alive. The shells should be closed or should close tightly when handled. To test a mollusk, with your forefinger above and thumb underneath, gently squeeze the mollusk, as if to push the top shell forward. If the shell doesn't firmly close, discard the mollusk immediately.

Slow Savvy

Removing bivalves from their shells is a labor-intensive process referred to as *shucking*. Increasingly, fish processors are doing this for us. Pints of shucked oysters, scallops by the pound, and minced fresh clams are becoming the rule rather than the exception, so look for preshucked mollusks when you're shopping.

Nantucket Clam Chowder

Fresh herbs and vegetables add flavor and aroma to this classic chowder—and this version was a prize winner on Nantucket!

2 pt. fresh minced clams or 4 (6.5-oz.) cans minced clams	2 large red-skinned potatoes, scrubbed and cut into ½-in. dice
3 TB. unsalted butter	3 TB. chopped fresh parsley
1 large onion, peeled and diced	1 TB. fresh thyme or 1 tsp. dried
3 TB. all-purpose flour	1 bay leaf
2 (8-oz.) bottles clam juice	1 cup half-and-half
2 celery ribs, rinsed, trimmed, and sliced	Salt and freshly ground black pepper

> *Serves: 4 to 6*
>
> **Prep time:** 20 minutes
>
> **Minimum cook time:** 3 hours in a medium slow cooker

1. Drain clams, reserving juice, and refrigerate clams until ready to use.

2. Heat butter in a small skillet over medium heat. Add onion, and cook, stirring frequently, for 3 minutes or until onion is translucent. Reduce the heat to low, and stir in flour. Cook *roux* for 2 minutes, stirring constantly. Raise the heat to medium-high, and stir in 1 bottle clam juice. Bring to a boil, and simmer for 1 minute.

3. Pour mixture into the slow cooker. Stir in remaining 1 bottle clam juice, juice drained from clams, celery, potatoes, parsley, thyme, and bay leaf. Cook on low for 5 to 7 hours or on high for 2½ to 3 hours or until potatoes are almost tender.

4. If cooking on low, raise the heat to high. Stir in clams and half-and-half. Cook for an additional 30 to 40 minutes or until clams are cooked through and soup is bubbly. Remove and discard bay leaf, and season chowder with salt and pepper.

Slow Speak

Roux (pronounced *roo*, like kangaroo) is the French term for flour that is cooked in fat and is used to thicken sauces and soups. For delicate cream sauces, the goal is to keep the mixture white, but it's the deep brown roux that gives Cajun and Creole foods their characteristic nutty taste. A dark roux is made with oil or lard instead of butter because butter would burn long before the right color is reached.

Manhattan Clam Chowder

The Manhattan version of chowder is made with a tomato base but still includes potatoes and other chowder vegetables.

Serves: 4 to 6	
Prep time: 15 minutes	
Minimum cook time: 3 hours in a medium slow cooker	

2 pt. minced fresh clams or 4 (6.5-oz.) cans minced clams

2 TB. bacon fat or vegetable oil

1 large onion, peeled and diced

2 celery ribs, rinsed, trimmed, and diced

1 carrot, peeled and finely chopped

½ green bell pepper, seeds and ribs removed, and finely chopped

2 large red-skinned potatoes, scrubbed and cut into ½-in. dice

6 bacon slices, cooked and crumbled (optional)

1 (28-oz.) can crushed tomatoes

2 (8-oz.) bottles clam juice

3 TB. chopped fresh parsley

1 TB. fresh thyme or 1 tsp. dried

2 tsp. fresh oregano or ½ tsp. dried

1 bay leaf

Salt and freshly ground black pepper

1. Drain clams, reserving juice, and refrigerate clams until ready to use.

2. Heat bacon fat in a medium skillet over medium heat. Add onion, celery, carrot, and green bell pepper. Cook, stirring frequently, for 3 minutes or until onion is translucent and pepper has begun to soften. Scrape mixture into the slow cooker.

3. Add potatoes, bacon (if using), tomatoes, clam juice, juice drained from clams, parsley, thyme, oregano, and bay leaf to the slow cooker. Cook on low for 5 to 7 hours or on high for 2½ to 3 hours or until potatoes are almost tender.

4. If cooking on low, raise the heat to high. Add clams and continue to cook for an additional 30 to 40 minutes or until clams are cooked through. Remove and discard bay leaf, and season chowder with salt and pepper. Serve immediately.

Variation: If you'd prefer finfish to shellfish, cut 1 pound of a firm-fleshed whitefish like cod or halibut into ⅓-inch dice and use that instead of the clams.

Crock Tales

In Melville's *Moby Dick,* Ishmael and Queequeg land on Nantucket and are sent to Hosea Hussey's Try Pots Inn. The name of the inn comes from the iron cauldrons used to melt blubber into whale oil. Melville writes that the two had "chowder for breakfast, chowder for dinner, and chowder for supper."

Caribbean Shrimp Chowder

Spicy chorizo sausage adds its flavor to this zesty stew cooked with healthful orange juice. Serve it over white or brown rice.

2 TB. olive oil

1 large onion, peeled and diced

4 garlic cloves, peeled and minced

1 celery rib, rinsed, trimmed, and thinly sliced

1 carrot, peeled and thinly sliced

½ lb. *chorizo*, finely chopped

5 cups shrimp stock, fish stock, or bottled clam juice

1 cup freshly squeezed orange juice

1 (14.5-oz.) can diced tomatoes, undrained

¼ cup coconut milk

2 tsp. ground cumin

Salt and crushed red pepper flakes

2 lb. extra-large (16 to 20 per lb.) raw shrimp, peeled and deveined

5 cups Swiss chard, rinsed, stemmed, and thinly sliced

¼ cup fresh cilantro, chopped

Serves: 6	
Prep time: 20 minutes	
Minimum cook time: 3 hours in a medium slow cooker	

1. Heat olive oil in a medium skillet over medium-high heat. Add onion, garlic, celery, and carrot. Cook, stirring frequently, for 3 minutes or until onion is translucent. Add chorizo, and cook, stirring frequently, for 2 minutes. Scrape mixture into the slow cooker.

2. Add stock, orange juice, tomatoes, coconut milk, and cumin to the slow cooker. Cook on low for 4 to 6 hours or on high for 2 or 3 hours or until vegetables are almost tender.

3. If cooking on low, raise the heat to high. Season broth with salt and red pepper flakes. Add shrimp, Swiss chard, and cilantro. Cook for 1 hour or until shrimp are cooked through and Swiss chard wilts. Serve immediately.

Variation: Not in a shrimp mood? Try 2 pounds bay scallops or any firm-fleshed whitefish like cod, halibut, or swordfish cut into ¼-inch cubes instead.

Slow Speak

Chorizo (*chore-EAT-zoh*) is a highly seasoned pork sausage flavored with garlic, chili powder, and other spices and used in both Mexican and Spanish cooking. The best substitute is linguiça.

Creole Crab and Corn Chowder

Both corn and crab have inherently sweet flavors, so their pairing in this chowder reflects well on both.

Serves: 6

Prep time: 25 minutes

Minimum cook time: 2½ hours in a medium slow cooker

---

1 lb. crabmeat

2 leeks, white part only

4 TB. unsalted butter

2 celery ribs, rinsed, trimmed, and chopped

1 yellow or orange bell pepper, seeds and ribs removed, and chopped

2 garlic cloves, peeled and minced

1 TB. Creole seasoning

¼ cup all-purpose flour

4 cups seafood stock or bottled clam juice

½ cup dry sherry

2 large red-skinned potatoes, scrubbed and cut into ½-in. dice

1 (8-oz.) can creamed corn

3 TB. chopped fresh parsley

2 tsp. fresh thyme or ½ tsp. dried

1 bay leaf

¾ cup heavy cream

1½ cups fresh corn kernels or frozen corn, thawed

Salt and freshly ground black pepper

1. Place crabmeat on a dark-colored plate, and pick it over gently with your fingertips to discard all shell and cartilage fragments. Refrigerate crab until ready to use.

2. Trim leeks, split lengthwise, and slice thinly. Place leek slices in a colander and rinse well under cold running water, rubbing with your fingers to dislodge all dirt. Shake leeks in the colander.

3. Heat butter in a large skillet over medium-high heat. Add leeks, celery, yellow bell pepper, and garlic. Cook, stirring frequently, for 3 minutes or until leeks are translucent. Add Creole seasoning, and stir for 30 seconds.

4. Reduce the heat to low and stir in flour. Cook, stirring constantly, for 2 minutes. Raise the heat to medium, and whisk in seafood stock and sherry. Bring to a boil, stirring occasionally, and transfer mixture to the slow cooker.

5. Add potatoes, creamed corn, parsley, thyme, and bay leaf to the slow cooker. Cook on low for 4 to 6 hours or on high for 2 or 3 hours or until potatoes are tender.

6. If cooking on low, raise the heat to high. Add crabmeat, cream, and corn. Cook for 20 to 30 minutes or until corn is cooked and chowder is bubbling. Remove and discard bay leaf, and season chowder with salt and pepper. Serve immediately.

Variation: You can use 1 pound small shrimp in this chowder, or to make it vegetarian, use 1 pound yellow squash, cut into ¼-inch dice and substitute vegetable stock. Add any of these foods at the same time you'd add the crab.

Slow Savvy

Shrimp are sold both raw and cooked, but crabmeat is only sold cooked. That's why it's always added at the end of the cooking time; it basically just heats up and absorbs flavor from the soup or sauce it's in.

San Francisco Seafood Soup (Cioppino)

If you're looking for a seafood dish to serve with a light red wine, this is the one. Serve it with thick slices of garlic toast to mop up the broth.

1½ lb. red snapper, halibut, or any firm-fleshed whitefish

1 lb. king crab leg, thawed if frozen

½ lb. extra-large (16 to 20 per lb.) raw shrimp

3 TB. olive oil

2 medium onions, peeled and diced

1 red bell pepper, seeds and ribs removed, and finely chopped

2 celery ribs, rinsed, trimmed, and diced

3 garlic cloves, peeled and minced

2 TB. chopped fresh oregano or 2 tsp. dried

2 tsp. fresh thyme or ½ tsp. dried

1 (28-oz.) can diced tomatoes, undrained

1½ cups dry red wine

1 (8-oz.) bottle clam juice

2 TB. tomato paste

1 bay leaf

Salt and freshly ground black pepper

¼ cup chopped fresh parsley

3 TB. chopped fresh basil or 2 tsp. dried

Serves: 6
Prep time: 25 minutes
Minimum cook time: 3 hours in a medium slow cooker

1. Rinse fish and pat dry with paper towels. Remove and discard any skin or bones, and cut fish into 1-inch cubes. Hack crab leg into 2-inch pieces with a large, heavy knife. Peel and devein shrimp. Refrigerate all seafood until ready to use, covered with plastic wrap.

2. Heat olive oil in a medium skillet over medium-high heat. Add onions, red bell pepper, celery, garlic, oregano, and thyme. Cook, stirring frequently, for 3 minutes or until onions are translucent. Scrape mixture into the slow cooker.

3. Add tomatoes, wine, clam juice, tomato paste, and bay leaf to the slow cooker, and stir well to dissolve tomato paste. Cook on low for 5 to 7 hours or on high for 2½ to 3 hours or until vegetables are almost tender. Season broth with salt and pepper.

4. If cooking on low, raise the heat to high. Add seafood, parsley, and basil. Cook for 30 to 45 minutes or until fish is cooked through. Serve immediately.

Variation: To keep this a shellfish-only stew, use 1½ pounds sea scallops instead of red snapper.

Crock Tales

Like many seafood soups, this one was born as a way to use up the bits and pieces of the day's catch. In the San Francisco area, it's a Christmas Eve tradition within the Italian community because it can contain the "Seven Fishes" that are part of the tradition, and it comes at the high point of the Dungeness crab season.

Provençal Fish Soup

Orange juice is part of the broth, so this is a soup that appeals even to people who don't like "fishy food" because its sweetness covers up some of the inherent fish taste.

1½ lb. halibut, swordfish, or any firm-fleshed whitefish

½ lb. large (21 to 30 per lb.) raw shrimp

¼ cup olive oil

1 large onion, peeled and diced

2 garlic cloves, peeled and minced

1 TB. paprika

1 celery rib, rinsed, trimmed, and sliced

1 carrot, peeled and sliced

2 large potatoes, peeled and cut into ½-in. dice

1 (14.5-oz.) can diced tomatoes, undrained

3 cups seafood stock or bottled clam juice

1 cup dry white wine

½ cup freshly squeezed orange juice

2 TB. chopped fresh parsley

1 TB. fresh thyme or 1 tsp. dried

1 TB. grated orange zest

Salt and freshly ground black pepper

4 to 6 thick slices of toasted French or Italian bread

Serves: 4 to 6	
Prep time: 25 minutes	
Minimum cook time: 3½ hours in a medium slow cooker	

1. Rinse fish and pat dry with paper towels. Remove and discard any skin or bones, and cut fish into 1-inch cubes. Peel and devein shrimp. Refrigerate fish and shrimp until ready to use, covered with plastic wrap.

2. Heat olive oil in a medium skillet over medium heat. Add onion and garlic, and cook, stirring frequently, for 3 minutes or until onion is translucent. Reduce the heat to low, and stir in paprika. Stir for 1 minute, and scrape mixture into the slow cooker.

3. Add celery, carrot, potatoes, tomatoes, stock, wine, orange juice, parsley, thyme, and orange zest to the slow cooker. Cook on low for 6 to 8 hours or on high for 3 or 4 hours or until vegetables are tender.

Cooker Caveats

It's important to refrigerate fish or seafood destined for the slow cooker. The length of time it would sit at room temperature before being cooked would place it in the "danger zone" of food safety.

4. If cooking on low, raise the heat to high. Add fish and shrimp to the slow cooker, and cook for 20 to 40 minutes or until fish is just cooked through. Season with salt and pepper. To serve, ladle soup over slices of toast.

Variation: Clams, oysters, scallops, shrimp, and stronger fish such as tuna all work well in this dish if you want to add or substitute. Keep fish at least ¾ inch thick.

⊂~

Curried Fish Soup

The creaminess in this lightly seasoned broth comes from flavorful coconut milk, and the seasonings give it a lovely yellow color.

Serves: 4 to 6
Prep time: 15 minutes
Minimum cook time: 3½ hours in a medium slow cooker

1½ lb. cod, halibut, swordfish, seas bass, or any firm-fleshed whitefish

2 TB. sesame oil

1 large onion, peeled and chopped

½ red bell pepper, seeds and ribs removed, and chopped

2 garlic cloves, peeled and minced

2 TB. grated fresh ginger

2 TB. freshly squeezed lemon juice

1 TB. ground coriander

1 TB. turmeric

1 TB. *curry powder*

3 cups seafood stock or bottled clam juice

¼ cup slivered almonds

1 cup coconut milk

1 (10-oz.) pkg. frozen cut green beans, thawed

Salt and cayenne

3 cups cooked white rice

½ cup chutney

¼ cup raisins

4 scallions, trimmed and thinly sliced

¼ cup grated sweetened coconut

1. Rinse fish and pat dry with paper towels. Remove and discard any skin or bones, and cut fish into 1-inch cubes. Refrigerate fish until ready to use, covered with plastic wrap.

2. Heat sesame oil in a medium skillet over medium heat. Add onion, red bell pepper, and garlic. Cook, stirring frequently, for 3 minutes or until onion is translucent. Scrape mixture into the slow cooker. Stir in ginger, lemon juice, coriander, turmeric, curry powder, and stock.

3. Cook on low for 5 or 6 hours or on high for 2½ to 3 hours or until mixture is bubbly and onions are soft.

4. While soup is cooking, toast almonds. Preheat the oven to 350°F. Spread almonds in a single layer on a cookie sheet, and bake for 5 minutes or until browned. Set aside.

5. If cooking on low, raise the heat to high. Stir in coconut milk, fish, and green beans. Cook on high for 1 hour or until soup is simmering and fish is cooked through. Season with salt and cayenne. Serve spooned over rice. Pass chutney, raisins, scallions, coconut, and toasted almonds separately.

Variation: Try turning this into a poultry soup by using 1½ pounds chicken or turkey cut into ½-inch cubes and also chicken stock. Add the poultry at the beginning of the cooking process.

Slow Speak

Curry powder is a blend of up to 20 spices, including dried red chiles, coriander seed, fenugreek seed, mustard seed, ground ginger, and cinnamon. The yellow color comes from turmeric.

Spanish Fish Soup with Potatoes, Greens, and Aioli (*Caldo de Perro*)

Swiss chard adds color and texture to this soup, and the garlicky topping enriches the flavorful broth.

> *Serves: 4 to 6*
>
> **Prep time:** 20 minutes
> **Minimum cook time:**
> 3½ hours in a medium
> slow cooker

1½ lb. halibut, cod, monkfish, snapper, sea bass, or any firm-fleshed whitefish

2 TB. olive oil

2 onions, peeled and diced

7 garlic cloves, peeled

4 cups fish stock or bottled clam juice

½ cup dry white wine

2 TB. freshly squeezed lemon juice

1 lb. red-skinned potatoes, scrubbed and cut into ½-in. dice

2 TB. chopped fresh parsley

1 tsp. dried thyme

1 bay leaf

½ lb. Swiss chard

Salt and freshly ground black pepper

½ cup mayonnaise

4 garlic cloves, peeled and crushed

1 tsp. grated lemon zest

4 to 6 thick slices of toasted French or Italian bread

1. Rinse fish and pat dry with paper towels. Remove and discard any skin or bones, and cut fish into 1-inch cubes. Refrigerate fish until ready to use, covered with plastic wrap.

2. Heat olive oil in a small skillet over medium heat. Add onions and garlic. Cook, stirring frequently, for 3 minutes or until onion is translucent. Scrape mixture into the slow cooker.

3. Add stock, wine, lemon juice, potatoes, parsley, thyme, and bay leaf to the slow cooker. Cook on low for 6 to 8 hours or on high for 3 or 4 hours or until potatoes are tender.

4. While soup is cooking, prepare Swiss chard. Rinse leaves and discard stems, and cut leaves crosswise into ½-inch slices.

5. If cooking on low, increase the heat to high. Add fish and Swiss chard. Cook for 20 to 45 minutes or until fish is just cooked through. Season with salt and pepper, and discard bay leaf.

6. Mix mayonnaise with garlic and lemon zest in a small bowl. Ladle soup over toast slices, and pass *aioli* separately.

Variation: This recipe works as well with seafood as with fish. Use extra-large shrimp, sea scallops, or some combination.

 Slow Speak

Aioli is a garlicky mayonnaise sauce that hails from Provence.

Asian Red Snapper Soup

This light and healthful soup is faster to make than most because the Asian vegetables are meant to remain crisp and, thus, don't have to cook as long.

1½ lb. red snapper or other firm-fleshed whitefish such as halibut or cod

2 TB. Asian sesame oil

4 scallions, rinsed, trimmed, and chopped

3 garlic cloves, peeled and minced

2 TB. grated fresh ginger

3 baby bok choy, rinsed, trimmed, and cut into quarters

2 carrots, peeled and thinly sliced

2 celery ribs, rinsed, trimmed, and sliced

4 cups seafood stock or bottled clam juice

1 cup coconut milk

2 TB. oyster sauce

2 TB. soy sauce

2 tsp. *Chinese chili paste with garlic*

⅓ cup half-and-half

¼ cup chopped fresh cilantro leaves

Salt and freshly ground black pepper

6 TB. black sesame seeds (optional)

> *Serves: 6*
>
> **Prep time:** 20 minutes
> **Minimum cook time:** 2 hours in a medium slow cooker

1. Rinse fish and pat dry with paper towels. Remove and discard any skin or bones, and cut fish into 1-inch cubes. Refrigerate fish until ready to use, covered with plastic wrap.

2. Heat sesame oil in a small skillet over medium-high heat. Add scallions, garlic, and ginger. Cook, stirring constantly, for 1 minute or until fragrant. Scrape mixture into the slow cooker.

3. Add snapper, bok choy, carrots, celery, stock, coconut milk, oyster sauce, soy sauce, and Chinese chili paste to the slow cooker, and stir well. Cook on low for 3 to 5 hours or on high for 1½ to 2 hours or until fish is cooked through.

4. If cooking on low, raise the heat to high. Add half-and-half and cilantro to the slow cooker. Cook for 30 minutes or until bubbling. Season with salt and pepper, and serve immediately, garnished with sesame seeds (if using).

Variation: This recipe is also delicious as a pork soup. Use pork tenderloin, trimmed and cut into ½-inch dice, and substitute chicken stock for the seafood stock.

Slow Speak

Chinese chili paste with garlic is a fiery thick paste made from fermented fava beans, red chiles, and garlic. It's available in jars in the Asian aisle of supermarkets.

Chapter 7

Poultry Soups Around the World

In This Chapter

- ◆ International noodle soups
- ◆ Soups with poultry meatballs
- ◆ Varied vegetable soups

More than just an old wives' tale, medical proof exists that there's curative value to chicken soup. But for centuries, we've known that steaming soups made with poultry are the quintessential comfort food, and those are the recipes you'll find in this chapter.

Chicken soups are part of every cuisine, and they can take different forms. Most of these soups contain nuggets of chicken or turkey, but in some, I've included poultry meatballs that float in the broth.

Because poultry is so delicate in flavor, almost any seasoning is compatible. You'll find everything from delicate Italian fare to assertive Mexican flair amongst these soups.

Versatile Veggies

Sturdy vegetables like carrots, potatoes, and celery are staples for the soup pot and, by extension, the slow cooker. And believe it or not, it takes longer for these vegetables to cook in the slow cooker than it takes most meats or chicken. When prepping hard vegetables, peel and trim them as usual and then cut them into bite-size pieces so they'll cook faster.

Add more delicate vegetables like green beans, peas, and snow peas for the last hour of the cooking time. If you're anxious to serve food as soon as you walk in the door, it's better to cook these tender vegetables in the microwave and then stir them into the slow cooker. If they cook for the whole time, they will be an unappealing gray color and very mushy.

You'll see that in most recipes one of the first steps is to *sauté* the onions and garlic before being adding them to the slow cooker. This preliminary cooking makes the onions and garlic sweeter and less sharp. (I've skipped this step in recipes where this doesn't matter.)

Slow Speak _____

Sauté is a common cooking term taken from French. It literally means "to jump." The idea is to keep food moving in the pan by stirring it frequently, if not constantly. Sautéed food is cooked in a little hot fat in a shallow pan over medium-high or high heat. This causes the food to release its natural sugars and intensify in flavor.

Mediterranean Chicken and Vegetable Soup

This chicken soup has all the hallmarks of Italian cooking, including a wide range of vegetables and pasta.

3 (6-oz.) boneless, skinless chicken breast halves

3 TB. olive oil

1 large onion, peeled and diced

3 garlic cloves, peeled and minced

5 cups chicken stock

1 (14.5-oz.) can diced tomatoes, drained

1 TB. tomato paste

1 carrot, peeled and sliced

2 celery ribs, trimmed and sliced

1 TB. dried oregano

1 (10-oz.) pkg. frozen lima beans, thawed

1 (10-oz.) pkg. frozen Italian-style green beans, thawed

2 cups cooked small pasta, such as macaroni or small shells

Salt and freshly ground black pepper

> *Serves: 4 to 6*
>
> **Prep time:** 15 minutes
> **Minimum cook time:** 3 hours in a medium slow cooker

1. Rinse chicken and pat dry with paper towels. Trim chicken of all visible fat, and cut into ½-inch cubes. Set aside.

2. Heat olive oil in a medium skillet over medium heat. Add onion and garlic, and cook, stirring frequently, for 3 minutes or until onion is translucent. Scrape mixture into the slow cooker. Stir in stock, tomatoes, tomato paste, chicken, carrot, celery, and oregano. Stir well.

3. Cook on low for 6 to 8 hours or on high for 3 or 4 hours. Add lima beans and green beans during the last hour of cooking. Once beans are cooked, stir in cooked pasta, and continue to cook until pasta is hot. Season with salt and pepper, and serve immediately.

Variation: Feel free to experiment with the vegetables in this soup. You can add zucchini or yellow squash, as well as any sort of canned beans. You can also omit the chicken and use vegetable stock for a vegetarian feast.

 Cooker Caveats

Don't add green vegetables to slow cooked dishes until the last hour of cooking. These tender foods will take on a dull, gray-green color and mushy texture if they're added sooner. Also, frozen vegetables, once thawed, have already been partially cooked, so a brief time in the slow cooker is all they need.

Mexican Tortilla Soup

The vegetables for this soup's broth are puréed to create a complex flavor profile. The crispy strips of fried tortilla on top add some fun texture.

Serves: 4 to 6	
Prep time: 25 minutes	
Minimum cook time: 3 hours in a medium slow cooker	

3 boneless, skinless chicken breast halves, or 6 boneless, skinless chicken thighs

2 TB. olive oil

2 medium onions, peeled and diced

4 garlic cloves, peeled and minced

1 TB. dried oregano

1 TB. dried basil

2 tsp. ground cumin

1 (14.5-oz.) can diced tomatoes

5 cups chicken stock

2 TB. tomato paste

1 celery rib, rinsed, trimmed, and sliced

1 small zucchini, rinsed, trimmed and cut into ¾-in. dice

1 carrot, peeled and sliced

1 medium potato, peeled and cut into ½-in. dice

Salt and freshly ground black pepper

½ cup vegetable oil

4 corn tortillas, cut into ½-in. strips

1 ripe avocado, peeled and diced

⅔ cup grated Monterey Jack cheese

1. Rinse chicken and pat dry with paper towels. Trim chicken of all visible fat, and cut into ½-inch cubes. Set aside.

2. Heat olive oil in a large skillet over medium heat. Add onions and garlic, and cook, stirring frequently, for 3 minutes or until onions are translucent. Add oregano, basil, and cumin. Cook for 1 minute, stirring constantly. Add tomatoes and stir well.

3. Transfer mixture to a food processor fitted with a steel blade or a blender and purée. Scrape purée back into the slow cooker, and add stock and tomato paste. Stir well.

4. Add diced chicken, celery, zucchini, carrot, and potato to the slow cooker. Cook on low for 6 to 8 hours or on high for 3 or 4 hours or until chicken is cooked through and no longer pink and potatoes are tender. Season with salt and pepper.

5. About 30 minutes before soup is finished, heat vegetable oil in a medium skillet over high heat. Add tortilla strips, and fry until crisp. Remove strips from the pan with a slotted spoon, and drain on paper towels.

6. To serve, ladle soup into bowls, and garnish each serving with fried tortilla strips, avocado, and cheese.

Slow Savvy

Like potatoes and apples, avocados turn brown when exposed to air. It's best to peel and dice this delicate fruit just before eating it. If you're only using half, keep the pit in the unused half and coat the cut surface with lemon juice to keep it green.

Old-Fashioned Chicken Noodle Soup

Now this soup is what Grandma had in mind for that cold! Thick with healthful vegetables, it's perfect for any winter night to keep from getting the cold, too.

Serves: 4 to 6
Prep time: 15 minutes
Minimum cook time: 3 hours in a medium slow cooker

2 boneless, skinless chicken breast halves or 4 boneless, skinless chicken thighs

3 TB. unsalted butter

2 medium onions, peeled and diced

2 garlic cloves, peeled and minced

5 cups chicken stock

1 carrot, peeled and sliced

1 parsnip, peeled and sliced, or 1 additional carrot

1 celery rib, trimmed and sliced

2 ripe tomatoes, rinsed, cored, seeded, and diced

2 TB. chopped fresh parsley

1 TB. fresh thyme or 1 tsp. dried

1 bay leaf

Salt and freshly ground black pepper

1 cup frozen peas, thawed

2 cups cooked egg noodles

 Slow Savvy

Although bay leaves add a pungent and woodsy flavor and aroma to dishes, they can be quite a bitter mouthful if you accidentally eat one, so be sure to remove them before serving. That's also why bay leaves are always added whole. If they were broken into pieces, it would be a real scavenger hunt to retrieve them.

1. Rinse chicken and pat dry with paper towels. Trim chicken of all visible fat, and cut into ½-inch cubes. Set aside.

2. Heat butter in a medium skillet over medium heat. Add onions and garlic, and cook, stirring frequently, for 3 minutes or until onion is translucent. Scrape mixture into the slow cooker.

3. Add chicken, stock, carrot, parsnip, celery, tomatoes, parsley, thyme, and bay leaf to the slow cooker, and stir well. Cook on low for 6 to 8 hours or on high for 3 or 4 hours or until chicken is cooked through and no longer pink and vegetables are tender. Remove and discard bay leaf, and season with salt and pepper.

4. If cooking on low, raise the heat to high. Add peas and egg noodles. Cook an additional 15 to 20 minutes or until soup is bubbling. Serve immediately.

Variation: There's almost an infinite list of vegetables you can include in Chicken Noodle Soup, and feel free to use up the leftovers from the night before, too. Add corn kernels, green beans, lima beans, or even asparagus tips.

Chinese Chicken Noodle Soup

By cutting the chicken into thin slices, it cooks through while the cabbage retains some texture in this Asian version of the classic soup.

3 (6-oz.) boneless, skinless chicken breast halves	6 cups chicken stock
3 TB. soy sauce	2 TB. tahini
2 TB. dry sherry	1 TB. rice wine vinegar
2 TB. Asian sesame oil	1 TB. granulated sugar
1 TB. vegetable oil	1 tsp. Chinese chili paste with garlic
4 scallions, rinsed, trimmed, and sliced	2 cups cooked Chinese noodles or medium egg noodles
3 garlic cloves, peeled and minced	3 TB. chopped fresh cilantro
1 TB. grated fresh ginger	Salt and freshly ground black pepper
4 cups chopped Napa or bok choy cabbage	

> *Serves: 4 to 6*
>
> **Prep time:** 20 minutes
> **Minimum cook time:** 2½ hours in a medium slow cooker

1. Rinse chicken and pat dry with paper towels. Trim chicken of all visible fat, and cut into very thin slices. Place chicken into the slow cooker, and toss it with soy sauce, sherry, and 1 tablespoon sesame oil.

2. Heat remaining 1 tablespoon sesame oil and vegetable oil in a small skillet over medium-high heat. Add scallions, garlic, and ginger. Cook, stirring constantly, for 30 seconds or until fragrant. Scrape mixture into the slow cooker.

3. Add cabbage, stock, tahini, vinegar, sugar, and chili paste to the slow cooker, and stir well. Cook on low for 4½ to 6 hours or on high for 2¼ to 3 hours or until chicken is cooked through and no longer pink.

4. If cooking on low, raise the heat to high. Add noodles and cilantro to soup, and season with salt and pepper. Cook for an additional 15 to 20 minutes or until noodles are heated through and soup is bubbly. Serve immediately.

Variation: Try this soup with either raw duck breast or trimmed pork tenderloin. The cooking time will be the same.

 Cooker Caveats

Regardless of brand, tahini has a tendency to separate with the sesame oil rising to the top and the paste setting below. Be sure to stir it well before measuring.

Chicken Soup with Fennel and Escarole

The licorice flavor of fresh fennel is reinforced by fennel seeds in this healthful and easy Italian chicken soup.

Serves: 4 to 6	
Prep time: 20 minutes	
Minimum cook time: 3 hours in a medium slow cooker	

3 (6-oz.) boneless, skinless chicken breast halves

1 *fennel* bulb

3 TB. olive oil

2 large onions, peeled and diced

3 garlic cloves, peeled and minced

5 cups chicken stock

1 (14.5-oz.) can diced tomatoes, undrained

2 tsp. fennel seed, crushed

1 head escarole

Salt and freshly ground black pepper

½ cup freshly grated Parmesan cheese

Slow Speak

Fennel is a plant native to the Mediterranean that looks like celery and has a mild anise flavor. It's called *finocchio* in Italian markets, but it's also called *fresh anise* in many supermarkets. The stalks can be used raw in place of celery in salads, and the bulb is usually cooked at least partially.

1. Rinse chicken and pat dry with paper towels. Trim chicken of all visible fat, and cut into ½-inch cubes. Rinse fennel and cut in half lengthwise. Discard core and all but 3 inches of ribs. Slice remaining ribs and dice bulb into ¾-inch pieces. Place chicken and fennel into the slow cooker.

2. Heat olive oil in a medium skillet over medium-high heat. Add onions and garlic, and cook, stirring frequently, for 3 minutes or until onions are translucent. Scrape mixture into the slow cooker. Stir stock, tomatoes, and fennel seed into the slow cooker, and stir well. Cook on low for 5 to 7 hours or on high for 2½ to 3 hours or until chicken is cooked through and no longer pink.

3. While soup is cooking, rinse escarole and discard core. Slice escarole into strips 1 inch wide.

4. If cooking on low, raise the heat to high. Add escarole to the slow cooker, and cook for an additional 30 to 40 minutes or until escarole is wilted. Season with salt and pepper, and serve immediately, passing cheese separately.

Mexican Meatball Soup (Sopa Albondigas)

Cornmeal gives these hearty turkey balls texture, and the chili powder in the broth underscores the Mexican nature of this soup.

1½ lb. lean ground turkey

¼ cup yellow cornmeal

¼ cup milk

1 large egg, lightly beaten

2 TB. chili powder

Salt and freshly ground black pepper

2 TB. olive oil

1 large onion, peeled and diced

4 garlic cloves, peeled and minced

1 tsp. ground cumin

½ tsp. dried oregano

1 (28-oz.) can diced tomatoes, undrained

3 cups chicken stock

½ cup refrigerated commercial tomato salsa

2 TB. chopped fresh cilantro

> *Serves: 4 to 6*
>
> **Prep time:** 20 minutes
> **Minimum cook time:**
> 3 hours in a medium slow cooker

1. Preheat the oven to 500°F. Line a broiler pan with heavy-duty aluminum foil, and grease the foil with vegetable oil spray or vegetable oil.

2. Combine turkey, cornmeal, milk, egg, 1 tablespoon chili powder, salt, and pepper in a mixing bowl, and mix well. Form mixture into 1-inch balls, and place them on the greased foil. Brown meatballs in the oven for 10 minutes or until lightly browned.

3. While meatballs are browning, heat olive oil in a medium skillet over medium heat. Add onion and garlic, and cook, stirring frequently, for 3 minutes or until onion is translucent. Reduce the heat to low, and stir in remaining 1 tablespoon chili powder, cumin, and oregano. Cook for 1 minute.

4. Scrape mixture into the slow cooker. Stir in tomatoes, stock, salsa, and cilantro. Stir well. Transfer meatballs to the slow cooker with a slotted spoon. Cook on low for 6 to 8 hours or on high for 3 or 4 hours or until meatballs are cooked through. Season with salt and pepper, and serve immediately.

Cooker Caveats

Refrigerated salsa, usually found in the produce section, is like the good stuff you make yourself—but easier because it's already made for you! Don't substitute the bottled stuff you can find in the aisle with the Mexican foods. It just won't taste as good.

Chinese Hot and Sour Duck Soup

Different varieties of dried mushrooms make this rich soup visually appealing. Serve it over white rice.

Serves: 4 to 6
Prep time: 20 minutes
Minimum cook time: 3 hours in a medium slow cooker

1 oz. dried *black tree fungus mushrooms*

½ oz. dried *lily buds*

6 large dried shiitake mushrooms

1 cup hot tap water

1 lb. boneless duck breast

5 cups chicken stock

½ lb. firm tofu, well drained and cut into ½-in. dice

1 (8-oz.) can sliced water chestnuts, drained and rinsed

¼ cup rice wine vinegar

2 TB. soy sauce

1 TB. Asian sesame oil

½ tsp. Chinese chili oil

3 TB. cornstarch

2 TB. cold water

2 large eggs, lightly beaten

2 scallions, rinsed, trimmed, and thinly sliced

1. Soak black tree fungus mushrooms, lily buds, and shiitake mushrooms in hot water for 10 minutes, pressing mushrooms down to keep them submerged.

2. Discard skin and fat from duck breast, and cut into ½-inch slices. Cut slices into thin shreds. Place duck into the slow cooker.

3. Remove mushrooms from the cup, and strain liquid through a coffee filter into the slow cooker. Rinse mushrooms well to remove any grit. Discard stems from shiitake mushrooms, and slice shiitake and black tree fungus mushrooms into thin slices; leave lily buds whole. Add mushrooms and lily buds to the slow cooker.

4. Add stock, tofu, water chestnuts, vinegar, soy sauce, sesame oil, and chili oil to the slow cooker. Cook on low for 6 to 8 hours or on high for 3 or 4 hours or until duck is cooked through.

5. If cooking on low, raise the heat to high. Combine cornstarch and cold water in a small cup, and stir cornstarch mixture into soup. Cook on high for 10 to 20 minutes or until liquid has thickened and is bubbly.

6. Stir eggs into soup, and continue to stir so eggs form thin strands. Cover the pan and bring soup back to a simmer. Serve over rice, garnished with scallion slices.

Variation: You can use pork tenderloin or chicken in this recipe instead of duck. The cooking time will be the same.

Slow Speak

Black tree fungus and lily buds are dried mushrooms traditionally used in hot and sour soup. Find them in the Asian food aisle of some supermarkets or in Asian markets. If you can't find them, use dried shiitake mushrooms.

Italian Wedding Soup

Delicate turkey meatballs moistened with mozzarella cheese float in this broth laced with spinach, fennel, and orzo.

Serves: 6
Prep time: 25 minutes
Minimum cook time: 3 hours in a medium slow cooker

2 large eggs, lightly beaten

⅓ cup Italian breadcrumbs

¼ cup milk

¼ cup grated mozzarella cheese

5 garlic cloves, peeled and minced

1½ lb. lean ground turkey

Salt and freshly ground black pepper

6 cups chicken stock

1 fennel bulb, rinsed, trimmed, and thinly sliced

1 (10-oz.) pkg. frozen whole-leaf spinach, thawed

¾ cup uncooked orzo or other small pasta

1. Preheat the oven to 500°F. Line a broiler pan with heavy-duty aluminum foil, and grease the foil with vegetable oil spray or vegetable oil.

2. Place eggs, breadcrumbs, milk, cheese, and 2 minced garlic cloves into a mixing bowl, and stir well. Add turkey, mix well, and season with salt and pepper. Form mixture into 1-inch balls, and place them on the greased foil. Brown meatballs in the oven for 10 minutes or until lightly browned. Transfer meatballs to the slow cooker with a slotted spoon.

3. Add stock to the slow cooker along with fennel and garlic. Cook on low for 6 to 8 hours or on high for 3 or 4 hours or until meatballs are cooked through and fennel is soft.

4. If cooking on low, raise the heat to high. Place spinach into a strainer, and press with the back of a spoon to extract as much liquid as possible. Add spinach and orzo to the slow cooker. Cook on high for 20 to 30 minutes or until orzo is cooked *al dente*. Season with salt and pepper.

Variation: Want a heartier soup? Try making the meatballs with beef or a combination of beef and veal.

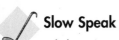

Slow Speak

Al dente literally means "against the teeth" in Italian. In cooking, it means that pasta or rice is cooked to the point that it's still chewy. It's that magical point between hard and mushy.

Chapter 8

Soups for Carnivore Cravings

In This Chapter

- Hearty beef soups
- Rich and filling lamb soups
- Pork, ham, and sausage soups

These recipes you'll find in this chapter are for filling soups for a cold winter night. When cooked in the slow cooker, you'll have hours while the soups simmer to anticipate the flavor and joy of the final dish. You'll find cuisines around the world represented, from Italian to Chinese, too.

Many of these soups contain heart-healthy beans. Because meat soups take a long time to cook and have the meat reach total tenderness, meats and beans—which also need a while to cook—seem to go well together, as you'll see when cooking these recipes.

"Meating" the Challenge

It's a happy coincidence that the cuts of meat best suited for slow cooking are also the least expensive ones. Even when set on high, a slow cooker is still cool enough to slowly convert the meat's connective tissue from collagen to gelatin. (That's why slow cooked meat is described as "fork-tender.")

The well-*marbled* meat with the collagen comes from the parts of the animals that get the most exercise. Imagine you're running around in a field. Your leg muscles get much more of a workout than your back muscles. And if you're running around on four legs, you can count your front legs and shoulders amongst those well-used muscles, too.

When shopping for meat destined for your slow cooker, look for, shanks, shoulder, round, and rump. Even if they're not labeled as such, you'll know you've selected the proper slow cooker cuts when you compare the price of these cuts with cuts such as tenderloin, sirloin, and rib. And there's no need to go for the high-priced Prime grade meats. Choice and Standard quality are just fine.

The Benefits of Browning

Whether or not to brown meat before putting it in the slow cooker is a matter of choice. I suggest it for all ground meat because browning also rids the meat of inherent fat and keeps it from clumping. This has to be done in a skillet on the stove.

If you're preparing a stew or roast, you can brown the meat under a preheated oven broiler in a broiler pan lined with aluminum foil. Turn the meat so it browns on all sides. The juices that seep out go into the pot and add flavor to the dish. Brown all beef and lamb before slow cooking. Browning adds a rich color to both the meat and the finished sauce. Browning is optional for pork, veal, and chicken. These lighter foods absorb color from the sauce.

Sweet and Sour Beef and Cabbage Soup

This hearty soup dotted with zesty raisins and dried currants is good ladled over cooked egg noodles.

1 small head green cabbage (about 1½ lb.)

1½ lb. stewing beef

¼ cup vegetable oil

1 large onion, peeled and diced

3 garlic cloves, peeled and minced

6 cups beef stock

1 (14.5-oz.) can diced tomatoes, undrained

¼ cup cider vinegar

¼ cup firmly packed dark brown sugar

¼ cup golden raisins

¼ cup dried currants

1 tsp. dried thyme

1 bay leaf

Salt and freshly ground black pepper

Serves: 4 to 6
Prep time: 25 minutes
Minimum cook time: 4 hours in a medium slow cooker

1. Rinse and core cabbage. Shred cabbage, and set aside.

2. Preheat the oven broiler, and line a broiler pan with heavy-duty aluminum foil.

3. Rinse beef and pat dry with paper towels. Cut beef into 1-inch cubes, if necessary, and arrange on the broiler pan. Broil cubes for 3 minutes per side or until browned. Spoon meat into the slow cooker, along with any juices that have collected in the pan.

4. Heat oil in a medium skillet over medium-high heat. Add onion and garlic, and cook, stirring frequently, for 3 minutes or until onion is translucent. Scrape mixture into the slow cooker.

5. Add cabbage, stock, tomatoes, vinegar, brown sugar, raisins, currants, thyme, and bay leaf. Stir well. Cook on low for 8 to 10 hours or on high for 4 or 5 hours or until meat is tender. Remove and discard bay leaf, and season soup with salt and pepper. (You can do this up to 3 days in advance and refrigerate soup tightly covered. Reheat over low heat, stirring occasionally.)

Variation: Want to make this a vegetarian dish? Omit the beef, use vegetable stock, and add 2 (15-ounce) cans white beans, drained and rinsed, for the last hour of cooking.

Slow Savvy

When cooking bulky foods like cabbage, chances are good that not all the cabbage will be covered with broth at the beginning of the cooking process. About midway through, push it down; by then, it'll have wilted considerably.

Italian Beef, Vegetable, and Pasta Soup (*Minestrone*)

This thick and rich soup contains a cornucopia of vegetables as well as pasta. It's a delicious and well-balanced meal.

Serves: 6
Prep time: 25 minutes
Minimum cook time: 4 hours in a medium slow cooker

1½ lb. stewing beef

2 TB. olive oil

1 large onion, peeled and diced

3 garlic cloves, peeled and minced

1½ cups shredded green cabbage

1 (28-oz.) can diced tomatoes, undrained

3 cups beef stock or chicken stock

1 carrot, peeled and thinly sliced

1 celery rib, rinsed, trimmed, and sliced

1 tsp. dried thyme

1 tsp. dried oregano

1 bay leaf

2 small zucchini, rinsed, trimmed, and cut into ½-in. dice

1 (10-oz.) pkg. frozen Italian green beans, thawed

1 (15-oz.) can white cannellini beans, drained and rinsed

½ cup small elbow macaroni or small pasta shells

Salt and freshly ground black pepper

Freshly grated Parmesan cheese

1. Preheat the oven broiler, and line a broiler pan with heavy-duty aluminum foil.

2. Rinse beef and pat dry with paper towels. Cut beef into 1-inch cubes, if necessary, and arrange on the broiler pan. Broil cubes for 3 minutes per side or until browned. Spoon meat into the slow cooker along with any juices that have collected in the pan.

3. Heat olive oil in a medium skillet over medium-high heat. Add onion and garlic, and cook, stirring frequently, for 3 minutes or until onion is translucent. Scrape mixture into the slow cooker.

4. Add cabbage, tomatoes, stock, carrot, celery, thyme, oregano, and bay leaf to the slow cooker. Cook on low for 6 to 8 hours or on high for 3 or 4 hours or until vegetables are tender.

5. If cooking on low, raise the heat to high. Stir in zucchini, green beans, cannellini beans, and pasta. Cook for 1 to 1½ hours or until pasta is cooked. Remove and discard bay leaf, season with salt and pepper, and serve soup topped with grated Parmesan cheese.

Crock Tales

If you think this hearty Italian soup changes from pot to pot, you're right. *Minestrone* is the Italian word for "big soup"; it comes from the Latin *ministro,* which means "to serve." As a big soup, it always contains a number of different vegetables, depending on what the chef has on hand or what's in season.

Beef, Mushroom, and Barley Soup

The combination of fresh white mushrooms and woodsy dried mushrooms creates an intense flavor to match the heartiness of the beef.

Serves: 6
Prep time: 25 minutes
Minimum cook time: 4 hours in a medium slow cooker

½ oz. dried *porcini* mushrooms

1 cup hot water

1½ lb. stewing beef

2 TB. unsalted butter

2 TB. vegetable oil

1 large onion, peeled and diced

1 celery rib, rinsed, trimmed, and diced

1 carrot, peeled and diced

½ lb. white mushrooms, rinsed, stemmed, and sliced

5 cups beef stock

1 cup pearl barley, rinsed

4 TB. chopped fresh parsley

2 tsp. fresh thyme or ½ tsp. dried

1 bay leaf

Salt and freshly ground black pepper

Slow Speak

Dried **porcini** mushrooms are extremely flavorful and aromatic. If you can't find porcini mushrooms, dried Polish mushrooms are a good substitute. Dried shiitake mushrooms don't have the same flavor, but they can be used in a pinch.

1. Preheat the oven broiler, and line a broiler pan with heavy-duty aluminum foil.

2. Soak porcini mushrooms in hot water for 15 minutes. Strain liquid through a sieve lined with a coffee filter into the slow cooker. Finely chop porcinis in a food processor fitted with a steel blade or by hand. Add porcinis to the slow cooker.

3. While mushrooms are soaking, rinse beef and pat dry with paper towels. Cut beef into 1-inch cubes, if necessary, and arrange on the broiler pan. Broil cubes for 3 minutes per side or until browned. Spoon meat into the slow cooker, along with any juices that have collected in the pan.

4. Heat butter and oil in a large skillet over medium-high heat. Add onion, celery, and carrot. Cook, stirring frequently, for 3 minutes or until onion is translucent. Add sliced white mushrooms. Cook for an additional 3 minutes or until mushrooms begin to soften. Scrape mixture into the slow cooker.

5. Stir in stock, barley, parsley, thyme, and bay leaf. Cook on low for 8 to 10 hours or on high for 4 or 5 hours or until barley is soft. Remove and discard bay leaf, and season soup with salt and pepper. (You can do this up to 3 days in advance and refrigerate soup tightly covered. Reheat over low heat, stirring occasionally.)

Moroccan Lamb and Garbanzo Bean Soup

Subtle yet aromatic spices like cumin and coriander characterize much of North African cooking, and you'll find them in this thick soup, too.

1 cup dried garbanzo beans

1½ lb. lamb stew meat

2 TB. olive oil

2 large onions, peeled and diced

3 garlic cloves, peeled and minced

½ tsp. ground cumin

½ tsp. ground coriander

1 carrot, peeled and sliced

3 cups beef stock or chicken stock

1 (14.5-oz.) can diced tomatoes, undrained

¼ cup chopped fresh cilantro

Salt and cayenne

2 cups hot *couscous*

Serves: 4 to 6	
Prep time: 20 minutes	
Minimum cook time: 4 hours in a medium slow cooker	

1. Rinse garbanzo beans in a colander, and place them into a mixing bowl covered with cold water. Allow garbanzo beans to soak overnight. Or place beans into a saucepan and bring to a boil over high heat. Boil 1 minute. Turn off the heat, cover the pan, and soak beans for 1 hour. Drain, discard soaking water, and place garbanzo beans into the slow cooker.

2. Preheat the oven broiler, and line a broiler pan with heavy-duty aluminum foil. Arrange lamb cubes on the broiler pan, and broil lamb cubes for 3 minutes per side or until browned. Spoon lamb into the slow cooker, along with any juices that have collected in the pan.

3. Heat olive oil in a medium skillet over medium-high heat. Add onions and garlic, and cook, stirring frequently, for 3 minutes or until onions are translucent. Reduce the heat to low, and stir in cumin and coriander. Cook for 1 minute, stirring constantly. Scrape mixture into the slow cooker.

4. Add carrot, stock, and tomatoes to the slow cooker. Cook on low for 9 to 11 hours or on high for 4 or 5 hours or until garbanzo beans and lamb are tender.

5. Transfer ½ garbanzo beans to a food processor fitted with a steel blade or a blender. Purée until smooth, and stir mixture back into soup. Stir in cilantro, and season soup with salt and cayenne. (You can do this up to 3 days in advance and refrigerate soup tightly covered. Reheat over low heat, stirring occasionally.) Ladle soup over hot couscous, and serve immediately.

Variation: Not fond of lamb? You can make this soup with either beef or turkey. The cooking time remains the same.

 Slow Speak _____

Couscous is not a grain even though it's cooked like one. It's a fine pasta made from semolina. Many instant couscous mixes miraculously fluff up in tap water, but you'll have a much fluffier product if you buy regular couscous and steam it for 15 to 20 minutes.

 ⌒

Red Lentil Soup with Lamb Meatballs

These oven-browned meatballs are the star of this soup, made with crunchy almonds, raisins, and herbs.

Serves: 4 to 6
Prep time: 25 minutes
Minimum cook time: 3½ hours in a medium slow cooker

1 cup slivered almonds

2 small onions, peeled

1½ lb. lean ground lamb

½ cup breadcrumbs

¼ cup milk

1 large egg, lightly beaten

½ cup raisins, coarsely chopped

4 garlic cloves, peeled and minced

3 TB. chopped fresh parsley

Salt and freshly ground black pepper

1 TB. turmeric

2 tsp. ground cumin

1 lb. red lentils, rinsed

6 cups beef stock or chicken stock

2 celery ribs, rinsed, trimmed, and sliced

1 TB. fresh thyme or 1 tsp. dried

1. Preheat the oven to 350°F. Place almonds on a baking sheet and toast for 5 to 7 minutes or until lightly browned. Chop almonds finely, and set aside.

2. Chop ½ onion finely, and set aside. Dice remaining 1½ onions, and set aside.

3. Increase the oven to 500°F. Line a broiler pan with heavy-duty aluminum foil, and grease the foil with vegetable oil spray or vegetable oil.

4. Combine almonds, lamb, breadcrumbs, milk, egg, raisins, chopped onion, 2 garlic cloves, parsley, salt, and pepper in a mixing bowl, and mix well. Form mixture into 1-inch balls, and place them on the greased foil. Brown meatballs in the oven for 10 minutes or until lightly browned.

5. While meatballs are browning, heat olive oil in a medium skillet over medium-high heat. Add diced onion and remaining 2 garlic cloves, and cook, stirring frequently, for 3 minutes or until onions are translucent. Reduce the heat to low and stir in turmeric and cumin. Cook for 1 minute, stirring constantly.

6. Scrape mixture into the slow cooker. Add lentils, stock, celery, and thyme. Stir well. Transfer meatballs to the slow cooker with a slotted spoon. Cook on low for 7 to 9 hours or on high for 3½ to 4 hours or until lentils have disintegrated. Season with salt and pepper. (You can do this up to 3 days in advance and refrigerate soup tightly covered. Reheat over low heat, stirring occasionally.)

Variation: You can use either ground beef, ground turkey, or some combination of meats instead of lamb if you prefer.

Slow Savvy

To save time, make this or any meatball mixture a day in advance and refrigerate it. But brown the meatballs the day they're to be cooked. Bacteria can grow in meat that's only partially cooked.

Portuguese Kale Soup with Linguiça

Garlicky sausage and healthful greens are combined with potatoes in this hearty soup.

Serves: 4 to 6
Prep time: 20 minutes
Minimum cook time: 5 hours in a medium slow cooker

2 TB. olive oil

1 large onion, peeled and diced

2 garlic cloves, peeled and minced

1 lb. Portuguese *linguiça* sausage, cut into ½-in. dice

1½ lb. boiling potatoes, peeled and diced

5 cups chicken stock or vegetable stock

¾ lb. kale

Salt and freshly ground black pepper

1. Heat olive oil in a medium skillet over medium heat. Add onion and garlic, and cook, stirring frequently, for 3 minutes or until onion is translucent. Scrape mixture into the slow cooker.

2. Add sausage to the pan, and cook over medium heat for 5 to 7 minutes, stirring frequently. Turn off the heat, transfer sausage to a covered storage container, and refrigerate until ready to use.

3. Add potatoes and stock to the slow cooker. Cook on low for 8 to 10 hours or on high for 4 or 5 hours or until potatoes are tender.

4. While soup is cooking, rinse kale and discard stems and center of ribs. Cut leaves crosswise into thin slices.

5. Drain soup through a sieve over a mixing bowl. Purée solids in a food processor fitted with a steel blade or in a blender. Return soup to the slow cooker, and stir in purée.

6. Add sausage and kale to the slow cooker. Cook on high for 1 or 2 hours or until kale is cooked and tender. Season with salt and pepper. (You can do this up to 3 days in advance and refrigerate soup tightly covered. Reheat over low heat, stirring occasionally.)

Variation: Having trouble finding linguiça? You can also use chorizo or even plain Italian sausage.

Slow Speak

Linguiça sausage is Portuguese and often spiced with garlic, cumin, and cinnamon. The best substitute for it is Spanish or Mexican chorizo.

Split Pea Soup with Ham

A great split pea soup is so thick the spoon stands up in it, and that's what this recipe makes, with fresh herbs adding nuances of flavor.

2 TB. vegetable oil

1 large onion, peeled and finely chopped

1 carrot, peeled and finely chopped

2 garlic cloves, peeled and minced

1 lb. green split peas, rinsed

1 (1-lb.) boneless ham steak, cut into ½-in. dice

6 cups ham stock or chicken stock

2 TB. chopped fresh parsley

1 TB. fresh thyme or 1 tsp. dried

1 bay leaf

Salt and freshly ground black pepper

Serves: 4 to 6
Prep time: 15 minutes
Minimum cook time: 3 hours in a medium slow cooker

1. Heat oil in a medium skillet over medium-high heat. Add onion, carrot, and garlic. Cook, stirring frequently, for 3 minutes or until onion is translucent. Scrape mixture into the slow cooker.

2. Add split peas, ham, stock, parsley, thyme, and bay leaf to the slow cooker. Cook on low for 6 to 8 hours or on high for 3 or 4 hours or until split peas have disintegrated. Remove and discard bay leaf, and season soup with salt and pepper. (You can do this up to 3 days in advance and refrigerate soup tightly covered. Reheat over low heat, stirring occasionally.)

Variation: Make this a vegetarian soup by omitting the ham, adding vegetable stock, and doubling the amount of parsley and thyme to boost the flavor.

 Slow Savvy

Extra fresh parsley? Rinse the bunch, trim off the stems, wrap it in bundles, and freeze it. When you need some, you can "chop" it with the blunt side of a chef's knife. It will chop easily when frozen.

Tuscan Fava Bean and Sausage Soup

This Italian soup enriched with Parmesan cheese contains lots of healthful vegetables, including colorful Swiss chard.

Serves: 4 to 6
Prep time: 20 minutes
Minimum cook time: 4 hours in a medium slow cooker

2 cups dried fava beans

1½ lb. bulk Italian sausage (sweet or hot)

2 large onions, peeled and diced

4 garlic cloves, peeled and minced

4 celery ribs, rinsed, trimmed, and diced

2 carrots, peeled and diced

5 cups chicken stock

½ cup chopped fresh parsley

1½ tsp. dried thyme

2 bay leaves

¾ lb. Swiss chard, rinsed, stemmed, and thinly sliced

⅔ cup freshly grated Parmesan cheese

Salt and freshly ground black pepper

Cooker Caveats

If you can't find bulk sausage, you can always find sausage links at the market, but push the sausage out of the casings before browning it. You'll think you're chewing rubber bands if the casings end up in the soup.

1. Rinse fava beans in a colander, place them in a mixing bowl, and cover with cold water. Allow beans to soak overnight. Or place beans in a saucepan, and bring to a boil over high heat. Boil 1 minute. Turn off the heat, cover the pan, and soak beans for 1 hour. Drain and discard the soaking water, and place beans into the slow cooker.

2. Place a heavy large skillet over medium-high heat. Add sausage, breaking up lumps with a fork. Cook, stirring occasionally, for 3 minutes or until sausage is browned and no longer pink. Remove sausage from the skillet with a slotted spoon, and place it into the slow cooker. Discard all but 2 tablespoons sausage fat from the skillet.

3. Add onions, garlic, celery, and carrots to the skillet. Cook, stirring frequently, for 3 minutes or until onions are translucent. Scrape mixture into the slow cooker.

4. Add stock, parsley, thyme, and bay leaves, and stir well. Cook on low for 6 to 8 hours or on high for 3 or 4 hours or until beans are almost tender.

5. If cooking on low, raise the heat to high. Add Swiss chard, and cook for 1 hour or until Swiss chard is wilted. Remove and discard bay leaves, and stir Parmesan cheese into soup. Season with salt and pepper, and serve immediately. (You can do this up to 3 days in advance and refrigerate soup tightly covered. Reheat over low heat, stirring occasionally.)

White Bean Soup with Prosciutto and Spinach

Salty ham, aromatic rosemary, and bright green spinach enliven this thick and rich bean soup.

2 cups dried navy beans or other small dried white beans

3 TB. olive oil

1 large onion, peeled and diced

6 garlic cloves, peeled and minced

1 (14.5-oz.) can diced tomatoes, drained

½ cup carrots finely chopped

½ cup celery finely chopped

1 (½-lb.) slice prosciutto

6 cups chicken stock or ham stock

1 TB. fresh thyme or 1 tsp. dried

1 TB. chopped fresh rosemary, or 1 tsp. dried

1 (10-oz.) pkg. frozen leaf spinach, thawed

Salt and freshly ground black pepper

Serves: 6
Prep time: 15 minutes
Minimum cook time: 4 hours in a medium slow cooker

1. Rinse beans in a colander, place them in a mixing bowl, and cover with cold water. Allow beans to soak overnight. Or place beans in a saucepan, and bring to a boil over high heat. Boil 1 minute. Turn off the heat, cover the pan, and soak beans for 1 hour. Drain and discard the soaking water, and place beans into the slow cooker.

2. Heat olive oil in a medium skillet over medium heat. Add onion and garlic, and cook, stirring frequently, for 3 minutes or until onion is translucent. Add mixture to the slow cooker, and stir in tomatoes, carrots, celery, prosciutto, stock, thyme, and rosemary. Cook on low for 7 to 9 hours or on high for 3½ to 4 hours or until beans are tender.

3. Remove prosciutto with tongs from the slow cooker, dice, and set aside.

4. Using a slotted spoon, transfer ½ of solids to a food processor fitted with a metal blade or a blender, and purée until smooth.

5. Place spinach in a colander and press with the back of a spoon to extract as much water as possible.

6. If cooking on low, raise the heat to high. Return prosciutto and purée to the soup, and add spinach. Cook soup on high for 20 to 30 minutes or until spinach is cooked. Season with salt and pepper. (You can do this up to 3 days in advance and refrigerate soup tightly covered. Reheat over low heat, stirring occasionally.)

Crock Tales

Prosciutto has been made for more than 2,000 years in the region of Italy near Parma and must come from Parma, San Daniele, or Veneto to be authentic. If you've wondered why prosciutto seems to go so well with Parmesan cheese, it might be because the whey from Parmigiano Reggiano is one of the foods fed to the pigs prosciutto comes from

Part 4

Stews to Savor

The first food almost everyone makes in a slow cooker is some sort of stew. Stews are meals in a bowl. Most of the time every component you need for a balanced meal is right in the pot, or it's just minutes to cook a dish that completes the meal.

The only common denominator for the recipes in Part 4 is that they're all for foods that come out in bite-size pieces. There are vegetarian bean stews from the Middle East and seafood stews from the American Southwest. You'll find Italian poultry stews and Chinese meat stews. There are also a number of variations of ever-popular chili. Some are made with meat or poultry, but there are also vegetarian versions.

"Y'all aware of the variety of scrumptious vegetable and fish dishes you can make in that slow cooker?"

9

Versatile and Vegetarian

In This Chapter

- ◆ International vegetable stews
- ◆ Hearty chilies
- ◆ Filling vegetable and legume stews

More and more Americans—me included—are realizing that increasing the number of servings of vegetables in the course of a day is important, and a delicious vegetable stew is one way to do it. Those are the recipes you'll be cooking in this chapter, and there's quite a range of options. There are stews from cuisines that span the globe—everything from the sunny flavors of Provence to the aromatic curries of India.

In addition to vegetables, many of these stews contain healthful beans, which, when paired with a carbohydrate like rice, become a complete protein.

Not only are these dishes delicious, they're also versatile. The serving sizes listed assume the vegetable stew is your entrée for the evening. But these dishes can also augment your repertoire of side dishes (you'll find chapters devoted to those in Part 6). You can double the number of servings as a side dish and then either omit the rice listed or serve some of the "soupy" vegetables over rice.

Provençal Vegetable Stew

This mix of peppers, squash, and tomatoes is seasoned with sunny herbs.

Serves: 4 to 6
Prep time: 20 minutes
Minimum cook time: 2½ hours in a medium slow cooker

1 (1-lb.) eggplant

Salt

⅓ cup olive oil

1 large onion, peeled and diced

3 garlic cloves, peeled and minced

2 red bell peppers, seeds and ribs removed, and thinly sliced

2 small zucchini, rinsed, trimmed, and cut into ¾-in. cubes

1 small summer squash, trimmed and cut into ¾-in. cubes

1 (14.5-oz.) can crushed tomatoes

1 cup vegetable stock

2 TB. tomato paste

1 TB. herbes de Provence, or 1 tsp. dried thyme, 1 tsp. dried oregano, and 1 tsp. dried rosemary

Freshly ground black pepper

2 or 3 cups cooked brown rice

Cooker Caveats

Even though the eggplant is rinsed, it still brings a fair amount of salt to the dish. Taste the stew before adding additional salt.

1. Rinse and trim eggplant, and cut into ½-inch cubes. Put eggplant in a colander, and sprinkle it liberally with salt. Place a plate on top of eggplant cubes, and weight the plate with cans. Place the colander in the sink or on a plate, and allow eggplant to drain for 30 minutes. Rinse eggplant cubes, and wring them dry with paper towels.

2. Heat half of olive oil in a medium skillet over medium-high heat. Add onion, garlic, and red bell peppers. Cook, stirring frequently, for 3 minutes or until onion is translucent. Scrape mixture into the slow cooker. Add remaining olive oil to the skillet, along with eggplant cubes. Cook, stirring frequently, for 3 minutes or until eggplant is starting to soften. Scrape eggplant into the slow cooker.

3. Add zucchini, summer squash, tomatoes, stock, tomato paste, and herbes de Provence to the slow cooker, and stir well. Cook on low for 5 to 7 hours or on high for 2½ to 3½ hours or until vegetables are tender. Season with salt and pepper, and serve immediately over brown rice.

Italian Tomato and Bread Stew (Pappa al Pomodoro)

This is a rich and creamy stew flavored with fresh basil and two cheeses.

3 lb. ripe plum tomatoes

1 lb. loaf Italian or French bread

¼ cup olive oil

1 large onion, peeled and chopped

2 garlic cloves, peeled and chopped

3 or 4 cups whole milk

½ cup firmly packed fresh chopped basil

½ cup grated whole milk mozzarella cheese

½ cup freshly grated Parmesan cheese

Salt and freshly ground black pepper

Serves: 4 to 6
Prep time: 20 minutes
Minimum cook time: 2 hours in a medium slow cooker

1. Grease a slow cooker liberally with vegetable oil spray.

2. Rinse tomatoes and discard core. Cut tomatoes in half and squeeze over the sink to remove seeds. Cut tomatoes into 1-inch dice, and set aside.

3. Cut bread into ½-inch cubes, and place cubes in the slow cooker.

4. Heat olive oil in a medium skillet over medium-high heat. Add onion and garlic, and cook, stirring frequently, for 3 minutes or until onion is translucent. Add tomatoes and cook an additional 5 minutes or until tomatoes soften. Scrape mixture into the slow cooker.

5. Add milk and basil to the slow cooker, and stir well. Cook on low for 4 to 6 hours or on high for 2 to 3 hours, stirring midway through the cooking time, or until mixture is thick and creamy.

6. If cooking on low, raise the heat to high. Stir mozzarella and Parmesan cheeses into the slow cooker, and cook for an additional 5 to 10 minutes or until cheeses melt. Season with salt and pepper, and serve immediately.

Cooker Caveats

There's a tremendous difference in flavor between whole milk mozzarella and the more popular part–skim milk version. The dish will suffer if you use the latter cheese.

Variation: If you want to make this dish in the middle of winter when tomatoes aren't so great, use 2 (28-oz.) cans diced tomatoes, drained. And try it with fresh oregano in place of basil; both work very well.

Creole Vegetable Stew

This hearty stew lists okra, tomatoes, and sweet potato amongst its ingredients, so it's both visually interesting and delicious.

Serves: 4 to 6

Prep time: 20 minutes

Minimum cook time:
3 hours in a medium slow cooker

---

2 TB. olive oil

1 large onion, peeled and diced

3 garlic cloves, peeled and minced

2 celery ribs, rinsed, trimmed, and sliced

2 TB. paprika

1 TB. fresh thyme or 1 tsp. dried

2 tsp. dried oregano

2 bay leaves

1 lb. sweet potato, peeled and cut into ½-in. cubes

½ lb. fresh okra, rinsed, trimmed, and cut into ½-in. slices

2 (14.5-oz.) cans diced tomatoes, undrained

2 cups vegetable stock

3 TB. chopped fresh parsley

1 (10-oz.) pkg. frozen black-eyed peas, thawed

1 cup fresh corn or frozen corn, thawed

Salt and hot red pepper sauce

2 or 3 cups cooked white or brown rice

Cooker Caveats

If fresh okra isn't available, it's alright to substitute frozen okra, thawed. But add it along with the black-eyed peas and corn; it will fall apart if it's cooked longer.

1. Heat olive oil in a medium skillet over medium-high heat. Add onion, garlic, and celery, and cook, stirring frequently, for 3 minutes or until onion is translucent. Reduce the heat to low, and add paprika, thyme, oregano, and bay leaves. Cook, stirring constantly, for 1 minute. Scrape mixture into the slow cooker.

2. Add sweet potato, okra, tomatoes, stock, and parsley to the slow cooker. Cook on low for 5 to 7 hours or on high for 2½ to 3 hours or until potatoes are almost tender.

3. If cooking on low, raise the heat to high. Add black-eyed peas and corn. Cook for 30 to 45 minutes or until vegetables are tender.

4. Remove and discard bay leaves, season stew with salt and red pepper sauce, and serve immediately over rice.

Chinese "Chili" with Beans

A range of Asian spices flavor the black beans cooked in the style of a traditional chili in this dish.

1½ cups dried black beans	¼ cup tamari
2 TB. Asian sesame oil	2 TB. Chinese black bean sauce
8 scallions, rinsed, trimmed, and cut into ½-in. pieces	2 TB. white wine vinegar
3 garlic cloves, peeled and minced	2 tsp. Chinese chili paste with garlic
2 TB. grated fresh ginger	2 tsp. granulated sugar
3 (14.5-oz.) cans vegetable stock	Salt and freshly ground black pepper
½ cup dry sherry	½ cup chopped fresh cilantro
¼ cup hoisin sauce	2 or 3 cups cooked jasmine rice

Serves: 4 to 6

Prep time: 15 minutes

Minimum cook time: 3 hours in a medium slow cooker

---

1. Rinse beans in a colander, place them in a mixing bowl, and cover with cold water. Allow beans to soak overnight. Or place beans in a saucepan and bring to a boil over high heat. Boil 1 minute. Turn off the heat, cover the pan, and soak beans for 1 hour. Drain, and discard soaking water. Place beans in the slow cooker.

2. Heat sesame oil in a small skillet over medium-high heat. Add scallions, garlic, and ginger, and cook for 30 seconds, stirring constantly. Scrape mixture into the slow cooker.

3. Add stock, sherry, hoisin sauce, tamari, black bean sauce, vinegar, chili paste, and sugar to the slow cooker. Stir well. Cook on low for 6 to 8 hours or on high for 3 or 4 hours or until beans are tender. Season with salt and pepper, and stir in cilantro. Serve immediately on top of rice.

 Slow Savvy

You can prolong the life of leafy herbs like cilantro, parsley, and dill with good storage. Treat them like a bouquet of flowers: trim the stems when you get home from the market and then stand the bunch in a glass of water in the refrigerator.

Zucchini Chili

Cubes of tender zucchini take the place of meat or poultry in this authentically seasoned Texas chili.

<table>
<tr><td>

Serves: 4 to 6

Prep time: 20 minutes
Minimum cook time:
3 hours in a medium slow cooker
</td></tr>
</table>

3 small zucchini (about 1 lb.)

2 TB. vegetable oil

1 large onion, peeled and diced

½ green or red bell pepper, seeds and ribs removed, and chopped

3 garlic cloves, peeled and minced

4 TB. chili powder

1 TB. ground cumin

2 tsp. dried oregano

1 (15-oz.) can red kidney beans, drained and rinsed

1 (28-oz.) can crushed tomatoes in tomato purée

1 (4-oz.) can diced mild green chiles, drained

2 TB. tomato paste

1 TB. granulated sugar

Salt and cayenne

2 cups hot cooked white or brown rice

Chopped scallions

Sour cream or plain yogurt

Grated Monterey Jack cheese

Slow Savvy

An easy way to cut vegetables like zucchini into even quarters is to trim both ends and then cut it in half horizontally. It will sit securely on the counter for you to cut, and it's easy to gauge what a quarter would be.

1. Rinse and trim zucchini. Cut into quarters lengthwise and then into ½-inch slices. Set aside.

2. Heat vegetable oil in a medium skillet over medium-high heat. Add onion, green bell pepper, and garlic, and cook, stirring frequently, for 3 minutes or until onion is translucent. Reduce the heat to low, and stir in chili powder, cumin, and oregano. Cook for 1 minute, stirring constantly. Scrape mixture into the slow cooker.

3. Add zucchini, kidney beans, tomatoes, green chiles, tomato paste, and sugar to the slow cooker, and stir well. Cook on low for 6 to 8 hours or on high for 3 or 4 hours or until zucchini is tender. Season with salt and cayenne. Serve over rice, and pass scallions, sour cream, and cheese separately.

Variation: Want to try some different vegetables? Yellow squash, green beans cut into 1-inch segments, and thinly sliced carrots can all be used in this recipe, and the cooking time remains the same. Use about 1 pound any or all.

Butternut Squash Stew with Black Beans

This is such a visually pretty stew, with pieces of bright dried apricot and leaves of baby spinach punctuating the squash and beans.

3 TB. olive oil

1 medium onion, peeled and diced

2 garlic cloves, peeled and minced

1 TB. paprika

2 tsp. ground coriander

2 tsp. ground cumin

Red pepper flakes

1 (2-lb.) butternut squash, peeled and cut into ¾-in. cubes

3 cups vegetable stock

1 (14.5-oz.) can diced tomatoes, drained

1 (15-oz.) can black beans, drained and rinsed

¾ cup chopped dried apricots

2 TB. freshly squeezed lemon juice

1 (3-in.) strip lemon zest

½ cup slivered almonds

4 cups firmly packed baby spinach leaves, rinsed

Salt

2 or 3 cups cooked couscous

Serves: 4 to 6
Prep time: 20 minutes
Minimum cook time: 3 hours in a medium slow cooker

1. Heat olive oil in a small skillet over medium-high heat. Add onion and garlic, and cook, stirring frequently, for 3 minutes or until onion is translucent. Add paprika, coriander, cumin, and red pepper flakes. Cook, stirring constantly, for 1 minute. Scrape mixture into the slow cooker.

2. Add squash, stock, tomatoes, beans, apricots, lemon juice, and lemon zest to the slow cooker, and stir well. Cook on low for 5 to 7 hours or on high for 2½ to 3 hours or until squash is almost tender.

3. While squash is cooking, preheat the oven to 350°F. Toast almonds in a single layer on a baking sheet for 5 to 7 minutes or until lightly browned. Set aside.

4. If cooking on low, raise the heat to high. Add spinach and season with salt. Cook for 20 to 30 minutes or until spinach is tender. Remove and discard lemon zest, and serve immediately over couscous.

Variation: To vary the taste, use dried currants instead of apricots and substitute sliced Swiss chard for the spinach.

 **Cooker Caveats**

If you're using baby spinach, there's no need to stem the leaves; the stems are tiny and tender. But if you're using more mature spinach, be sure to stem the leaves and also cut the leaves into 2-inch strips.

Moroccan Garbanzo Bean Stew

Turmeric gives this stew a vivid yellow color, and cinnamon adds its aromatic flavor to the meaty garbanzo beans.

Serves: 4 to 6	
Prep time: 15 minutes	
Minimum cook time: 3½ hours in a medium slow cooker	

2 cups dried garbanzo beans	4 cups vegetable stock
3 TB. vegetable oil	1 tsp. *turmeric*
2 large onions, peeled and diced	½ tsp. ground cinnamon
3 garlic cloves, peeled and minced	Salt and freshly ground black pepper
1 (28-oz.) can diced tomatoes, drained	2 or 3 cups cooked couscous

1. Rinse beans in a colander, place them in a mixing bowl, and cover with cold water. Allow beans to soak overnight. Or place beans into a saucepan and bring to a boil over high heat. Boil 1 minute. Turn off the heat, cover the pan, and soak beans for 1 hour. Drain, and discard soaking water. Place beans in the slow cooker.

2. Heat vegetable oil in a medium skillet over medium-high heat. Add onions and garlic, and cook, stirring frequently, for 3 minutes or until onions are translucent. Scrape mixture into the slow cooker.

3. Add drained garbanzo beans, tomatoes, stock, turmeric, and cinnamon to the slow cooker, and stir well. Cook on low for 7 or 8 hours or on high for 3½ to 4 hours or until garbanzo beans are soft. Season with salt and pepper prior to the last hour of cooking time. Serve immediately on top of couscous.

Slow Speak

Turmeric is sometimes called "poor man's saffron." Although it doesn't have the same fragrance as saffron, it has its own stronger flavor and imparts the same rich yellow color in foods. Turmeric is the root of a tropical plant, and it's what gives American mustard its distinctive yellow color.

Spicy Garbanzo Bean and Kale Stew

Iron-rich kale adds texture and color to this bean stew flavored with chili powder.

1½ lb. *kale*

¼ cup olive oil

2 large onions, peeled and diced

3 garlic cloves, peeled and minced

2 green bell peppers, seeds and ribs removed, and chopped

3 TB. chili powder

1 tsp. dried thyme

1 tsp. dried oregano

½ to 1 tsp. dry hot red pepper flakes or to taste

1 tsp. ground cumin

1 tsp. sugar

1 bay leaf

3 (15-oz.) cans garbanzo beans, drained and rinsed

2 (28-oz.) cans diced plum tomatoes, undrained

1 (14.5-oz.) can vegetable stock

1 (6-oz.) can tomato paste

Salt

3 or 4 cups cooked brown rice

Serves: 4 to 6
Prep time: 15 minutes
Minimum cook time: 1½ hours in a medium slow cooker

1. Discard coarse stems from kale and rinse and chop leaves. Place leaves in the slow cooker.

2. Heat olive oil in a small skillet over medium-high heat. Add onions and garlic, and cook, stirring frequently, for 3 minutes or until onion is translucent. Add green bell peppers, and cook for an additional 2 minutes. Add chili powder, thyme, oregano, red pepper flakes, cumin, sugar, and bay leaf. Cook, stirring constantly, for 1 minute. Scrape mixture into the slow cooker.

3. Add garbanzo beans, tomatoes, stock, and tomato paste to the slow cooker. Cook on low for 3 to 5 hours or on high for 1½ to 2 hours or until kale is tender.

4. Remove and discard bay leaf, and season stew with salt. Serve immediately over rice.

 Slow Speak

Kale is the renegade cousin of the cabbage family. Its flavor is very mild, and it has frilly deep green leaves that look like a bouquet of flowers rather than a tight head. For best results, buy small heads that are perky and not limp.

Mexican Mixed-Bean Stew

Using canned beans means this stew is one of the fastest recipes in this book to prepare. Your diners might be surprised to find the zucchini, too.

Serves: 4 to 6
Prep time: 15 minutes
Minimum cook time: 1½ hours in a medium slow cooker

3 TB. olive oil

1 large onion, peeled and diced

3 garlic cloves, peeled and minced

1 red bell pepper, seeds and ribs removed, and finely chopped

2 TB. chili powder

1 TB. ground cumin

1 tsp. dried oregano, preferably Mexican

¾ cup refrigerated tomato salsa

1 (15-oz.) can tomato sauce

2 medium zucchini, rinsed, trimmed, and cut into ½-in. dice

1 (15-oz.) can red kidney beans, drained and rinsed

1 (15-oz.) can garbanzo beans, drained and rinsed

Salt and freshly ground black pepper

2 or 3 cups cooked brown rice

1. Heat olive oil in a medium skillet over medium-high heat. Add onion, garlic, and red bell pepper, and cook, stirring frequently, for 3 minutes or until onion is translucent. Stir in chili powder, cumin, and oregano. Cook for 1 minute, stirring constantly. Scrape mixture into the slow cooker.

2. Stir in salsa, tomato sauce, zucchini, kidney beans, and garbanzo beans. Cook on low for 3 to 5 hours or on high for 1½ to 2½ hours or until zucchini is tender. Season with salt and pepper, and serve over rice.

Cooker Caveats

Different dried beans require varied cooking times, but all canned beans cook at the same rate. They are completely cooked when you take them out of the can and should not be subjected to long cooking times or they'll fall apart. Cook canned beans only long enough that they absorb the flavor of the sauce, but not for more than a few hours.

Spicy Curried Lentil Stew with Cashew Nuts

This stew, which also contains tomatoes and zucchini, is one of the most aromatic dishes you'll ever eat. It contains a range of spices as well as curry powder.

¼ cup vegetable oil

2 onions, peeled and chopped

3 garlic cloves, peeled and minced

1 jalapeño chili, seeds and ribs removed, and finely chopped

1 TB. curry powder

1 tsp. ground cumin

1 tsp. ground coriander

½ tsp. turmeric

2 medium tomatoes, rinsed, cored, seeded, and chopped

1½ cups brown lentils

2 (14.5-oz.) cans vegetable stock

2 (3-in.) cinnamon sticks

2 *cardamom* pods

1 cup cashew nuts

3 medium zucchini, rinsed, trimmed, and cut into ½-in. dice

¼ cup chopped fresh cilantro

Salt and freshly ground black pepper

2 to 3 cups cooked basmati rice

Serves: 4 to 6	
Prep time: 20 minutes	
Minimum cook time: 2 hours in a medium slow cooker	

1. Heat vegetable oil in medium skillet over medium-high heat. Add onions, garlic, and jalapeño, and cook, stirring frequently, for 3 minutes or until onion is translucent. Stir in curry powder, cumin, coriander, and turmeric. Cook, stirring constantly, for 1 minute. Scrape mixture into the slow cooker.

2. Add tomatoes, lentils, stock, cinnamon sticks, and cardamom pods to the slow cooker. Cook on low for 3 to 5 hours or on high for 1½ to 2 hours or until lentils are almost soft.

3. While lentils are cooking, preheat the oven to 350°F. Toast cashew nuts in a single layer on a baking sheet for 5 to 7 minutes or until lightly browned. Set aside.

4. If cooking on low, raise the heat to high. Remove and discard cinnamon sticks and cardamom pods, and add zucchini and cilantro to the slow cooker. Cook for 30 to 45 minutes or until zucchini is tender. Season with salt and pepper, and serve immediately over rice.

Slow Speak

Cardamom, an aromatic spice native to tropical countries, is a member of the ginger family. Each dried pod contains about 20 seeds, which are the size of a cranberry. The pod shells can be lightly crushed and will disintegrate while the dish cooks. If not, they're easy to remove.

Fishy Business

In This Chapter

◆ Saucy shrimp stews

◆ International fish stews

◆ Fish stews with varied vegetables

Any species of fish that comes from an ocean or lake has probably ended up in some culture's stew pot, and those aquatic options are the recipes you'll find in this chapter.

Fish stews are essentially healthful, and all the recipes in this chapter contain vegetables, too. You'll also find serving suggestions for which a carbohydrate goes well with the recipes if they don't contain one as an ingredient.

The Dilemma of Deveining

To devein a shrimp means to remove the gray-black vein (the intestinal tract) from the back of a shrimp. You can do this with the tip of a sharp knife or a special tool called a deveiner. In one hand, hold the shrimp with its back facing up. With the other hand, cut gently down the back with a small paring knife. If there is a thin black line, scrape it out. That's the "vein"— actually the intestinal tract, which can be bitter and gritty.

On small and medium shrimp, deveining is more for cosmetic purposes. However, because the intestinal vein of large shrimp contains grit, you should always remove it. For these recipes, devein the shrimp before cooking, and discard all peel, which is actually the shrimp's paperlike shell.

If you're cooking shrimp for a shrimp cocktail, it's better to peel and devein them after cooking because they won't shrink as much during the cooking process and will present a more pleasing shape.

Shrimp Creole

This famed dish from New Orleans is made with herbs and very
little spice in a rich tomato sauce.

3 TB. olive oil

6 scallions, rinsed, trimmed,
and chopped

2 celery ribs, rinsed,
trimmed, and sliced

½ green bell pepper, seeds
and ribs removed, and finely
chopped

3 garlic cloves, peeled and
minced

1 TB. dried oregano

1 TB. paprika

1 tsp. ground cumin

½ tsp. dried basil

2 (8-oz.) cans tomato sauce

½ cup seafood stock or
bottled clam juice

2 bay leaves

1½ lb. extra large (16 to 20
per lb.) raw shrimp, peeled
and deveined

Salt and cayenne

2 or 3 cups cooked white rice

Serves: 4 to 6
Prep time: 20 minutes
Minimum cook time: 2½ hours in a medium slow cooker

1. Heat olive oil in a medium skillet over medium-high heat.
   Add scallions, celery, green bell pepper, and garlic. Cook,
   stirring frequently, for 3 minutes or until scallions are translucent. Reduce the heat to low, and stir in oregano, paprika,
   cumin, and basil. Cook 1 minute, stirring constantly. Scrape
   mixture into the slow cooker.

2. Stir tomato sauce, stock, and bay leaves into the slow cooker.
   Cook on low for 4 to 6 hours or on high for 2 or 3 hours or
   until vegetables are soft.

3. If cooking on low, raise the heat to high. Remove and discard
   bay leaves, and stir in shrimp. Cook for 15 to 30 minutes or
   until shrimp are pink and cooked through. Season with salt and
   cayenne, and serve over white rice.

Variation: Try 1½ pounds bay scallops, sea scallops cut into quarters, or 1-inch cubes of firm-fleshed whitefish as a change from the
traditional shrimp.

 Cooker Caveats

It's a great time-
saver to double
or triple many of
the recipes in this
chapter—including
this one—to freeze
some of the base
for a future meal.
However, do not
freeze the seafood.
It will be mushy
when it's thawed and
reheated. Freezing
makes all liquids
expand, and when
this happens to fish, it
breaks down its deli-
cate cell walls.

Chinese Shrimp in Black Bean Sauce

The colorful vegetables remain crisp in this dish flavored with ginger and garlic as well as heady black beans.

Serves: 4 to 6
Prep time: 15 minutes
Minimum cook time: 2 hours in a medium slow cooker

3 TB. Chinese *fermented black beans*, coarsely chopped but not rinsed

⅓ cup dry sherry

2 TB. Asian sesame oil

6 scallions, rinsed, trimmed, and thinly sliced

4 garlic cloves, peeled and minced

3 TB. grated fresh ginger

½ lb. bok choy, rinsed, trimmed, and cut into ½-in. slices

1 red bell pepper, seeds and ribs removed, and thinly sliced

2 cups seafood stock or bottled clam juice

¼ cup soy sauce

3 TB. Chinese oyster sauce

1 TB. Chinese chili sauce or ½ tsp. hot red pepper sauce

1½ lb. large (21 to 30 per lb.) raw shrimp, peeled and deveined

1 TB. cornstarch

2 TB. cold water

Salt and freshly ground black pepper

2 or 3 cups cooked Chinese noodles or linguine

Slow Speak

Fermented black beans are small black soybeans with a pungent flavor that have been preserved in salt before being packed. Chop and soak them in liquid to soften them and release their flavor prior to cooking.

1. Stir black beans into sherry to plump for 10 minutes.

2. Heat sesame oil in a small skillet over medium-high heat. Reserve 3 tablespoons scallions, and add remaining scallions, garlic, and ginger. Cook, stirring constantly, for 1 minute. Scrape mixture into the slow cooker.

3. Add bok choy, red bell pepper, bean–sherry mixture, stock, soy sauce, oyster sauce, and chili sauce to the slow cooker, and stir well. Cook on low for 3 to 5 hours or on high for 1½ to 2 hours or until vegetables are crisp-tender.

4. If cooking on low, raise the heat to high. Stir in shrimp, and cook for 15 to 30 minutes or until shrimp are pink and cooked through. Mix cornstarch and cold water in a small cup, and stir cornstarch mixture into stew. Cook for an additional 5 to 10 minutes or until juices are bubbling and slightly thickened.

5. Season with salt and pepper, sprinkle with remaining 3 table-spoons scallions, and serve over noodles.

Spicy Southwest Shrimp

Chorizo sausage and jalapeño chiles flavor this shrimp dish made with pinto beans.

¼ lb. chorizo sausage, thinly sliced

2 medium onions, peeled and diced

5 garlic cloves, minced

3 jalapeño chiles, seeds and ribs removed, and finely chopped

1 TB. ground cumin

2 medium tomatoes, cored, seeded, and diced

2 (15-oz.) cans pinto beans, drained and rinsed

2½ cups seafood stock or bottled clam juice

1½ lb. large (21 to 30 per lb.) raw shrimp, peeled and deveined

3 TB. chopped fresh cilantro

2 tsp. fresh thyme or ½ tsp. dried

Salt and freshly ground black pepper

2 to 3 cups cooked brown rice

Serves: 4 to 6
Prep time: 15 minutes
Minimum cook time: 2½ hours in a medium slow cooker

1. Place chorizo in a medium skillet over medium-high heat. Cook, stirring frequently, for 3 minutes. Add onions and garlic to the skillet, reduce heat to medium, and cook, stirring frequently, for 2 minutes. Add jalapeño and cumin, and continue to cook for 1 minute. Scrape mixture into the slow cooker.

2. Add tomatoes, beans, and stock to the slow cooker, and cook on low for 4 to 6 hours or on high for 2 or 3 hours or until vegetables are soft.

3. If cooking on low, raise the heat to high. Stir in shrimp, cilantro, and thyme. Cook for 15 to 30 minutes or until shrimp are pink and cooked through. Season with salt and pepper, and serve over brown rice.

Variation: This recipe is also delicious as a vegetarian entrée; substitute 2 pounds 1-inch cubes of firm tofu for the shrimp and sausage, and use vegetable stock.

Cooker Caveats

Be careful when cooking hot chiles that the steam from the pan doesn't get in your eyes. The potent oils in the peppers can be transmitted in the vapor.

Italian Shrimp with Dried Currants, Pine Nuts, and Capers

Crunchy nuts, salty capers, and sweet dried currants make this a distinctive tomato sauce for shrimp.

Serves: 4 to 6

Prep time: 15 minutes

Minimum cook time: 3½ hours in a medium slow cooker

---

3 TB. olive oil

1 large onion, peeled and diced

4 garlic cloves, peeled and minced

2 celery ribs, rinsed, trimmed, and sliced

2 carrots, peeled and sliced

1 (8-oz.) can tomato sauce

1 (14.5-oz.) can diced tomatoes, undrained

¾ cup dry white wine

2 TB. chopped fresh parsley

2 TB. chopped fresh oregano or 2 tsp. dried

2 tsp. fresh thyme or ½ tsp. dried

1 bay leaf

½ cup dried currants

¼ cup capers, drained and rinsed

¼ cup *pine nuts*

1½ lb. extra large (16 to 20 per lb.) raw shrimp, peeled and deveined

Salt and freshly ground black pepper

2 or 3 cups cooked brown rice

Slow Speak

Pine nuts, also called *piñon* in Spanish and *pignoli* in Italian, are the nuts located inside the pine cones of various species of evergreen. To remove them, you must heat the pine cones and then pull out the nuts, which are in thin shells, by hand. This labor-intensive method is what makes them so expensive.

1. Heat olive oil in a medium skillet over medium-high heat. Add onion, garlic, celery, and carrot, and cook, stirring frequently, for 3 minutes or until onions are translucent. Scrape mixture into the slow cooker.

2. Stir in tomato sauce, tomatoes, wine, parsley, oregano, thyme, bay leaf, currants, and capers. Cook on low for 6 to 8 hours or on high for 3 or 4 hours or until vegetables are soft.

3. While sauce is simmering, place pine nuts in a heavy small skillet over medium heat. Toast nuts, swirling the pan, for 3 minutes or until lightly browned. Remove nuts from the pan and set aside.

4. If cooking on low, raise the heat to high. Stir in shrimp, and cook for 15 to 30 minutes or until shrimp are pink and cooked through. Remove and discard bay leaf. Season dish with salt and pepper, and serve over brown rice. Garnish each serving with pine nuts.

Variation: Use 1½ pounds bay scallops, sea scallops cut into quarters, or ¾-inch cubes of firm-fleshed whitefish in place of shrimp.

Seafood Gumbo

This recipe is straight out of the bayous of Louisiana, with okra and spices flavoring the broth.

¼ cup plus 3 TB. vegetable oil

¼ cup all-purpose flour

1 cup water

3 medium onions, peeled and diced

1 green or red bell pepper, seeds and ribs removed, and diced

2 celery ribs, rinsed, trimmed, and sliced

4 garlic cloves, peeled and minced

1 lb. fresh okra, rinsed, stemmed, and cut into ½-in. slices

1 (14.5-oz.) can diced tomatoes, undrained

3 cups seafood stock or bottled clam juice

1 TB. fresh thyme or 1 tsp. dried

1 TB. fresh chopped basil or 1 tsp. dried

2 bay leaves

1 lb. snapper, cod, halibut, or other firm-fleshed whitefish, cut into 1-in. cubes

¾ lb. large (21 to 30 per lb.) raw shrimp, peeled and deveined

½ pt. shucked oysters or ¼ lb. additional shrimp

Salt and cayenne

3 cups cooked white rice

Serves: 4 to 6
Prep time: 20 minutes
Minimum cook time: 3½ hours in a medium slow cooker

1. Heat ¼ cup vegetable oil in a small saucepan over medium-high heat. Whisk in flour, and reduce the heat to medium. Whisk flour constantly for 5 to 7 minutes or until roux is walnut brown. Whisk in water, and whisk until the mixture is thick and smooth. Scrape mixture into the slow cooker.

2. Heat remaining 3 tablespoons oil in a medium skillet over medium-high heat. Add onions, green bell pepper, celery, and garlic. Cook, stirring frequently, for 3 minutes or until onion is translucent. Scrape mixture into the slow cooker, and add okra, tomatoes, stock, thyme, basil, and bay leaves. Cook on low for 6 to 8 hours or on high for 3 or 4 hours or until vegetables are tender.

3. If cooking on low, raise the heat to high. Add fish, shrimp, and oysters to the slow cooker, and cook for 15 to 30 minutes or until fish is cooked through and oyster edges have curled. Remove and discard bay leaves, and season gumbo with salt and cayenne. Serve over white rice.

Variation: One pound smoked chicken or smoked turkey, cut into 1-inch cubes, is an excellent substitution for seafood, and use chicken stock instead of seafood stock.

Sweet and Sour Fish Stew

Sweet and sour is a time-honored flavor combination in many cuisines, and this Chinese fish stew includes a cornucopia of colorful vegetables, too.

Serves: 4 to 6
Prep time: 20 minutes
Minimum cook time: 3½ hours in a medium slow cooker

2 TB. Asian sesame oil

1 large red onion, peeled, halved, and sliced

3 scallions, rinsed, trimmed, and thinly sliced

4 garlic cloves, peeled and minced

2 TB. grated fresh ginger

½ tsp. red pepper flakes plus more to taste

1½ cups seafood stock or bottled clam juice

2 TB. balsamic vinegar

2 TB. soy sauce

2 TB. firmly packed dark brown sugar

4 bok choy ribs, rinsed, trimmed, and sliced

2 celery ribs, rinsed, trimmed, and sliced

2 carrots, peeled and thinly sliced

¼ lb. fresh shiitake mushrooms, stemmed and sliced, if large

½ lb. large (21 to 30 per lb.) raw shrimp, peeled and deveined

½ lb. bay scallops or sea scallops (cut into quarters), rinsed

½ lb. snapper, cod, halibut, or other firm-fleshed whitefish, rinsed and cut into 1-in. cubes

½ lb. snow peas, rinsed and trimmed

2 TB. cornstarch

2 TB. cold water

Salt

2 or 3 cups cooked white rice or jasmine rice

1. Heat sesame oil in a medium skillet over medium-high heat. Add onion, scallions, garlic, ginger, and ½ teaspoon red pepper flakes. Cook, stirring frequently, for 3 minutes or until onion is translucent. Scrape mixture into the slow cooker.

2. Stir in stock, vinegar, soy sauce, and brown sugar. Add bok choy, celery, carrots, and mushrooms. Cook on low for 5 to 7 hours or on high for 2½ to 3 hours or until vegetables are tender-crisp.

3. If cooking on low, raise the heat to high. Add shrimp, scallops, fish, and snow peas to the slow cooker. Cook for 30 to 45 minutes or until fish is cooked through. Mix cornstarch and cold water in a small cup, and stir cornstarch mixture into stew. Cook for an additional 5 to 10 minutes or until juices are bubbling and slightly thickened. Season with salt and additional red pepper flakes, and serve stew over rice.

Slow Savvy

For this or any Chinese dish, you can vary the cooking time to make the vegetables the texture you like them. This timing renders the vegetables soft, but if you want them crisper, cut back by as much as 1 or 2 hours.

Caribbean Curried Seafood Pilau with Black Beans

Creamy coconut milk tempers the fiery curry and hot chiles in this colorful and healthful stew.

Serves: 4 to 6
Prep time: 15 minutes
Minimum cook time: 3 hours in a medium slow cooker

½ lb. lump crabmeat

2 TB. olive oil

2 medium onions, peeled and diced

4 garlic cloves, peeled and minced

1 jalapeño or Scotch bonnet chile, seeds and ribs removed, and finely chopped

2 TB. curry powder

2 ripe plum tomatoes, rinsed, cored, and diced

2 (14-oz.) cans light coconut milk

Salt and freshly ground black pepper

1 (15-oz.) can black beans, drained and rinsed well

1 (10-oz.) pkg. frozen peas, thawed

1 lb. large (21 to 30 per lb.) raw shrimp, peeled and deveined

2 or 3 cups cooked white or brown rice

Cooker Caveats

There's very little difference in taste or texture between light coconut milk and the high-fat variety, but using the light version cuts down substantially on fat.

1. Place crabmeat on a dark-colored plate, and pick it over gently with your fingertips to discard all shell and cartilage fragments. Refrigerate crab, covered with plastic wrap, until ready to use.

2. Heat olive oil in a medium skillet over medium-high heat. Add onions, garlic, and jalapeño chile. Cook, stirring frequently, for 3 minutes or until onion is translucent. Reduce the heat to low, add curry powder, and cook, stirring constantly, for 1 minute. Scrape mixture into the slow cooker.

3. Add tomatoes and coconut milk to the slow cooker, and season with salt and pepper. Cook on low for 6 to 8 hours or on high for 3 or 4 hours or until vegetables are soft.

4. If cooking on low, raise the heat to high. Stir in beans, peas, and shrimp. Cook for 15 to 30 minutes or until shrimp are pink and cooked through. Season with salt and pepper, and serve over rice.

Variation: Try bay scallops or ½-inch cubes of swordfish or cod for a different combination.

Cod Stew with Summer Squash and Rosemary

Aromatic rosemary flavors this delicate stew also made with potatoes and woodsy shiitake mushrooms.

½ lb. fresh shiitake mushrooms

3 TB. olive oil

3 shallots, peeled and minced

2 garlic cloves, peeled and minced

¼ cup chopped fresh parsley

3 TB. chopped fresh rosemary or 1 TB. dried

1 bay leaf

1 cup dry white wine

2 cups fish stock or bottled clam juice

1 lb. small new potatoes, scrubbed and cut into quarters

2 yellow summer squash, trimmed, halved lengthwise, and thinly sliced

1½ lb. cod fillets, rinsed

Salt and freshly ground black pepper

2 tsp. cornstarch

2 TB. cold water

Serves: 4 to 6
Prep time: 15 minutes
Minimum cook time: 3½ hours in a medium slow cooker

1. Discard mushroom stems. Wipe mushrooms with a damp paper towel, slice thinly, and set aside.

2. Heat olive oil in a Dutch oven over medium-high heat. Add shallots and garlic, and cook, stirring frequently, for 2 minutes. Add mushrooms and cook, stirring frequently, for 3 minutes or until mushrooms are soft and shallots are translucent. Scrape mixture into the slow cooker.

3. Add parsley, rosemary, bay leaf, white wine, stock, and potatoes to the slow cooker. Cook on low for 6 to 8 hours or on high for 3 or 4 hours or until vegetables are soft.

4. If cooking on low, raise the heat to high. Add squash and cod, and cook for 20 to 30 minutes or until fish is cooked through. Season with salt and pepper, and remove and discard bay leaf. Mix cornstarch and cold water in a small cup, and stir cornstarch mixture into stew. Cook for an additional 5 to 10 minutes or until juices are bubbling and slightly thickened. Serve immediately.

Variation: Salmon is also delicious in this recipe, and its pink color makes the dish pretty, too.

 Slow Savvy

Squash is a tender vegetable that cooks in the same amount of time as the fish, so you add it later in the cooking process. The same is true for zucchini, snow peas, and sugar snap peas.

Portuguese Seafood Stew with Red Pepper Aioli

Aioli is a garlicky mayonnaise sauce, and it enlivens this fish stew made with red wine, orange juice, and linguiça sausage.

Serves: 4 to 6
Prep time: 20 minutes
Minimum cook time: 3½ hours in a medium slow cooker

2 oranges

¼ lb. bacon, cut into 1-in. pieces

1 medium onion, peeled and diced

1 carrot, trimmed, peeled, and thinly sliced

1 celery stalk, trimmed and thinly sliced

6 garlic cloves, peeled and minced

½ lb. mild linguiça sausage, diced

1 (14.5-oz.) can diced tomatoes, undrained

½ cup dry red wine

3 cups fish stock or bottled clam juice

3 TB. chopped fresh basil or 1 tsp. dried

2 TB. chopped fresh parsley

2 tsp. fresh thyme or ½ tsp. dried

1 bay leaf

3 large boiling potatoes, scrubbed and cut into ½-in. dice

½ cup mayonnaise

¼ cup pimiento, drained

1 TB. freshly squeezed lemon juice

Salt and freshly ground black pepper

¾ lb. thick cod fillet, rinsed and cut into 1-in. cubes

½ lb. swordfish fillet, rinsed, skin discarded, and cut into 1-in. cubes

1. Rinse oranges, grate off zest, and squeeze oranges for juice. Set aside.

2. Cook bacon in a heavy skillet over medium-high heat for 5 to 7 minutes or until crisp. Remove bacon from the pan with a slotted spoon, and place it in the slow cooker. Discard all but 2 tablespoons fat.

3. Add onion, carrot, celery, and 3 garlic cloves to the skillet. Cook, stirring frequently, for 3 minutes or until onion is translucent. Add linguiça and cook for 3 minutes more. Scrape mixture into the slow cooker.

4. Add tomatoes, orange zest, orange juice, red wine, stock, basil, parsley, thyme, bay leaf, and potatoes to the slow cooker. Cook on low for 6 to 8 hours or on high for 3 or 4 hours or until vegetables are soft.

5. While stew base is cooking, combine remaining 3 garlic cloves, mayonnaise, pimiento, and lemon juice in a blender. Purée until smooth. Scrape sauce into a serving bowl, and season with salt and pepper. Refrigerate until ready to serve.

6. If cooking on low, raise the heat to high. Add cod and swordfish, and cook for 15 to 30 minutes or until fish is cooked through. Season with salt and pepper, and remove and discard bay leaf. Serve immediately, passing sauce separately.

Crock Tales

George Brown Goode's *History of the American Fisheries* was a landmark book when the government published it in 1887. Goode writes that fishing for swordfish dates back to the 1840s in New England's waters. "Its flesh is excellent food, and it is captured by harpoon according an exciting and even dangerous sport … with the harpooner taking a position at the end of the bowsprit."

Chapter 11

The Best of the Barnyard

In This Chapter

- ◆ Old-fashioned American chicken stews
- ◆ Chicken and turkey stews from Mexico to Morocco to China
- ◆ Hearty dumpling-topped stews

Lean skinless, boneless chicken and turkey breasts are becoming the mainstays of many diets today. There are endless ways to prepare this poultry, and as an added bonus, they cook in less time than beef, lamb, or pork.

Pounding to Perfection

Some recipes tell you to pound the breast to an even thickness so it will cook evenly and quickly. To do so, place the breast between two sheets of wax paper and pound with the smooth side of a meat mallet or the bottom of a small, heavy skillet or saucepan. However, don't do this unless instructed.

After you have boned and pounded the chicken breasts, you can keep a supply frozen. Wrap each breast separately in plastic wrap, and lay the wrapped breasts flat in a heavy resealable plastic bag. Once frozen, you can easily separate the individual breasts and defrost only the number required for a recipe.

Chicken Marengo

This is a delicate chicken dish, with lots of low-calorie mushrooms in the white wine sauce.

Serves: 4 to 6
Prep time: 20 minutes
Minimum cook time: 3¼ hours in a medium slow cooker

4 (6-oz.) boneless, skinless chicken breast halves

All-purpose flour for dredging

¼ cup olive oil

1 large onion, peeled and diced

3 garlic cloves, peeled and minced

1 orange, washed

1 (14.5-oz.) can diced tomatoes, undrained

½ cup dry white wine

½ cup chicken stock

½ lb. white mushrooms, rinsed, stemmed, and sliced

1 tsp. dried thyme

1 bay leaf

Salt and freshly ground black pepper

2 cups cooked buttered egg noodles or rice

Crock Tales

This dish was invented to celebrate a victory. When Napoleon's troops won the Battle of Marengo on June 14, 1800, his cook, Dunand, produced this in the camp kitchen.

1. Rinse chicken and pat dry with paper towels. Trim fat, and cut chicken into 1-inch cubes. Coat chicken with flour, shaking off any excess.

2. Heat oil in a large skillet over medium-high heat. Add chicken, and brown cubes on all sides. Remove chicken from the pan, and place it in the slow cooker. Add onion and garlic to the skillet. Cook, stirring frequently, for 3 minutes or until onion is translucent. Scrape mixture into the slow cooker.

3. Grate zest from orange, and squeeze juice out of orange. Add zest and orange juice to the slow cooker along with tomatoes, wine, stock, mushrooms, thyme, and bay leaf. Cook on low for 6 to 8 hours or on high for 3 or 4 hours or until chicken is tender. Remove and discard bay leaf, and season stew with salt and pepper. Serve on top of buttered egg noodles or rice.

Variation: You'll frequently see veal used as the meat in this dish. It's fine to turn it into a veal stew; the cooking time remains the same.

Chicken Stew with Wild Mushrooms

The woodsy flavor of wild mushrooms adds interest to the creamy sauce for this easy recipe.

4 (6-oz.) boneless, skinless chicken breast halves

¾ lb. fresh shiitake mushrooms

2 TB. unsalted butter

2 TB. vegetable oil

1 onion, peeled and chopped

3 garlic cloves, peeled and minced

2 carrots, peeled and sliced

1 celery rib, rinsed, trimmed, and sliced

1 cup chicken stock

½ cup dry white wine

2 TB. chopped fresh parsley

1 TB. fresh thyme or 1 tsp. dried

1 TB. cornstarch

½ cup heavy cream

Salt and freshly ground black pepper

Cooked white or brown rice

Serves: 4 to 6
Prep time: 15 minutes **Minimum cook time:** 3¼ hours in a medium slow cooker

1. Rinse chicken and pat dry with paper towels. Trim fat, and cut chicken into 1-inch cubes. Wipe mushrooms with a damp paper towel, discard stems, and cut mushrooms in half if large.

2. Heat butter and oil in a medium skillet over medium-high heat. Add onion and garlic, and cook, stirring frequently, for 2 minutes. Add mushrooms, and cook, stirring frequently, for 3 or 4 minutes or until mushrooms begin to soften. Scrape mixture into the slow cooker.

3. Add chicken, carrots, celery, stock, wine, parsley, and thyme to the slow cooker. Stir well. Cook for 6 to 8 hours on low or 3 or 4 hours on high or until chicken is cooked through and no longer pink and vegetables are tender.

4. If cooking on low, raise the heat to high. Stir cornstarch into cream, and stir cream mixture into the slow cooker. Cook for an additional 15 to 20 minutes or until juices are bubbling and slightly thickened. Season with salt and pepper, and serve over rice.

Variation: This can become an excellent vegetarian stew. Substitute 1½ pounds white mushrooms for the chicken, and use vegetable stock. The cooking time will be the same.

Cooker Caveats

Dairy products like cream and cheese tend to curdle if cooked in a slow cooker for the entire cooking time. Add them at the end and let them cook for no more than 1 hour, unless otherwise directed in the recipe.

Mexican Chicken Stew

This easy to make, hearty stew contains kidney beans in a spicy tomato sauce.

Serves: 4
Prep time: 15 minutes
Minimum cook time: 4 hours in a medium slow cooker

4 (6-oz.) boneless, skinless chicken breast halves

3 TB. vegetable oil

1 large onion, peeled and diced

3 garlic cloves, peeled and minced

½ green bell pepper, seeds and ribs removed, and finely chopped

1 TB. chili powder

1 tsp. ground cumin

1 cup refrigerated tomato salsa

1 (8-oz.) can tomato sauce

1 (15-oz.) can kidney beans, drained and rinsed

Salt and freshly ground black pepper

Cooked white or brown rice

1. Rinse chicken and pat dry with paper towels. Trim fat, and cut chicken into 1-inch cubes.

2. Heat oil in a medium skillet over medium-high heat. Add onion, garlic, and green bell pepper. Cook, stirring frequently, for 3 minutes or until onion is translucent. Stir in chili powder and cumin. Cook 1 minute, stirring constantly. Scrape mixture into the slow cooker.

3. Add chicken, salsa, tomato sauce, and kidney beans. Cook on low for 4 to 6 hours or on high for 2 or 3 hours. Season with salt and pepper, and serve over rice.

Variation: Want to make this a vegetarian stew? Easy: add 3 more cans of kidney or your favorite beans instead of the chicken.

Slow Savvy _____

To easily remove the seeds and ribs from bell peppers, cut a slice off the bottom so the pepper stands up straight. You'll see that there are natural curves to the sections. Holding the pepper by its stem, cut down those curves, and you'll be left with a skeleton of ribs and seeds. Throw it out, and you're ready to chop the pepper.

Moroccan Chicken Stew with Dried Apricots

This is a North African version of sweet and sour chicken, with green olives added to balance the sweetness of the dried apricots.

4 (6-oz.) boneless, skinless chicken breast halves

4 garlic cloves, peeled and minced

¾ cup dry white wine

¾ cup chicken stock

⅓ cup white wine vinegar

2 TB. olive oil

¼ lb. dried apricots, finely chopped

½ cup sliced pimiento-stuffed green olives

¼ cup firmly packed dark brown sugar

3 TB. dried oregano

2 tsp. ground cumin

2 TB. cornstarch

2 TB. cold water

Salt and freshly ground black pepper

2 cups hot couscous or rice

Serves: 4 to 6
Prep time: 15 minutes
Minimum cook time: 3¼ hours in a medium slow cooker

1. Rinse chicken and pat dry with paper towels. Trim fat, and cut chicken into 1-inch cubes. Arrange chicken in the slow cooker.

2. Combine garlic, wine, stock, vinegar, oil, apricots, olives, brown sugar, oregano, and cumin in a bowl. Pour over chicken. Cook on low for 6 to 8 hours or on high for 3 or 4 hours or until chicken is cooked through and no longer pink.

3. If cooking on low, raise the heat to high. Mix cornstarch and cold water in a small cup. Stir mixture into chicken. Cook for an additional 15 to 20 minutes or until juices are bubbling and slightly thickened. Season with salt and pepper. Serve stew over couscous or rice.

Variation: I've made this stew with both veal and pork, and the cooking time is almost the same. Add about 1 hour on low or 30 minutes on high.

 Slow Savvy

An easy way to chop dried apricots is in a food processor fitted with a steel blade, using the on-and-off pulsing action. The dried apricots won't stick to the blade if you chop them with the brown sugar. In recipes that call for flour, you can chop the apricots with that as well.

Chicken Provençal with Olives

Vibrant seasoning, colorful red bell peppers, and the fresh taste of orange juice are all part of this easy dish.

Serves: 4 to 6
Prep time: 20 minutes
Minimum cook time: 3 hours in a medium slow cooker

4 leeks

2 oranges

4 (6-oz.) boneless, skinless chicken breast halves

½ cup all-purpose flour

3 TB. olive oil

4 garlic cloves, peeled and minced

2 red bell peppers, seeds and ribs removed, and thinly sliced

1 (14.5-oz.) can diced tomatoes, drained

1 cup dry white wine

1 cup chicken stock

¾ cup pitted oil-cured black olives

3 TB. chopped fresh parsley

1 TB. herbes de Provence

1 bay leaf

Salt and freshly ground black pepper

2 cups cooked rice or buttered egg noodles

Cooker Caveats

It's always worth the time to look over pitted olives carefully and not just dump them into a pot. More than one dentist has been called late at night because a patient bit down on an olive to discover a molar-cracking pit.

1. Trim leeks, split lengthwise, and slice thinly. Place slices in a colander and rinse well under cold running water, rubbing with your fingers to dislodge all dirt. Shake leeks in the colander.

2. Grate zest and squeeze juice out of oranges. Set aside.

3. Rinse chicken and pat dry with paper towels. Trim fat, and cut chicken into 1-inch cubes. Coat chicken with flour, shaking off any excess.

4. Heat oil in a large skillet over medium-high heat. Add chicken and brown cubes on all sides. Remove chicken from the pan, and place it in the slow cooker. Add leeks, garlic, and red bell peppers. Cook, stirring frequently, for 3 minutes or until leeks are translucent. Scrape mixture into the slow cooker.

5. Add tomatoes, orange juice and zest, wine, stock, olives, parsley, herbes de Provence, and bay leaf to the slow cooker. Cook on low for 6 to 8 hours or on high for 3 or 4 hours or until chicken is cooked through and no longer pink. Remove and discard bay leaf, and season with salt and pepper. Serve on top of rice or buttered egg noodles.

Variation: Feel like meat tonight? Try this recipe with ¾-inch cubes pork loin, and cook for 7 to 9 hours on low or 3¼ to 4 hours on high.

Chinese Curried Chicken

Creamy coconut milk is the base for this lightly seasoned stew that includes silken cabbage and red bell pepper.

4 (6-oz.) boneless, skinless chicken breast halves

1 carrot, peeled and sliced

½ red bell pepper, seeds and ribs removed, and cut into 1-in. squares

1 cup sliced *bok choy* or Napa cabbage

1 TB. grated fresh ginger

3 scallions, rinsed, trimmed, and chopped

3 garlic cloves, peeled and minced

1 cup chicken stock

1 cup canned unsweetened coconut milk

2 TB. rice wine vinegar

2 TB. firmly packed dark brown sugar

1 TB. soy sauce

1½ tsp. curry powder or to taste

2 TB. cornstarch

2 TB. cold water

Cooked white rice

Condiments: chutney, raisins, thinly sliced scallions, sweetened coconut, slivered almonds

Serves: 4 to 6
Prep time: 20 minutes
Minimum cook time: 3¼ hours in a medium slow cooker

1. Rinse chicken and pat dry with paper towels. Trim fat, and cut chicken into 1-inch cubes.

2. Place chicken, carrot, red bell pepper, and bok choy into the slow cooker.

3. Combine ginger, scallions, garlic, stock, coconut milk, vinegar, brown sugar, soy sauce, and curry powder in a mixing bowl and stir well. Pour mixture over chicken and vegetables. Cook on low for 6 to 8 hours or on high for 3 to 4 hours or until chicken is cooked through and no longer pink.

4. If cooking on low, raise the heat to high. Mix cornstarch with cold water, and stir cornstarch mixture into the slow cooker. Cook for an additional 15 to 20 minutes or until juices are bubbling and slightly thickened. Serve over cooked rice, and pass condiments separately.

Variation: Try 1-inch cubes firm tofu and vegetable stock to make this a vegetarian stew.

 Slow Speak

Bok choy is part of the family of Asian cabbages and is the one with the most delicate flavor. Select small heads with snowy white stalks, and use just the stalks when cooking. Save the leaves for a salad or toss them into a soup.

Turkey Molé

Unsweetened cocoa powder and peanut butter add richness to this easy dish's ancient sauce.

Serves: 4 to 6
Prep time: 20 minutes
Minimum cook time: 3¼ hours in a medium slow cooker

1 (1½-lb.) boneless, skinless turkey breast

3 TB. vegetable oil

2 large onions, peeled and diced

3 garlic cloves, peeled and minced

3 TB. chili powder

2 TB. unsweetened cocoa powder

2 TB. peanut butter

1 tsp. *Chinese five-spice powder*

½ tsp. ground coriander

1 (14.5-oz.) can diced tomatoes, drained

1¼ cups chicken stock

1 TB. cornstarch

2 TB. cold water

Salt and cayenne

2 cups cooked white or brown rice

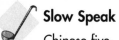

Slow Speak

Chinese five-spice powder is a spice mixture I use in place of cinnamon in dishes from many cultures. Cinnamon is one of the ingredients, along with anise, ginger, fennel, and pepper.

1. Rinse turkey and pat dry with paper towels. Trim fat, and cut turkey into 1-inch cubes.

2. Heat oil in a medium skillet over medium-high heat. Add onions and garlic. Cook, stirring frequently, for 3 minutes or until onions are translucent. Reduce the heat to low, and stir in chili powder, cocoa powder, peanut butter, Chinese five-spice powder, and coriander. Cook for 1 minute, stirring constantly. Scrape mixture into the slow cooker.

3. Stir in turkey, tomatoes, and stock. Cook on low for 6 to 8 hours or on high for 3 or 4 hours or until turkey is cooked through and no longer pink.

4. If cooking on low, raise the heat to high. Mix cornstarch and water in a small cup, and stir it into the slow cooker. Cook for 15 to 20 minutes or until juices are bubbling and slightly thickened. Season with salt and cayenne, and serve over rice.

Variation: Pork loin, cut into 1-inch cubes, is another approach to this dish. Cook it for an extra 1 hour on low or 30 minutes on high.

Turkey Chili

This chili has all the seasonings and flavors you'd expect, but it's leaner and lighter because of the turkey base.

1½ lb. ground turkey

1 onion, peeled and chopped

1 red bell pepper, seeds and ribs removed, and chopped

3 garlic cloves, peeled and minced

3 TB. chili powder

2 TB. ground cumin

2 (14.5-oz.) cans diced tomatoes, undrained

1 (15-oz.) can red kidney beans, drained and rinsed

Salt and cayenne

2 cups cooked white or brown rice

Serves: 4 to 6
Prep time: 15 minutes
Minimum cook time: 3¼ hours in a medium slow cooker

1. Combine turkey, onion, red bell pepper, garlic, chili powder, cumin, and tomatoes in the slow cooker. Stir well. Cook on low for 6 to 8 hours or on high for 3 or 4 hours.

2. If cooking on low, raise the heat to high. Add beans and cook for an additional 20 minutes or until bubbling. Season with salt and cayenne, and serve over rice.

Slow Savvy

Any chili can become a finger food by turning it into nachos. Pile the chili on large nacho corn chips, top with some grated Monterey Jack cheese, and pop under the broiler until the cheese is melted.

Turkey Stew with Cornmeal Dumplings

Apples and dried fruit are part of this stew that's topped with delicious light and fluffy dumplings.

Serves: 4 to 6

Prep time: 20 minutes
Minimum cook time: 5 hours in a medium slow cooker

1 (1½-lb.) boneless, skinless turkey breast

2 TB. vegetable oil

1 onion, peeled and diced

2 garlic cloves, peeled and minced

1 carrot, peeled and sliced

2 Granny Smith apples, peeled, cored, and thinly sliced

¼ cup chopped dried apricots

¼ cup raisins

1½ cups chicken stock

½ cup apple cider

2 TB. chopped fresh parsley

1 TB. chopped fresh sage or 1 tsp. dried

2 tsp. fresh thyme or ½ tsp. dried

½ tsp. ground cinnamon

1 (10-oz.) pkg. frozen mixed vegetables, thawed

Salt and freshly ground black pepper

½ cup all-purpose flour

½ cup yellow cornmeal

1 tsp. baking powder

½ tsp. salt

1 large egg, lightly beaten

¼ cup milk

3 TB. unsalted butter, melted

1. Rinse turkey and pat dry with paper towels. Trim fat, and cut turkey into 1-inch cubes.

2. Heat oil in a medium skillet over medium-high heat. Add onion and garlic, and cook, stirring frequently, for 3 minutes or until onion is translucent. Scrape mixture into the slow cooker.

3. Add turkey, carrot, apples, apricots, raisins, stock, cider, parsley, sage, thyme, and cinnamon to the slow cooker. Stir well. Cook on low for 7 to 9 hours or on high for 3½ to 4 hours or until turkey is cooked through and no longer pink.

4. If cooking on low, raise the heat to high. Stir in mixed vegetables, and cook for 30 minutes. Season with salt and pepper.

5. To make dumplings, combine flour, cornmeal, baking powder, and salt in a mixing bowl. Stir in egg, milk, and melted butter, and mix well. Drop batter by 1 tablespoon measures onto stew. Cover the slow cooker, and cook on high for 35 to 45 minutes or until a toothpick inserted into the center of a dumpling comes out clean.

Slow Savvy

When you're making a pretty apple tart, how the apples look matters. But in a stew like this one, who cares? They fall apart anyway. Here's an easy way to slice them: peel the apples, and, turning the apple, slice off the sides. Soon all you'll be left with is the core to throw away.

Mexican Turkey with Chili and Raisins (*Picadillo*)

While flavored like a traditional chili, the addition of cinnamon and raisins gives this adaptation a distinctive character.

Serves: 4 to 6
Prep time: 15 minutes
Minimum cook time: 3 hours in a medium slow cooker

2 TB. vegetable oil

1 large onion, peeled and diced

3 garlic cloves, peeled and minced

2 TB. chili powder

½ tsp. ground cinnamon

1½ lb. ground turkey

1 (14.5-oz.) can diced tomatoes

½ cup beef stock

1 (4-oz.) can diced mild green chiles

2 TB. cider vinegar

½ cup raisins

Salt and freshly ground black pepper

2 cups hot cooked white or yellow rice

1. Heat oil in a medium skillet over medium-high heat. Add onion and garlic, and cook, stirring frequently, for 3 minutes or until onion is translucent. Reduce the heat to low, and stir in chili powder and cinnamon. Cook for 1 minute, stirring constantly. Scrape mixture into the slow cooker.

2. Add turkey, tomatoes, stock, green chiles, vinegar, and raisins to the slow cooker. Cook on low for 6 to 8 hours or on high for 3 or 4 hours or until turkey is cooked through and no longer pink. Season with salt and pepper, and serve over rice.

Slow Savvy

Use Picadillo—or any recipes in this chili section—as the stuffing for bell peppers or the base for a "tamale pie." Steam or microwave the peppers until tender and fill them. For the pie, make a batch of cornbread batter. Place the hot Picadillo in a 9×13-inch pan, spread the batter over the top, and bake it according to the cornbread directions.

Meaty Morsels

In This Chapter

- ◆ Beef stews from plain to fancy
- ◆ Stews starring pork and ham
- ◆ European lamb stews
- ◆ Delicate veal stews

The term *stew* is almost synonymous with "hearty meats." The stew pot has always been the repository of meat odds and ends left over from sectioning larger cuts. It's only in the past few decades that stew meat has found its way into the meat case in its own name. In this chapter, you'll find a wide variety of ways to season and sauce stews. Many of these are historic dishes that have been enjoyed for centuries.

The key to the success of these stews is patience. You can't rush the cooking time. Although pork and veal become tender before beef or lamb, all these dishes need many hours to reach the perfect tenderness level.

Choosing Your Cuts

Many cuts on a cow require long, slow cooking; others are meant to be grilled, broiled, or roasted. Even if you know nothing about beef and what the various parts are called, you can still pick the right ones for a stew. Just look at the price tags. Look at the cost of a tenderloin roast and then look at the cost of a brisket. Buy the brisket for the slow cooker.

Price is a good guideline, but there are others. Anything that says *chuck, rump,* or *shank* is a good slow cooker choice. One of the best cuts of beef for the slow cooker is the short ribs, also called *flanken* in some parts of the country. The terminology for the major cuts of meat is similar for beef, lamb, pork, and veal.

The cuts of meat from the legs, shoulders, and hind-quarters are the best cuts for slow cooking.

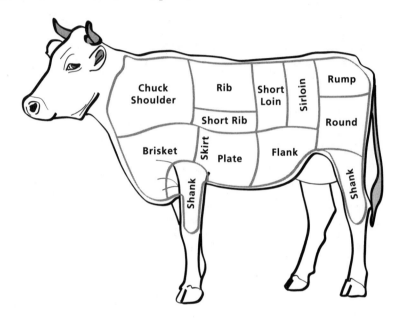

The shape of your slow cooker is another important consideration. If your slow cooker is round, a rump roast is your best bet. If it's oval, go with a chuck roast or a brisket.

Beef Stew in Red Wine with Mushrooms (*Boeuf Bourguignon*)

This dish is a classic of French cooking, with mushrooms and herbs flavoring the aromatic red wine sauce.

2 lb. stewing beef, fat trimmed and cut into 1-in. cubes

2 TB. olive oil

1 large onion, peeled and diced

3 garlic cloves, peeled and minced

½ lb. white mushrooms, rinsed, stemmed, and sliced

2 cups dry red wine

½ cup beef stock

1 TB. tomato paste

1 TB. chopped fresh parsley

1 tsp. *herbes de Provence,* or 1 tsp. dried thyme

1 bay leaf

2 TB. cornstarch

2 TB. cold water

Salt and freshly ground black pepper

1½ lb. steamed new potatoes or 2 cups cooked buttered egg noodles

Serves: 6 to 8	
Prep time: 25 minutes	
Minimum cook time: 4 hours in a medium slow cooker	

1. Preheat the oven broiler, and line a broiler pan with heavy-duty aluminum foil. Arrange beef on the foil, and broil for 3 minutes per side or until browned. Transfer beef to the slow cooker, and pour in any juices that have collected in the pan.

2. Heat olive oil in a medium skillet over medium heat. Add onion, garlic, and mushrooms. Cook, stirring frequently, for 4 or 5 minutes or until onion is translucent and mushrooms are soft. Scrape mixture into the slow cooker.

3. Stir in wine, stock, tomato paste, parsley, herbes de Provence, and bay leaf. Cook on low for 8 to 10 hours or on high for 4 or 5 hours or until beef is tender.

4. If cooking on low, raise the heat to high. Mix cornstarch and cold water in a small cup, and stir cornstarch mixture into beef. Cook for an additional 15 to 20 minutes or until juices are bubbling and slightly thickened. Remove and discard bay leaf, and season stew with salt and pepper. (You can do this up to 3 days in advance and refrigerate stew tightly covered. Reheat over low heat, stirring occasionally.) Serve stew with steamed new potatoes or buttered egg noodles.

Slow Speak

Herbes de Provence is one of my favorite blended seasonings, and you can now find it in many supermarkets and specialty food stores. You can make it yourself by blending equal parts dried thyme, tarragon, chervil, rosemary, basil, and lavender.

Beef Stroganoff

The sour cream is what gives the tomato sauce its distinctive flavor in this classic comfort food dish.

Serves: 4 to 6
Prep time: 15 minutes
Minimum cook time: 4¼ hours in a medium slow cooker

2 lb. stewing beef, fat trimmed and cut into 1-in. cubes

3 TB. unsalted butter

3 TB. vegetable oil

2 large onions, peeled and diced

3 garlic cloves, peeled and minced

¾ lb. white mushrooms, rinsed, trimmed, and sliced

2 TB. paprika

1 (8-oz.) can tomato sauce

¾ cup beef stock

1 TB. prepared mustard

1 (1.2-oz.) pkg. dehydrated mushroom gravy mix

¾ cup sour cream

Salt and freshly ground black pepper

2 cups cooked buttered egg noodles

Crock Tales

Beef Stroganoff was named for a nineteenth-century Russian diplomat, Count Paul Stroganoff. It was one of the dishes that became a hallmark of what Americans years ago called "continental cuisine."

1. Preheat the oven broiler, and line a broiler pan with heavy-duty aluminum foil. Arrange beef on the foil, and broil for 3 minutes per side or until beef is lightly browned. Transfer beef to the slow cooker, and pour in any juices that have collected in the pan.

2. Heat butter and oil in a large skillet over medium-high heat. Add onions, garlic, and mushrooms. Cook, stirring frequently, for 4 minutes or until onion is translucent and mushrooms are soft. Reduce the heat to low, and stir in paprika. Cook for 1 minute, stirring constantly. Scrape mixture into the slow cooker.

3. Stir in tomato sauce, stock, mustard, and gravy mix. Cook on low for 8 to 10 hours or on high for 4 or 5 hours or until beef is tender.

4. If cooking on high, reduce the heat to low. Stir in sour cream, and season with salt and pepper. Cook for 15 to 20 minutes or until the mixture is hot. Do not let stew boil. (You can do this up to 3 days in advance and refrigerate stew tightly covered. Reheat over low heat, stirring occasionally.) Serve stew over buttered egg noodles.

Variation: This dish works well with chicken and turkey; just reduce the initial cooking time by 2 hours on low or 1 hour on high.

Guinness Beef Stew

Flavorful dark beer and sautéed onions make this a rich and hearty stew.

2 lb. stewing beef, fat trimmed and cut into 1-in. cubes

2 TB. vegetable oil

4 large onions, peeled and thinly sliced

2 garlic cloves, peeled and minced

1 (12-oz.) bottle Guinness Stout beer

1 cup beef stock

2 TB. firmly packed dark brown sugar

2 TB. chopped fresh parsley

1 TB. fresh thyme or 1 tsp. dried

1 bay leaf

2 TB. cornstarch

2 TB. cold water

Salt and black pepper

2 cups cooked buttered egg noodles

Serves: 6
Prep time: 20 minutes
Minimum cook time: 4 hours in a medium slow cooker

1. Preheat the oven broiler, and line a broiler pan with heavy-duty aluminum foil. Arrange beef in a single layer on the foil, and broil for 3 minutes per side or until beef is lightly browned. Place beef into the slow cooker along with any juices that have collected in the pan.

2. Heat oil in a medium skillet over medium-high heat. Add onions and garlic, and cook, stirring, for 3 minutes or until onion is translucent. Scrape mixture into the slow cooker.

3. Add beer, stock, brown sugar, parsley, thyme, and bay leaf. Stir well. Cook on low for 8 to 10 hours or on high for 4 or 5 hours or until beef is very tender.

4. If cooking on low, raise the heat to high. Mix cornstarch with cold water in a small cup. Add cornstarch mixture to the slow cooker, cover, and cook for an additional 10 to 15 minutes or until juices are bubbling and slightly thickened. Remove and discard bay leaf, and season stew with salt and pepper. (You can do this up to 3 days in advance and refrigerate stew tightly covered. Reheat over low heat, stirring occasionally.) Serve stew with buttered egg noodles.

Slow Savvy

The general ratio of fresh herbs to dried herbs is about three to one. So if a recipe doesn't give you an equivalent and calls for 1 tablespoon fresh herb, use 1 teaspoon dried herb.

Old-Fashioned Beef Stew

Here's a stew that might remind you of your childhood, with potatoes and colorful vegetables simmered with the beef in an herbed sauce.

Serves: 6
Prep time: 20 minutes
Minimum cook time: 4 hours in a large slow cooker

2 lb. stewing beef, fat trimmed and cut into 1-in. cubes

2 TB. vegetable oil

1 onion, peeled and chopped

2 garlic cloves, peeled and minced

½ lb. white mushrooms, rinsed, trimmed, and halved, if large

3 carrots, peeled, and cut into ½-in. slices

2 celery ribs, rinsed, trimmed, and sliced

4 large red-skinned potatoes, scrubbed and cut into 1-in. dice

1 large turnip, peeled and cut into 1-in. dice

1 (10-oz.) pkg. frozen pearl onions, thawed

3 cups beef stock

2 TB. Worcestershire sauce

2 TB. tomato paste

1 TB. fresh thyme or 1 tsp. dried

1 bay leaf

1 cup frozen peas, thawed

2 TB. unsalted butter, softened

3 TB. all-purpose flour

Salt and freshly ground black pepper

1. Preheat the oven broiler, and line a broiler pan with heavy-duty aluminum foil. Arrange beef in a single layer on the foil, and broil for 3 minutes per side or until beef is lightly browned. Place beef into the slow cooker along with any juices that have collected in the pan.

2. Heat oil in a medium skillet over medium-high heat. Add onion, garlic, and mushrooms. Cook, stirring frequently, for 3 to 5 minutes or until onion is translucent and mushrooms are soft. Scrape mixture into the slow cooker.

3. Add carrots, celery, potatoes, turnip, pearl onions, stock, Worcestershire sauce, tomato paste, thyme, and bay leaf. Cook on low for 8 to 10 hours or on high for 4 or 5 hours or until beef is very tender. Add peas for the last hour of cooking.

4. If cooking on low, raise the heat to high. Mix softened butter with flour in a small cup to make a thick paste. Stir butter-flour mixture in small bits into the slow cooker, cover, and cook for an additional 10 to 15 minutes or until juices are bubbling and slightly thickened. Remove and discard bay leaf, and season stew with salt and pepper. (You can do this up to 3 days in advance and refrigerate stew tightly covered. Reheat over low heat, stirring occasionally.)

Variation: I've also used lamb for this stew, with the same cooking time.

Chinese Beef Stew

Mushrooms, carrots, and asparagus round out the colors and textures of this slow cooker version of a Chinese "sand pot" casserole.

½ lb. fresh asparagus spears

2 lb. stewing beef, fat trimmed and cut into 1-in. cubes

2 TB. Asian sesame oil

3 scallions, trimmed and thinly sliced

2 TB. grated fresh ginger

4 garlic cloves, peeled and minced

1 small red onion, peeled and thinly sliced

½ lb. white mushrooms, rinsed, trimmed, and sliced

10 baby carrots, peeled and halved lengthwise

1½ cups beef stock

3 TB. soy sauce

2 TB. Chinese *oyster sauce*

1 TB. firmly packed dark brown sugar

1 TB. Chinese chili oil or ¼ tsp. red pepper flakes

2 TB. cornstarch

2 TB. cold water

Salt and freshly ground black pepper

2 cups cooked white rice or Chinese noodles

Serves: 6
Prep time: 25 minutes
Minimum cook time: 4½ hours in a medium slow cooker

1. Rinse asparagus and discard woody stems. Cut asparagus into ½-inch slices on the diagonal. Set aside.

2. Preheat the oven broiler, and line a broiler pan with heavy-duty aluminum foil. Arrange beef in a single layer on the foil, and broil for 3 minutes per side or until beef is lightly browned. Place beef into the slow cooker along with any juices that have collected in the pan.

3. Heat sesame oil in a medium skillet over medium-high heat. Add scallions, ginger, garlic, red onion, and mushrooms. Cook, stirring frequently, for 3 to 5 minutes or until mushrooms begin to soften. Scrape mixture into the slow cooker.

4. Stir in carrots, stock, soy sauce, oyster sauce, brown sugar, and Chinese chili oil. Cook on low for 8 to 10 hours or on high for 4 or 5 hours or until beef is very tender. Add asparagus for the last hour of cooking.

5. If cooking on low, raise the heat to high. Mix cornstarch with cold water in a small cup. Add cornstarch mixture to the slow cooker, cover, and cook for an additional 10 to 15 minutes or until juices are bubbling and slightly thickened. Season with salt and pepper. (You can do this up to 3 days in advance and refrigerate stew tightly covered. Reheat over low heat, stirring occasionally.) Serve stew over rice or Chinese noodles.

Variation: Try this stew with veal or pork, and reduce the initial cooking time by 2 hours on low or 1 hour on high.

Slow Speak _____

Oyster sauce is another seasoning staple of the Chinese pantry. It's made from oysters, brine, and soy sauce, and it's cooked until it's deep brown, thick, and concentrated. It gives dishes a rich flavor, and it's not as salty as soy sauce.

Chili Con Carne

There's nothing like a steaming bowl of chili on a cold winter's night or in front of a football game, and the slow cooker makes it so easy!

3 TB. vegetable oil

1 large onion, peeled and diced

4 garlic cloves, peeled and minced

1 jalapeño chile, seeds removed, and finely chopped

½ green bell pepper, seeds and ribs removed, and finely chopped

3 TB. *chili powder*

1 TB. ground cumin

1½ lb. lean ground beef

1 (8-oz.) can tomato sauce

2 (14.5-oz.) cans diced tomatoes, drained

1 (15-oz.) can red kidney beans, drained and rinsed

Salt and cayenne

Sour cream

Chopped onion

Grated Monterey Jack cheese

Serves: 4 to 6
Prep time: 20 minutes
Minimum cook time: 3 hours in a medium slow cooker

1. Heat vegetable oil in a medium skillet over medium-high heat. Add onion, garlic, jalapeño, and green bell pepper. Cook, stirring frequently, for 3 minutes or until onion is translucent. Stir in chili powder and ground cumin. Cook for 1 minute, stirring constantly. Spoon mixture into the slow cooker.

2. Place ground beef in the skillet, and break up lumps with a fork. Cook beef for 3 to 5 minutes or until browned. Remove beef from the pan with a slotted spoon, and place it in the slow cooker.

3. Stir in tomato sauce, tomatoes, and kidney beans. Cook on low for 6 to 8 hours or on high for 3 or 4 hours. Season with salt and cayenne. (You can do this up to 3 days in advance and refrigerate chili tightly covered. Reheat over low heat, stirring occasionally.) Serve, passing sour cream, onion, and cheese separately.

Slow Speak

Chili powder is a blend of herbs and spices, and if you make it yourself the base should be ground red chiles and ground cumin. Then add as much paprika, ground coriander, cayenne, and oregano as you like. Some brands also include garlic powder and onion powder.

Pork Stew with Dried Fruit

Root vegetables are joined by dried apricots and raisins in a light sauce flavored with Dijon mustard.

Serves: 4 to 6

Prep time: 15 minutes

Minimum cook time: 3¼ hours in a medium slow cooker

---

2 lb. pork shoulder, cut into 1-in. cubes

1 bunch scallions, trimmed and cut into 1-in. pieces

2 carrots, peeled and sliced

2 parsnips, peeled and sliced

½ cup chopped dried apricots

½ cup raisins

2 cups chicken stock

2 TB. *Dijon mustard*

1 TB. cornstarch

2 TB. cold water

Salt and freshly ground black pepper

2 cups cooked buttered egg noodles or rice

1. Rinse pork and pat dry with paper towels. Arrange pork, scallions, carrots, parsnips, apricots, and raisins in the slow cooker.

2. Stir together stock and Dijon mustard, and add to the slow cooker. Cook on low for 6 to 8 hours or on high for 3 or 4 hours or until meat is tender.

3. If cooking on low, raise the heat to high. Mix cornstarch with water in a small cup. Stir in cornstarch mixture, and cook for 15 to 20 minutes or until juices are bubbling and slightly thickened. Season with salt and pepper. (You can do this up to 3 days in advance and refrigerate stew tightly covered. Reheat over low heat, stirring occasionally.) Serve stew over buttered egg noodles or rice.

Variation: If you want to make this stew with chicken or turkey, reduce the cooking time by 1 hour on low or 30 minutes on high.

Slow Speak

Dijon mustard originated in Dijon, France, and is known for its clean, sharp flavor. Although it's made just about everywhere today, the only "must" is that it contain unfermented grape juice. Other than that, the mustard seeds can be brown or black, and it can have a taste from mild to hair-curling hot.

Cajun Stewed Red Beans and Ham

Red beans and rice are a classic in Louisiana, and the ham makes this version even heartier.

1 lb. dried red kidney beans, rinsed

1 (1½-lb.) boneless ham steak

2 medium onions, peeled and finely chopped

2 celery ribs, rinsed, trimmed, and finely chopped

1 green bell pepper, seeds and ribs removed, and finely chopped

2 bay leaves

2 tsp. dried thyme

4 cups water

Salt and cayenne

2 to 3 cups cooked white rice

Serves: 6
Prep time: 15 minutes
Minimum cook time: 4 hours in a medium slow cooker

1. Rinse beans in a colander and place them in a mixing bowl covered with cold water. Allow beans to soak overnight. Or place beans into a saucepan and bring to a boil over high heat. Boil 1 minute. Turn off the heat, cover the pan, and soak beans for 1 hour. Drain beans, discard soaking water, and place them in the slow cooker.

2. Trim ham of all visible fat, and cut ham into 1-inch cubes.

3. Add ham, onions, celery, green bell pepper, bay leaves, thyme, and water to the slow cooker. Stir well. Cook on low for 8 to 10 hours or on high for 4 or 5 hours or until beans are very tender. Remove and discard bay leaves. Season with salt and cayenne. (You can do this up to 3 days in advance and refrigerate stew tightly covered. Reheat over low heat, stirring occasionally.) Serve stew over rice.

Variation: This dish is a snap to make into a vegetarian feast by omitting the ham. You might need to add some additional salt to compensate.

 Crock Tales

Louis Armstrong, whose name is synonymous with New Orleans jazz, used to sign his letters "Red beans and ricely yours."

Veal Marsala

This garlicky Italian veal stew is fast to pull together and a real crowd-pleaser for parties.

Serves: 6
Prep time: 15 minutes
Minimum cook time: 3 hours in a medium slow cooker

¼ cup olive oil

2 lb. veal stew meat, fat trimmed, and cut into 1-in. cubes

All-purpose flour for dredging

6 garlic cloves, peeled and minced

⅓ cup chopped fresh parsley

¾ cup dry marsala wine

¼ cup chicken stock

Salt and freshly ground black pepper

2 cups cooked orzo, pasta, or rice

1. Heat oil in a large skillet over medium-high heat.

2. Coat veal with flour, shaking off any excess. Add veal cubes to the hot skillet, and brown on all sides. Remove veal from the pan, and place it in the slow cooker.

3. Add garlic to the skillet. Cook, stirring constantly, for 1 minute. Scrape garlic into the slow cooker.

4. Add parsley, wine, and stock to the slow cooker. Cook on low for 6 to 8 hours or on high for 3 or 4 hours or until veal is tender. Season with salt and pepper. (You can do this up to 3 days in advance and refrigerate stew tightly covered. Reheat over low heat, stirring occasionally.) Serve stew over orzo, pasta, or rice.

Variation: As is true with many dishes, you can substitute chicken or turkey for the veal and the cooking time won't change.

Cooker Caveats

When you're browning meat coated with flour, browning the flour is even more important than browning the meat. This step creates a sauce that thickens slightly but does not taste pasty. If you don't want to brown the veal, thicken the juices with 1 tablespoon cornstarch mixed with 2 tablespoons cold water instead.

Greek Lamb Stew

Pearl onions and dried currants punctuate this succulent stew's cinnamon-scented red wine sauce.

2 lb. lamb stew meat, fat trimmed, and cut into 1-in. cubes

2 TB. olive oil

2 onions, peeled and diced

3 garlic cloves, peeled and minced

1 TB. dried oregano

½ tsp. ground cinnamon

½ tsp. ground coriander

1 (14.5-oz.) can diced tomatoes

1 cup beef stock

½ cup dry red wine

¼ cup orange juice

2 TB. lemon juice

3 TB. firmly packed dark brown sugar

1 TB. grated orange zest

1 lb. frozen pearl onions, thawed

¼ cup dried currants

2 TB. cornstarch

1 TB. cold water

2 cups boiled *orzo* or brown rice

Serves: 4 to 6
Prep time: 20 minutes
Minimum cook time: 4 hours in a medium slow cooker

1. Preheat the oven broiler, and line a broiler pan with heavy-duty aluminum foil. Arrange lamb in a single layer on the foil, and broil for 3 minutes per side or until lamb is lightly browned. Place lamb in the slow cooker along with any juices that have collected in the pan.

2. Heat oil in a medium skillet over medium-high heat. Add onions and garlic, and cook, stirring frequently, for 3 minutes or until onions are translucent. Reduce the heat to low and stir in oregano, cinnamon, and coriander. Cook, stirring constantly, for 1 minute. Scrape mixture into the slow cooker.

3. Add tomatoes, stock, wine, orange juice, lemon juice, brown sugar, orange zest, pearl onions, and currants to the slow cooker. Stir well. Cook stew on low for 8 to 10 hours or on high for 4 or 5 hours or until lamb is very tender.

4. If cooking on low, raise the heat to high. Mix cornstarch with cold water in a small cup. Add cornstarch mixture to the slow cooker, cover, and cook for an additional 10 to 15 minutes or

Slow Speak

Orzo is a rice-shape pasta used a lot in Greek cooking that's now gaining fans on this side of the Atlantic. The best orzo is imported and has very long grains. Unlike most pastas, it absorbs the flavors of sauces beautifully.

until juices are bubbling and slightly thickened. (You can do this up to 3 days in advance and refrigerate stew tightly covered. Reheat over low heat, stirring occasionally.) Serve stew over orzo or brown rice.

Variation: Not a lamb fan? No problem. You can make the stew with beef and the cooking time will remain the same.

Classic French Lamb Stew (*Navarin d'Agneau*)

Aromatic thyme and rosemary flavor the delicate white wine sauce for this classic French dish.

Serves: 6
Prep time: 25 minutes
Minimum cook time: 4 hours in a medium slow cooker

2 lb. lamb stew meat, fat trimmed, and cut into 1-in. cubes

2 TB. olive oil

2 onions, peeled and diced

4 garlic cloves, peeled and minced

½ lb. mushrooms, rinsed, stemmed, and halved, if large

3 large carrots, peeled and cut into ½-in. pieces

2 cups beef stock

1 cup dry white wine

3 TB. tomato paste

2 TB. fresh thyme or 2 tsp. dried

2 TB. chopped fresh rosemary or 2 tsp. dried

2 bay leaves

3 TB. chopped fresh parsley

1 (10-oz.) pkg. frozen pearl onions, thawed

1 (10-oz.) pkg. frozen peas, thawed

2 TB. cornstarch

2 TB. cold water

Salt and freshly ground black pepper

1½ lb. boiled baby potatoes

1. Preheat the oven broiler, and line a broiler pan with heavy-duty aluminum foil. Arrange lamb in a single layer on the foil, and broil for 3 minutes per side or until lamb is lightly browned. Place lamb in the slow cooker along with any juices that have collected in the pan.

2. Heat oil in a medium skillet over medium-high heat. Add onions, garlic, and mushrooms. Cook, stirring frequently, for 3 minutes or until onions are translucent and mushrooms are soft. Scrape mixture into the slow cooker.

3. Add carrots, stock, wine, tomato paste, thyme, rosemary, bay leaves, parsley, and pearl onions to the slow cooker. Stir well. Cook stew on low for 8 to 10 hours or on high for 4 or 5 hours or until lamb is very tender. Add peas for the last hour of cooking.

4. If cooking on low, raise the heat to high. Mix cornstarch with cold water in a small cup. Add cornstarch mixture to the slow cooker, cover, and cook for an additional 10 to 15 minutes or until juices are bubbling and slightly thickened. Remove and discard bay leaves, and season stew with salt and pepper. (You can do this up to 3 days in advance and refrigerate stew tightly covered. Reheat over low heat, stirring occasionally.) Serve with boiled baby potatoes.

 **Slow Savvy**

I've been faithful to the classic French recipe for this stew, but if you want to put the potatoes right into the slow cooker and not cook them separately, go ahead. It will save you washing another pot.

Part 5

Main Dishes for All Times of Day

Until now, the pieces of food we've been cooking have been small. They've been in appetizers, soups, and stews. Now it's time to get larger. In Part 5, you'll find recipes for whole pieces of chicken still on the bone, as well as shanks and chops of meat. There's also a whole section of pot roasts and a chapter devoted to popular one-dish dinners. But don't think Part 5 is for carnivore cravings only. There's a wonderful chapter on fish and seafood entrées from around the world, too!

And because your slow cooker can't tell time, there's a whole chapter of recipes to serve for breakfast and brunch.

"I slime over to the other side of the room, and when I'm back six hours later the braised algae is ready to eat. Just amazing."

Chapter 3

Brightening Breakfast and Brunch

In This Chapter

◆ Filling hot cereals

◆ Savory bread puddings

◆ Egg dishes for a crowd

Do you shy away from inviting people for brunch because you think it's too much work early in the day? Or do you picture yourself endlessly cooking eggs? If so, you're not alone. I used to be one of you. The slow cooker—and the recipes in this chapter—can change all that. Many of these treats for early in the day can be prepared to be ready to cook the night before. Eggs are one exception to the rule that raw and cooked food should not be combined prior to cooking, so you can get everything ready to go!

As is true with bean dishes and other foods that tend to scorch on direct heat, homey thick and hot cereals are foolproof when made in the slow cooker. You'll find recipes for those in this chapter as well.

Egg-Cetera

The slow cooker is very successful with egg dishes because eggs need to cook at a low temperature to remain tender. The protein in an egg becomes hard at 165°F, which is just about what the slow cooker heats to on low. Eggs should be cooked to that temperature to make them totally safe and bacteria-free.

The scientific reality is that if eggs are cooked at a high temperature, they toughen. That might be the objective if you're making fried eggs, because you need them to be hard enough that you can flip them in the pan without breaking them. But the recipes in this chapter are tender egg dishes, and the slow cooker treats them kindly.

Cutting Cholesterol

Eggs have gotten a bad nutritional reputation because of the fat and cholesterol in the yolk. But the white is the "good egg." The white, made up primarily of protein and water, is what gives eggs their ability to bind.

If you want to be judicious about cutting cholesterol, you can use an egg substitute product like Egg Beaters. These products are essentially egg whites tinted yellow. But you can also make your own by using 2 egg whites for each whole egg, or if a recipe calls for several eggs, use 2 egg whites and 1 whole egg for every 2 whole eggs listed.

Creamy Oatmeal with Dried Fruit

Amber maple syrup joins tangy dried cranberries and apricots to flavor this hearty porridge.

2 cups old-fashioned rolled oats or Irish steel-cut oats

1 (12-oz.) can evaporated milk

1½ cups apple juice

¼ cup pure maple syrup

¼ cup chopped dried apricots

¼ cup dried cranberries

¼ cup raisins

¾ tsp. ground ginger

½ tsp. salt

Serves: 6 to 8
Prep time: 15 minutes
Minimum cook time: 2½ hours in a medium slow cooker

1. Grease the slow cooker liberally with vegetable oil spray or melted butter.

2. Add oats, evaporated milk, apple juice, maple syrup, apricots, cranberries, raisins, ginger, and salt to the slow cooker. Stir well.

3. Cook on low for 5 to 7 hours or on high for 2½ to 3 hours or until oatmeal is soft and mixture is creamy. Stir halfway through cooking time. Serve immediately.

Variation: Another morning, try serving this sweetened with dark brown sugar. Then use raisins in place of other dried fruit and substitute cinnamon for the ginger.

Cooker Caveats

It's important to use old-fashioned rolled oats or Irish steel-cut oats for this recipe. Quick-cooking or instant oats will turn into textureless mush.

Cornmeal Porridge with Raspberries

This is really a breakfast version of polenta, sweetened with brown sugar and spiced with cinnamon.

Serves: 4 to 6

Prep time: 10 minutes
Minimum cook time:
3 hours in a medium slow cooker

3½ cups water

1 (12-oz.) can evaporated milk

¼ cup firmly packed light brown sugar

1 cup yellow cornmeal or polenta

¼ tsp. ground cinnamon

¼ tsp. ground nutmeg

Pinch of salt

1 cup *mascarpone* cheese

1 pt. fresh raspberries, rinsed

 **Slow Speak**

Mascarpone (*mas-kar-POHN*) is a buttery rich triple-cream cheese from the Lombardy region of Italy with a very delicate flavor. If you can't find it, substitute equal parts butter and cream cheese.

1. Grease the slow cooker liberally with vegetable oil spray or melted butter.

2. Combine water, evaporated milk, and brown sugar in the slow cooker. Stir well to dissolve sugar. Whisk in cornmeal, cinnamon, nutmeg, and salt.

3. Cook on low for 6 to 8 hours or on high for 3 or 4 hours or until mixture is very thick. Stir every few hours after it comes to a boil.

4. If cooking on high, reduce the heat to low. Stir in mascarpone and whisk well. Gently fold in raspberries, and cook for 5 minutes to warm berries. Serve immediately.

Variation: Any type of berry is wonderful in this recipe, as are chopped ripe peaches or plums.

Hot Apple Muesli

This breakfast cereal is similar to an apple cobbler, with raisins added for additional flavor and texture.

4 Granny Smith apples, peeled, cored, and diced

¾ tsp. ground cinnamon

¼ cup granulated sugar

2 TB. freshly squeezed lemon juice

2 cups muesli cereal

½ cup raisins

4 TB. unsalted butter, melted

Serves: 4 to 6		
Prep time: 15 minutes		
Minimum cook time: 3 hours in a medium slow cooker		

1. Grease the inside of the slow cooker liberally with vegetable oil spray.

2. Place apples in a mixing bowl, and toss with cinnamon, sugar, and lemon juice until evenly coated. Stir in muesli cereal and raisins. Transfer mixture to the slow cooker. Drizzle top with melted butter.

3. Cook on low for 6 to 8 hours or on high for 3 or 4 hours or until apples are tender. Serve immediately.

Variation: This recipe works equally well with your favorite granola in place of the muesli, and feel free to substitute peaches for the apples.

Crock Tales

Muesli, German for "mixture," was developed at the end of the nineteenth century by Swiss nutritionist Dr. Maximilian Oskar Bircher-Benner. The doctor recognized the value of whole grains as well as fruits in the diet, and advocated both raw and toasted cereal grains be incorporated.

Scrambled Eggs for a Crowd

This recipe alone is enough reason to buy a slow cooker; you can feed a huge crowd out of one pot!

Serves: 12 to 18
Prep time: 15 minutes
Minimum cook time: 2 hours in a medium slow cooker

3 dz. large eggs

1 cup sour cream

Salt and freshly ground black pepper

1. Grease the inside of the slow cooker liberally with vegetable oil spray or melted butter.

2. Whisk eggs with sour cream, and season with salt and pepper. Pour mixture into the slow cooker.

3. Cook on low for 2 to 4 hours or until eggs are set. Stir eggs after 1½ hours of cooking to break up the cooked egg portion.

Variation: This recipe is open to endless additions. Add anything you'd use as filling for an omelet—from sautéed mushrooms, peppers, or onions to bits of cooked bacon or chopped ham—to the eggs as they cook.

Slow Savvy

If you're making a small amount of scrambled eggs, modify this preparation method by melting some butter in a skillet over low heat. Add the beaten eggs, cover the pan, and cook until the eggs begin to puff. Stir and turn off the heat.

Spinach and Cheese Strata

Kids love this for breakfast when it's paired with ham—just tell them it's "Green Eggs and Ham."

3 TB. unsalted butter

1 medium onion, peeled and diced

6 large eggs, lightly beaten

2 cups whole milk

1 TB. herbes de Provence, or 1 tsp. dried thyme, 1 tsp. dried rosemary, and 1 tsp. dried basil

Salt and freshly ground black pepper

⅔ lb. loaf white bread, broken into small pieces

1 (10-oz.) pkg. frozen chopped spinach, thawed

1½ cups grated mozzarella cheese

Serves: 4 to 6

Prep time: 15 minutes

Minimum cook time: 4 hours in a medium slow cooker

---

1. Heat butter in a small skillet over medium-high heat. Add onion and cook, stirring frequently, for 3 minutes or until onion is translucent. Remove the pan from the heat and set aside.

2. Grease the inside of the slow cooker liberally with vegetable oil spray or melted butter.

3. Combine eggs, milk, herbes de Provence, salt, and pepper in a large mixing bowl, and whisk well. Add bread pieces to the bowl, and stir so bread absorbs egg mixture.

4. Place spinach in a sieve and press with the back of a spoon to extract as much liquid as possible. Add onion, spinach, and cheese to bread mixture and stir well. Transfer mixture to the slow cooker.

5. Cook on low for 4 to 6 hours or until the mixture is puffed and an instant-read thermometer inserted in the center reads 165°F. Serve immediately.

Variation: Try this with chopped broccoli or chopped asparagus and cheddar cheese instead of spinach and mozzarella.

 Cooker Caveats

Never rinse eggs before using them. The water makes the shells porous and can cause the eggs to spoil faster and allow bacteria to enter.

Sausage, Apple, and Sage Raisin Bread Strata

This dish has a sweet and savory balance, with sweet apple and raisins in contrast to the hearty sausage.

Serves: 6 to 8
Prep time: 15 minutes
Minimum cook time: 4 hours in a medium slow cooker

1 large Golden Delicious apple

8 large eggs

3½ cups whole milk

Salt and freshly ground black pepper

1 cup grated mozzarella cheese

¾ lb. loaf raisin bread, cut into ½-in. cubes

¾ lb. bulk breakfast sausage

2 TB. unsalted butter

1 small onion, peeled and diced

3 TB. granulated sugar

¼ cup chopped fresh sage or 1 TB. dried

½ tsp. ground cinnamon

1. Peel apple and cut into quarters. Discard core and slice quarters into thin slices.

2. Grease the inside of the slow cooker liberally with vegetable oil spray.

3. Combine eggs, milk, salt, and pepper in a mixing bowl, and whisk well. Stir in mozzarella cheese and bread cubes, and stir so bread absorbs egg mixture.

4. Place a large skillet over medium-high heat. Add sausage, breaking up lumps with a fork. Cook sausage, stirring frequently, for 5 minutes or until browned. Remove sausage from the pan with a slotted spoon and add to bread mixture. Discard sausage grease.

5. Return the skillet to the stove, and reduce the heat to medium. Add butter and onion. Cook, stirring frequently, for 3 minutes or until onion is translucent. Add apple, sugar, sage, and cinnamon to the skillet. Cook, stirring frequently, for 5 minutes or until apple softens. Stir apple into bread mixture. Transfer mixture to the slow cooker.

6. Cook on low for 4 to 6 hours or until the mixture is puffed and an instant-read thermometer inserted in the center reads 165°F. Serve immediately.

Variation: If raisin bread isn't available, use a ¾-pound loaf French or Italian bread and add ½ cup raisins and an additional ½ teaspoon cinnamon to custard mixture.

Crock Tales

Although there isn't really a Jolly Green Giant, there certainly was a Johnny Appleseed. Named John Chapman, he was born in Massachusetts in 1774. Unlike the artistic depictions of his propagating apples by tossing seeds out of his backpack, he actually started nurseries for apple tree seedlings in the Allegheny Valley in 1800. By the time of his death in 1845, Chapman had pushed as far west as Indiana, establishing groves of apple trees as he went.

Blueberry French Toast Strata

Lemon zest is a wonderful flavor accent in this sweet and cheese-less strata.

Serves: 6 to 8

Prep time: 15 minutes

Minimum cook time: 4 hours in a medium slow cooker

---

8 large eggs

3½ cups whole milk

Salt

⅓ cup granulated sugar

1 TB. grated lemon zest

1 tsp. pure vanilla extract

¾ lb. loaf challah, Portuguese sweet bread, or white bread, cut into ½-in. cubes

1 pt. fresh blueberries, rinsed, or 2 cups dry-packed frozen blueberries, thawed

1. Grease the inside of the slow cooker liberally with vegetable oil spray or melted butter.

2. Combine eggs, milk, salt, sugar, lemon zest, and vanilla extract in a mixing bowl, and whisk well. Add bread cubes, and stir so bread absorbs egg mixture. Add blueberries, and stir again. Transfer mixture to the slow cooker.

3. Cook on low for 4 to 6 hours or until the mixture is puffed and an instant-read thermometer inserted in the center reads 165°F. Serve immediately.

Variation: Any berry works wonderfully in this dish. Try orange zest instead of or in addition to lemon, too.

Cooker Caveats

You can substitute half-and-half for the whole milk, but do not substitute 2 percent milk or skim milk. Milk with a lower fat content produces a strata that tastes watery rather than rich. If skim or 2 percent milk is all you have in the house, add 2 tablespoons melted butter to the custard mixture for each 1 cup milk.

Bacon, Corn, and Jalapeño Jack Strata

In addition to a hearty brunch dish, you can serve this strata to 10 to 12 people as a side dish with a grilled or broiled entrée.

8 large eggs

3½ cups whole milk

Salt and freshly ground black pepper

1½ cups grated jalapeño jack cheese

¾ lb. loaf French or Italian bread, cut into ½-in. cubes

1 lb. bacon, cut into 1-in. pieces

1 (10-oz.) pkg. frozen corn, thawed and drained

½ cup diced pimiento

Serves: 6 to 8
Prep time: 15 minutes
Minimum cook time: 4 hours in a medium slow cooker

1. Grease the inside of the slow cooker liberally with vegetable oil spray or melted butter.

2. Combine eggs, milk, salt, and pepper in a mixing bowl, and whisk well. Add cheese and bread cubes, and stir so bread absorbs egg mixture.

3. Place a large skillet over medium-high heat, and add bacon pieces. Cook, stirring occasionally, for 5 to 7 minutes or until bacon is crisp. Remove bacon from the pan with a slotted spoon, and add to bread mixture. Stir in corn and pimiento. Transfer mixture to the slow cooker.

4. Cook on low for 4 to 6 hours or until mixture is puffed and an instant-read thermometer inserted in the center reads 165°F. Serve immediately.

Variation: For a spicier version of this dish, substitute Mexican chorizo or Portuguese linguiça sausage for the bacon. Either one of those will really wake up your taste buds first thing in the morning!

Slow Savvy

The best place to store eggs is in their cardboard carton. The carton helps prevent moisture loss, and it shields the eggs from absorbing odors from other foods. If you're not sure if your eggs are fresh, submerge them in a bowl of cool water. If they stay on the bottom, they're fine. If they float to the top, it shows they're old because eggs develop an air pocket at one end as they age.

Potato, Onion, and Bacon Frittata

This combination of omelet additions comes from the Lyon region of France, and all the elements add great flavor to the dish.

Serves: 4 to 6

Prep time: 25 minutes

Minimum cook time: 2 hours in a medium slow cooker

½ lb. bacon, cut into 1-in. lengths

2 large red-skinned potatoes, scrubbed and cut into ¼-in. dice

1 large onion, peeled and diced

1 garlic clove, peeled and minced

8 large eggs

¼ cup half-and-half

2 TB. chopped fresh parsley

Salt and freshly ground black pepper

Slow Savvy

It makes sense to buy 1 pound of bacon rather than a ½ pound that sells for almost the same price. You can freeze the rest by rolling a few slices together and then placing the rolls in a plastic bag. That way you don't have to defrost the whole thing.

---

1. Place bacon in a large skillet over medium-high heat. Cook, stirring occasionally, for 5 to 7 minutes or until bacon is crisp. Remove bacon from the pan with a slotted spoon and drain on paper towels. Set aside.

2. Discard all but 3 tablespoons bacon fat from the skillet. Add potatoes and cook for 10 minutes or until tender, scraping them occasionally with a heavy spatula. Add onion and garlic to the skillet and cook, stirring frequently, for 5 minutes or until onion is soft.

3. Whisk eggs with half-and-half and parsley, and season with salt and pepper. Add vegetable mixture and bacon to eggs.

4. Grease the inside of the slow cooker liberally with vegetable oil spray or melted butter. Pour egg mixture into the slow cooker. Cook on high for 2 to 2½ hours or until eggs are set.

5. Run a spatula around the sides of the slow cooker and under the bottom of the frittata to release it. Slide it gently onto a serving platter, and cut it into wedges. Serve immediately.

Variation: You can substitute ham or sausage for the bacon, and ½ cup diced red bell pepper works well cooked along with the onion and garlic.

Vegetable Frittata with Pasta

This frittata with zucchini, scallions, and tomatoes is delicately flavored with herbs and olives.

1 (6-oz.) pkg. refrigerated fresh angel-hair pasta

3 TB. olive oil

2 small zucchini, rinsed, trimmed, and thinly sliced

4 scallions, trimmed and thinly sliced

3 garlic cloves, peeled and minced

2 ripe plum tomatoes, rinsed, cored, seeded, and finely chopped

3 TB. chopped fresh basil or 2 tsp. dried

1 TB. chopped fresh oregano or 1 tsp. dried

¼ cup sliced green olives

Salt and freshly ground black pepper

6 large eggs

½ cup freshly grated Parmesan cheese

Serves: 4 to 6
Prep time: 25 minutes
Minimum cook time: 1½ hours in a medium slow cooker

1. Cook pasta according to package directions until al dente. Drain and set aside to cool.

2. Heat olive oil in a large skillet over medium-high heat. Add zucchini, scallions, and garlic. Cook, stirring frequently, for 5 minutes or until zucchini is tender. Add tomatoes, basil, oregano, and olives. Cook mixture, stirring frequently, for 5 minutes or until liquid from tomatoes evaporates. Season with salt and pepper, and cool for 10 minutes.

3. Grease the inside of the slow cooker liberally with vegetable oil spray or melted butter. Whisk eggs with cheese, and stir in cooked pasta and vegetables. Pour mixture into the slow cooker.

4. Cook on high for 1½ to 2 hours or until eggs are set. Run a spatula around the sides of the slow cooker and under the bottom of the frittata to release it. Slide it gently onto a serving platter, and cut it into wedges. Serve hot or at room temperature.

Cooker Caveats

It's important that you cook the vegetables until they're dry. If they're not cooked to that point, the frittata will be watery and won't come out of the pan easily.

Sausage and Pepper Hash

Delicate shallots, multiple colors of sweet bell peppers, and numerous herbs make this hash a luscious base for baked eggs.

Serves: 6 to 8

Prep time: 25 minutes

Minimum cook time: 2 hours in a medium slow cooker

---

2 lb. bulk pork sausage

10 shallots, peeled and minced

6 garlic cloves, peeled and minced

3 yellow bell peppers, seeds and ribs removed, and finely chopped

3 red bell peppers, seeds and ribs removed, and finely chopped

3 green bell peppers, seeds and ribs removed, and finely chopped

1 jalapeño chile, seeds and ribs removed, and finely chopped

1 TB. chopped fresh sage or 1 tsp. dried

1 TB. fresh thyme or 1 tsp. dried

1 TB. chopped fresh rosemary or 1 tsp. dried

1 TB. chopped fresh oregano or 1 tsp. dried

½ cup chopped fresh parsley

3 bay leaves

Salt and freshly ground black pepper

12 to 16 large eggs

1. Place a large skillet over medium-high heat. Add sausage, breaking up any lumps with a fork, and cook, stirring frequently, for 6 to 8 minutes or until sausage is browned. Remove sausage from the pan with a slotted spoon, drain on paper towels, and place it in the slow cooker.

2. Add shallots, garlic, yellow bell peppers, red bell peppers, green bell peppers, and jalapeño to the skillet. Cook, stirring frequently, for 3 minutes or until shallots are translucent. Scrape vegetables into the slow cooker, and add sage, thyme, rosemary, oregano, parsley, and bay leaves.

3. Cook on low for 4 to 6 hours or on high for 2 or 3 hours or until vegetables are very soft. Tilt the slow cooker, and skim off as much grease as possible. Remove and discard bay leaves, and season with salt and pepper.

4. Preheat the oven to 350°F.

5. Spread sausage mixture in a 10×14-inch baking dish. Make 12 to 16 indentations in the mixture with the back of a spoon, and break 1 egg into each. Sprinkle eggs with salt and pepper, and bake for 12 to 15 minutes or until egg whites are set. Serve immediately.

Crock Tales

Hash is a general term for food that's finely chopped. The English word first appears in the mid-seventeenth century; it comes from the French word *hacher,* which means "to chop." Because hash was frequently made with leftovers, inexpensive restaurants became known as "hash houses."

Stuffed Brunch Peppers

Italian sausage moistened with tomato sauce and eggs are the filling for this easy-to-make brunch dish.

Serves: 4
Prep time: 20 minutes
Minimum cook time: 2½ hours in a medium slow cooker

4 bell peppers (any color) that sit evenly when placed on a flat surface

2 TB. olive oil

¼ cup Italian breadcrumbs

1 lb. bulk sweet Italian sausage

½ cup spaghetti sauce

4 large eggs

Salt and freshly ground black pepper

3 TB. freshly grated Parmesan cheese

1. Cut tops off peppers. Discard tops and seeds, and pull out ribs with your fingers. Set aside.

2. Heat olive oil in a medium skillet over medium-high heat. Add breadcrumbs and cook, stirring frequently, for 2 minutes or until browned. Scrape breadcrumbs into a small bowl, and set aside. Wipe the skillet clean with paper towels.

3. Add sausage to the skillet, breaking up any lumps with a fork. Cook, stirring frequently, for 6 to 8 minutes or until sausage is browned. Remove sausage from the pan with a slotted spoon, and drain on paper towels. Place sausage in a small mixing bowl, and stir in spaghetti sauce.

4. Spoon sausage mixture into the bottom of each pepper, dividing it evenly among them. Arrange peppers in the slow cooker. Cook on low for 4 to 6 hours or on high for 2 or 3 hours or until peppers soften.

5. If cooking on low, raise the heat to high. Break an egg into each pepper, and sprinkle egg with salt, pepper, toasted breadcrumbs, and cheese. Cook for 20 to 30 minutes or until eggs are cooked. Serve immediately.

Variation: To make this a more delicate dish, use ground beef or ground turkey in place of the sausage.

Chapter 14

Sensational Seafood

In This Chapter

◆ Slow cooked fish relatively fast

◆ Fish with crisp vegetables

◆ Slow cooked vegetable sauces for delicate fish dishes

Unlike meats, which can take a whole workday to cook in the slow cooker, fish and seafood need only a fraction of that time. In fact, overcooking seafood is more of a risk than undercooking. That's why the slow cooker plays a background role in creating delicious fish dishes.

What makes these dishes different from those in other chapters is that the seafood is cooked for a very brief time at the end of the cooking cycle. While this is also the case with the fish stew recipes in Chapter 10, many of the recipes in this chapter are intended to keep the vegetables on the crisp side so the overall cooking time is occasionally as little as 2 hours.

Fish Families

Although the recipes in this chapter call for specific fish, it's more important to use the freshest fish in the market rather than the particular species.

All finfish fall into three basic families, and you can easily substitute one species for another. Use the following table to make life at the fish counter easier.

A Guide to Fish

Description	Species	Characteristics
Firm, lean	black sea bass, cod family, flat fish (flounder, sole, halibut), grouper, lingcod, ocean perch, perch, pike, porgy, red snapper, smelt, striped bass, turbot, salmon, trout, drum family, tilefish, tilapia	low fat, mild to delicate flavor, firm flesh, flakes when cooked
Meaty	catfish, carp, eel, monkfish (anglerfish), orange roughy, pike, salmon, shark, sturgeon, swordfish, some tuna varieties, mahi-mahi (dolphinfish), whitefish, pompano, yellowtail	low to high fat, diverse flavors and textures, usually thick steaks or fillets
Fatty or strong-flavored	bluefish, mackerel, some tuna varieties	high fat, pronounced flavor

Slow Savvy

Fish is high in protein and low to moderate in fat, cholesterol, and sodium. A 3-ounce portion of fish has between 47 and 170 calories, depending on the species, and is an excellent source of B vitamins, iodine, phosphorus, potassium, iron, and calcium. The most important nutrient in fish may be the omega-3 fatty acids, the primary polyunsaturated fatty acids found in the fat and oils of fish. They lower low-density lipoprotein levels (LDL, the "bad" cholesterol) and raise high-density lipoprotein levels (HDL, the "good" cholesterol). Fatty fish that live in cold water, such as mackerel and salmon, seem to have the most omega-3 fatty acids.

Italian-Style Baked Bluefish

Tomatoes and other vegetables dotted with olives glorify this delicious oily fish.

¼ cup olive oil

2 celery ribs, rinsed, trimmed, and sliced

1 large onion, peeled and diced

6 garlic cloves, peeled and minced

1 (14.5-oz.) can diced tomatoes, undrained

½ cup dry white wine

¼ cup chopped pitted kalamata olives

4 TB. small capers, rinsed and drained

2 TB. chopped fresh parsley

2 tsp. fresh thyme or ½ tsp. dried

2 lb. bluefish fillets, skinned and cut into serving pieces

Salt and freshly ground black pepper

2 cups cooked white rice or pasta

Serves: 4 to 6
Prep time: 25 minutes
Minimum cook time: 3 hours in a medium slow cooker

1. Heat olive oil in a medium skillet over medium-high heat. Add celery, onion, and garlic. Cook, stirring frequently, for 3 minutes or until onion is translucent. Scrape mixture into the slow cooker, and add tomatoes, wine, olives, capers, parsley, and thyme. Cook on low for 5 to 7 hours or on high for 2½ to 3 hours or until vegetables are tender.

2. If cooking on low, raise the heat to high. Pour vegetable mixture into a mixing bowl. Season bluefish with salt and pepper. Place ½ of bluefish into the slow cooker and top with ½ of vegetable mixture. Repeat with the other ½ of bluefish and vegetable mixture. Cook fish on high for 20 to 30 minutes or until cooked through and flakes easily. Serve fish with rice or pasta.

Variation: If bluefish is a bit too strong for your taste, try tilapia, cod, or flounder for a milder flavor. If you don't live in a bluefish part of the country, try mackerel instead.

Cooker Caveats

Many people think of bluefish as a strong-smelling fish, but that's not the case when it's freshly caught. When buying bluefish, there should be no "fishy" smell to the fillets at all.

Chinese-Style Sea Bass with Mixed Vegetables

Delicate sea bass is joined with crisp vegetables in a light sauce flavored with ginger in this easy dish.

Serves: 4 to 6
Prep time: 15 minutes
Minimum cook time: 2 hours in a medium slow cooker

1 lb. fresh asparagus spears

3 TB. Asian sesame oil

6 scallions, trimmed and cut into 1-in. pieces

5 garlic cloves, peeled and minced

3 TB. grated fresh ginger

1 small jalapeño chile, seeds and ribs removed, and finely chopped

1 large red bell pepper, seeds and ribs removed, and thinly sliced

1 medium red onion, peeled and thinly sliced

¼ cup soy sauce

¼ cup plum wine or sweet sherry

¾ cup fish stock or chicken stock

1½ lb. sea bass fillets, rinsed and cut into 4 to 6 serving-size pieces

Salt and freshly ground black pepper

2 to 3 cups cooked jasmine rice

¼ cup black sesame seeds or toasted white sesame seeds

 Slow Savvy

Toasting sesame seeds is a quick process. Place them in a small dry skillet over medium-high heat, and shake the pan as they begin to brown. The entire process takes less than 1 minute.

1. Rinse asparagus and break off woody stems. Cut asparagus on the diagonal into 1-inch pieces. Set aside.

2. Heat sesame oil in a large skillet over medium-high heat. Add scallions, garlic, ginger, and jalapeño. Cook, stirring constantly, for 30 seconds. Add asparagus, red bell pepper, and red onion to the skillet. Cook, stirring frequently, for 2 minutes. Transfer mixture to the slow cooker.

3. Add soy sauce, plum wine, and stock to the slow cooker. Cook on low for 3 or 4 hours or on high for 1½ to 1¾ hours or until vegetables are tender-crisp.

4. If cooking on low, raise the heat to high. Season sea bass with salt and pepper, and place it on top of vegetables. Cook for 30 to 45 minutes or until fish is cooked through and flakes easily. Serve fish and vegetables over rice, and sprinkle with sesame seeds.

Variation: Try this recipe with jumbo shrimp instead of sea bass, and they'll be cooked in 15 to 20 minutes.

Halibut in White Wine with Pearl Onions and Oranges

Crispy sugar snap peas top this delicate dish with subtle fish cooked with oranges and herbs.

3 scallions

2 navel oranges

2 TB. olive oil

1 celery rib, trimmed and sliced

3 garlic cloves, peeled and minced

1 (1-lb.) pkg. frozen pearl onions, thawed and drained

1 (14.5-oz.) can diced tomatoes, undrained

¼ cup chopped fresh parsley

1½ cups fish stock or chicken stock

½ cup dry white wine

1 cup freshly squeezed orange juice

1 bay leaf

Salt and freshly ground black pepper

1½ to 2 lb. halibut fillets, cut into 6 to 8 pieces, rinsed

¾ lb. sugar snap peas, rinsed and stemmed

2 or 3 cups cooked couscous

Serves: 4 to 6
Prep time: 15 minutes **Minimum cook time:** 2¼ hours in a medium slow cooker

1. Rinse and trim scallions, discarding all but 2 inches of green tops. Slice scallions, and set aside.

2. Cut all rind and white pith from oranges, and cut into ½-inch dice.

3. Heat olive oil in a small skillet over medium-high heat. Add scallions, celery, and garlic, and cook, stirring frequently, for 3 minutes or until scallions are translucent. Scrape mixture into the slow cooker.

4. Add pearl onions, tomatoes, parsley, fish stock, white wine, orange juice, and bay leaf to the slow cooker. Season with salt and pepper, and stir well. Cook on low for 3 or 4 hours or on high for 1½ to 2 hours or until bubbling and vegetables are tender.

5. If cooking on low, raise the heat to high. Add orange pieces, halibut fillets, and sugar snap peas to the slow cooker. Cook for 30 to 50 minutes or until fish is cooked through and flakes easily. Remove and discard bay leaf. Serve immediately, spooning halibut and vegetables over couscous.

Variation: Try salmon in this recipe for a change of color as well as flavor.

 Slow Savvy

I've considered nominating frozen pearl onions for a Nobel Prize. They are such an incredible convenience and not at the sake of quality. It takes forever to peel baby pearl onions; it's just not worth it.

Cod with Tomatoes and Fennel

The slight licorice flavor of the fennel is enhanced by the inclusion of anise-flavored liqueur in this healthful recipe.

Serves: 4 to 6
Prep time: 15 minutes
Minimum cook time: 3 hours in a medium slow cooker

2 medium fennel bulbs

¼ cup olive oil

1 large onion, peeled and thinly sliced

3 garlic cloves, peeled and minced

1 (28-oz.) can diced tomatoes, drained

½ cup dry white wine

½ cup freshly squeezed orange juice

2 TB. Pernod, ouzo, or other anise-flavored liqueur

1 TB. grated orange zest

2 lb. thick cod fillets, cut into serving pieces

Salt and freshly ground black pepper

 Slow Savvy _____

This is one dish you can start the day before you want to serve it. Cook the vegetables and then refrigerate the mixture. The next day, reheat the vegetables and cook the cod as directed.

1. Discard stalks from fennel, and save for another use. Rinse fennel, cut in half lengthwise, and discard core and top layer of flesh. Slice fennel thinly, and set aside.

2. Heat olive oil in a large skillet over medium-high heat. Add onion and garlic, and cook, stirring frequently, for 3 minutes or until onion is translucent. Add fennel and cook for an additional 2 minutes. Scrape mixture into the slow cooker.

3. Add tomatoes, wine, orange juice, Pernod, and orange zest to the slow cooker. Cook on low for 5 to 7 hours or on high for 2½ to 3 hours or until fennel is tender-crisp.

4. If cooking on low, raise the heat to high. Season cod with salt and pepper, and place it on top of vegetables. Cook for 30 to 45 minutes or until fish is cooked through and flakes easily.

Variation: Try this recipe with jumbo shrimp instead of cod; they cook in 15 to 20 minutes.

Rare Tuna with Salsa Topping

As soon as I started reading about chefs cooking fish in a 200°F oven, I knew the slow cooker would be even better! This robust, meaty fish remains perfectly rare, and the salsa is a great topping.

4 to 6 (6-oz.) tuna steaks, at least ¾ in. thick

3 TB. olive oil

2 TB. ground cumin

2 TB. chili powder

Salt and freshly ground black pepper

4 ripe plum tomatoes, rinsed, cored, and diced

3 scallions, rinsed, trimmed, and chopped

3 TB. snipped fresh chives

2 TB. freshly squeezed lime juice

Serves: 4 to 6
Prep time: 15 minutes
Minimum cook time: 1 hour in a medium slow cooker

1. Rub tuna with 1 tablespoon olive oil. Combine cumin, chili powder, salt, and pepper in a small bowl. Rub mixture on both sides of tuna, and place tuna in the slow cooker. Cook on high for 40 minutes. Turn tuna gently with a slotted spatula.

2. Combine remaining olive oil with tomatoes, scallions, chives, and lime juice. Season with salt and pepper. Top tuna with salsa, and cook on high for an additional 20 to 30 minutes for rare tuna or longer for fish that's more done. Serve immediately.

Variation: Salmon is a good substitute for tuna, and it takes the same amount of time to cook.

 Cooker Caveats

As they do on restaurant menus, I feel obligated to tell you that some health authorities warn against eating uncooked and undercooked fish and seafood, along with meats.

Monkfish with Cabbage and Bacon

Monkfish is called "poor man's lobster" because of its sweet flavor and a texture similar to the prized crustacean. Blanched cabbage and hearty bacon are a great combination with it.

Serves: 4 to 6

Prep time: 25 minutes

Minimum cook time: 2 hours in a medium slow cooker

½ small (1½-lb.) head Savoy or green cabbage

¼ lb. bacon, diced

2 lb. monkfish fillets, trimmed and cut into serving pieces

3 garlic cloves, peeled and minced

1 cup fish stock or bottled clam juice

2 TB. snipped fresh chives

1 TB. chopped fresh parsley

1 TB. chopped fresh basil or 1 tsp. dried

2 tsp. fresh tarragon or ½ tsp. dried

2 tsp. grated lemon zest

Salt and freshly ground black pepper

2 TB. unsalted butter

1 to 1½ lb. steamed new potatoes

1. Rinse and core cabbage. Cut cabbage into wedges and then shred. Bring a large pot of salted water to a boil. Add cabbage and boil for 4 minutes. Drain cabbage and place it in the slow cooker.

2. Cook bacon in a heavy skillet over medium heat for 5 to 7 minutes or until crisp. Remove bacon from the pan with a slotted spoon, and place it in the slow cooker. Raise the heat to high, and *sear* monkfish in the bacon fat on all sides, turning the pieces gently with tongs, until browned. Refrigerate monkfish.

3. Add garlic, stock, chives, parsley, basil, tarragon, and lemon zest to the slow cooker. Cook on low for 3 or 4 hours or on high for 1½ to 2 hours or until cabbage is almost tender.

4. If cooking on low, raise the heat to high. Season monkfish with salt and pepper, and place it on top of vegetables. Cook monkfish for 30 to 45 minutes or until cooked through. Remove monkfish from the slow cooker and keep it warm. Add butter to cabbage, and stir to melt butter. Season with salt and pepper.

5. To serve, mound equal-size portions of cabbage on each plate. Slice monkfish into medallions, and arrange on top of cabbage. Serve with steamed new potatoes.

Variation: If monkfish is hard to find where you live, try thick fillets of halibut or cod instead. The cooking time is the same.

Slow Speak

To **sear** is to quickly brown food in very hot fat. In addition to browning the food, searing seals the outer layer so its juices don't escape as readily during cooking. When searing food, always turn it with tongs rather than a meat fork, which punctures the skin and lets all the juices escape.

Moroccan Fish Tagine

Aromatic Middle Eastern spices and olives flavor this lean and light dish.

Serves: 4 to 6

Prep time: 15 minutes

Minimum cook time: 2½ hours in a medium slow cooker

⅔ cup olive oil

¼ cup freshly squeezed lemon juice

¼ cup dry white wine

2 TB. chopped fresh cilantro

1 TB. paprika

1 tsp. ground cumin

1 tsp. ground ginger

½ tsp. salt

¼ tsp. cayenne

1½ lb. cod, halibut, or other firm-fleshed whitefish, rinsed and cut into serving pieces

2 large onions, peeled and diced

3 garlic cloves, peeled and minced

1 cup fish stock or bottled clam juice

½ cup sliced green olives

Salt and freshly ground black pepper

2 or 3 cups cooked couscous

Crock Tales

A tagine might sound exotic, but it's basically a Moroccan stew that can feature just about any sort of fish, meat, or poultry as long as it also contains olives and spices such as cumin.

1. Combine ½ cup olive oil, lemon juice, wine, cilantro, paprika, cumin, ginger, salt, and cayenne in a heavy, resealable plastic bag. Mix well and add fish. Marinate fish in the refrigerator for 2 to 4 hours, turning the bag occasionally so fish marinates evenly.

2. Heat remaining olive oil in a medium skillet over medium-high heat. Add onions and garlic, and cook, stirring frequently, for 3 minutes or until onion is translucent. Scrape mixture into the slow cooker.

3. Drain marinade from fish, and add liquid to the slow cooker along with stock and olives. Return fish to the bag and refrigerate. Cook on low for 4 or 5 hours or on high for 2 or 3 hours or until onion is tender.

4. If cooking on low, raise the heat to high. Add fish to the slow cooker, and cook for 30 to 40 minutes or until fish is cooked through and flakes easily. Season with salt and pepper, and serve fish with hot couscous.

Mexican Snapper

This spicy dish comes from Veracruz, and it's emblematic of the Mexican way to cook fish.

2 TB. olive oil

2 onions, peeled and thinly sliced

4 garlic cloves, peeled and minced

1 jalapeño chile, seeds and ribs removed, and finely chopped

1 TB. chili powder

2 tsp. dried oregano

1 (14.5-oz.) can diced tomatoes, undrained

1 cup fish stock or bottled clam juice

2 TB. freshly squeezed lemon juice

2 TB. tomato paste

1 tsp. grated lemon zest

¼ cup sliced green olives

2 lb. red snapper or other firm-fleshed whitefish fillets, cut into serving pieces

Salt and freshly ground black pepper

2 cups cooked white or brown rice

Serves: 4 to 6
Prep time: 15 minutes
Minimum cook time: 2½ hours in a medium slow cooker

1. Heat olive oil in a medium skillet over medium-high heat. Add onions, garlic, and jalapeño, and cook, stirring frequently, for 3 minutes or until onion is translucent. Stir in chili powder and oregano. Cook for 1 minute, stirring constantly. Scrape mixture into the slow cooker.

2. Add tomatoes, stock, lemon juice, tomato paste, and lemon zest to the slow cooker. Stir well. Cook for 4 to 6 hours on low or for 2 or 3 hours on high or until vegetables are tender.

3. If cooking on low, raise the heat to high. Stir in olives, and gently add fish. Cook for 20 to 40 minutes or until fish is cooked through and flakes easily. Season with salt and pepper, and serve fish with rice.

Variation: This recipe is also delicious made with 2 pounds boneless, skinless chicken breasts or slices of firm tofu. Add these foods to the slow cooker at the onset of cooking, and substitute either chicken or vegetable stock for the seafood stock.

 Slow Savvy

A chile pepper's seeds and ribs contain almost all the capsaicin, the chemical compound that delivers the peppers' punch. Because small chiles have proportionately more seeds and ribs to flesh, a general rule is the smaller the chili, the hotter.

Shrimp and Shiitake Bread Pudding

This bread pudding is topped with a creamy sauce, and the flavors of the shrimp and shiitake blend nicely with the herbs.

Serves: 4 to 6

Prep time: 25 minutes

Minimum cook time: 2 hours in a medium slow cooker

12 slices white bread

4 TB. unsalted butter

2 shallots, peeled and minced

1 garlic clove, peeled and minced

½ lb. fresh shiitake or crimini mushrooms, rinsed, stemmed, and sliced

¼ cup brandy

1 lb. cooked shrimp, peeled and deveined

3 large eggs

1 cup heavy cream

½ cup seafood stock or bottled clam juice

2 tsp. fresh chopped tarragon or ½ tsp. dried

Salt and freshly ground black pepper

½ cup dry white wine

1 (8-oz.) pkg. refrigerated Alfredo sauce

1 TB. tomato paste

2 TB. chopped fresh chives or 2 tsp. dried

Salt and freshly ground black pepper

1. Grease the inside of the slow cooker liberally with vegetable oil spray.

2. Toast bread slices. Break bread into small cubes, and place them in the slow cooker.

3. Heat butter in a medium skillet over medium-high heat. Add shallots, garlic, and mushrooms, and cook, stirring frequently, for 3 to 5 minutes until shallots are translucent. Increase the heat to high and add brandy. Cook for 2 or 3 minutes or until brandy has evaporated. Scrape mixture into the slow cooker along with shrimp.

4. Whisk together eggs, cream, stock, tarragon, salt, and pepper. Pour mixture into the slow cooker, and stir well. Press bread into liquid with the back of a spoon so it absorbs custard. Cook on low for 4 to 6 hours or on high for 2 or 3 hours or until a toothpick inserted into the center comes out clean.

5. While pudding is cooking, make sauce. Pour wine into a small saucepan, and boil over high heat until it's reduced in volume by ½. Add Alfredo sauce, tomato paste, and chives. Stir until smooth, and season with salt and pepper. Pass sauce separately.

Variation: Feel free to try cooked lobster, crabmeat, or cubes of leftover fish in place of the shrimp.

Slow Savvy

The oven broiler is the best way to toast large amounts of bread at the same time. Place the oven rack about ⅓ of the way down, and arrange the bread on baking sheets. Watch the bread carefully, though. You've only got a few seconds between nicely toasted and burned.

Spanish Seafood and Rice (*Paella*)

Precious aromatic saffron flavors and colors the rice that mixes with bell peppers and herbs in this classic dish from Valencia.

Serves: 6 to 8
Prep time: 20 minutes
Minimum cook time: 2½ hours in a medium slow cooker

---

2 TB. olive oil

1 onion, peeled and diced

3 garlic cloves, peeled and minced

½ red or green bell pepper, seeds and ribs removed, and cut into ½-in. dice

2 cups long-grain converted rice

4 cups seafood stock or bottled clam juice

1 tsp. dried oregano

1 tsp. dried thyme

1 bay leaf

½ tsp. crushed saffron threads

Salt and freshly ground black pepper

1 (10-oz.) pkg. frozen artichoke hearts, thawed

1 cup frozen peas, thawed

¾ lb. extra large (16 to 20 per lb.) raw shrimp, peeled and deveined

½ lb. sea scallops, rinsed and halved

½ lb. swordfish, rinsed and cut into 1-in. cubes

Crock Tales

Ounce for ounce, saffron is the most expensive food in the world. All the individual threads are harvested by hand from the purple crocus.

1. Heat olive oil in a medium skillet over medium-high heat. Add onion, garlic, and red bell pepper. Cook, stirring frequently, for 3 minutes or until onion is translucent. Scrape mixture into the slow cooker.

2. Add rice, stock, oregano, thyme, bay leaf, and saffron to the slow cooker, and stir well. Cook on low for 4 to 6 hours or on high for 2 or 3 hours or until rice is almost tender.

3. If cooking on low, raise the heat to high. Season mixture with salt and pepper, and remove and discard bay leaf. Stir in artichoke hearts, peas, shrimp, scallops, and swordfish. Cook for an additional 30 to 45 minutes or until shrimp are pink.

Variation: To augment the seafood with chicken, cut boneless, skinless breasts into 1-inch cubes and add them to the slow cooker for the initial cooking time.

Chapter **15**

Our Feathered Friends

In This Chapter

◆ An international collection of chicken recipes

◆ Delicious ways to eat turkey when it's not Thanksgiving

◆ Recipes for "other white meats"

Chicken in all forms is becoming the mainstay of many diets. And why not? It's a healthful and relatively inexpensive source of protein that can be prepared myriad ways. Chicken is like a blank canvas to cooking. Its natural delicacy means that it absorbs seasonings superbly, and a wide range of flavors at that. Perhaps that's another reason why Americans are eating so much chicken! It's impossible to be bored by it.

The slow cooker is the perfect pot for cooking chicken because there's almost no way the chicken can become dry with the way the slow cooker cooks. Turn the page; you'll find a wide range of recipes for treating this poultry pal in this chapter.

Safety First

Chicken and all meats should always be rinsed under cold running water after they're taken out of the package. If it's going to be prebrowned in the oven or in a skillet on the stove, pat the pieces dry with paper towels and then wash your hands. Chicken often contains salmonella, a naturally occurring bacteria that's killed by cooking, but you don't want to transfer this bacteria to other foods.

For the sake of food safety, if you're cooking a whole chicken in the slow cooker, it's best to cook it on high. The low heat might keep the meat of a whole bird in the bacterial danger zone for more than 2 hours. High is the way to go.

Chicken in Red Wine (*Coq au Vin*)

Go into any bistro in Paris, and you're likely to find this hearty dish of chicken, mushrooms, and pearl onions simmered in herbed wine on the menu.

1 (3- to 4-lb.) chicken or 6 chicken pieces of your choice (breasts, thighs, legs) with bones

2 cups dry red wine

½ cup chicken stock

3 garlic cloves, peeled and minced

1 tsp. dried thyme

1 bay leaf

1 (1-lb.) bag frozen pearl onions, thawed

½ lb. white mushrooms, rinsed, stemmed, and halved

1 TB. cornstarch

2 TB. cold water

Salt and freshly ground black pepper

1½ lb. oven-roasted or steamed potatoes

Serves: 4 to 6
Prep time: 20 minutes
Minimum cook time: 3½ hours in a medium slow cooker

1. Preheat the oven broiler, and line a broiler pan with heavy-duty aluminum foil.

2. If using a whole chicken, cut it into serving pieces. Rinse chicken, and pat dry with paper towels. Arrange chicken on the foil, and broil for 3 to 5 minutes or until browned. Turn pieces, and brown the other side. Arrange chicken in the slow cooker.

3. Combine wine, stock, garlic, thyme, bay leaf, pearl onions, and mushrooms in the slow cooker. Arrange chicken pieces in the cooker, skin side down. Cook on low for 6 to 8 hours or on high for 3 to 4 hours or until chicken is cooked through, tender, and no longer pink. Remove chicken and vegetables from the slow cooker with a slotted spoon, and cover with foil to keep them warm.

4. Pour cooking liquid from the slow cooker into a saucepan, and bring it to a boil over high heat. Boil until liquid is reduced in volume by half. Mix cornstarch and water in a small cup, and add cornstarch mixture to the boiling liquid. Reduce the heat to low, and simmer sauce for 2 minutes or until juices are bubbling and slightly thickened. Remove and discard bay leaf, season with salt and pepper, and pour sauce over chicken. Serve chicken with oven-roasted or steamed potatoes.

Variation: For a lighter-tasting and -toned dish, try this recipe with a dry white wine instead of the traditional red.

Cooker Caveats

When cooking with wine or any other acid such as lemon juice, it's important to use a stainless-steel or coated steel pan rather than aluminum. When mixed with the wine or acid, an aluminum pan can impart a metallic taste to the dish.

Chicken Fricassee with Wild Mushrooms

Woodsy wild mushrooms flavor the delicate cream sauce for this historic American dish.

Serves: 4 to 6

Prep time: 20 minutes

Minimum cook time: 3½ hours in a medium slow cooker

---

1 (3- to 4-lb.) chicken or 6 chicken pieces of your choice (breasts, thighs, legs), with bones	**1 TB. fresh thyme or 1 tsp. dried**
8 TB. unsalted butter	**1 TB. fresh rosemary or 1 tsp. dried**
3 shallots, peeled and diced	**¾ lb. wild mushrooms, rinsed, stemmed, and sliced**
2 garlic cloves, peeled and minced	**½ cup heavy cream**
3 TB. all-purpose flour	**Salt and freshly ground black pepper**
1½ cups chicken stock	**2 cups cooked white or brown rice**
3 TB. chopped fresh parsley	

Slow Speak

Fricassee (*frick-a-SEE*) is an old method for creating a tender chicken dish. The chicken is lightly cooked in butter before it's stewed with liquid and vegetables.

1. If using a whole chicken, cut it into serving pieces. Rinse chicken and pat dry with paper towels.

2. Heat 3 tablespoons butter in a large skillet over medium-high heat. Add chicken pieces, brown on both sides, and cover the pan. Cook for 5 minutes and then transfer chicken to the slow cooker.

3. Add shallots and garlic to the skillet. Cook, stirring frequently, for 3 minutes or until shallots are translucent. Reduce the heat to low, and stir in flour. Cook for 1 minute, stirring constantly. Raise the heat to medium-high, and stir in stock. Bring to a boil, and simmer for 2 minutes. Stir in parsley, thyme, and rosemary. Pour mixture over chicken in the slow cooker. Cook for 6 to 8 hours on low or 3 or 4 hours on high or until chicken is cooked through, tender, and no longer pink.

4. While chicken is cooking, heat remaining 5 tablespoons butter in a medium skillet over medium-high heat. Add mushrooms and cook, stirring frequently, for 5 minutes or until mushrooms are soft.

5. If cooking on low, raise the heat to high. Stir mushrooms and cream into the slow cooker, and season with salt and pepper. Cook for an additional 20 to 30 minutes or until sauce is bubbly. Serve chicken over rice.

Chicken Paprikash

Sour cream is used to finish this classic Hungarian chicken dish, usually prepared with thighs.

2 TB. vegetable oil

1 TB. unsalted butter

1 large onion, peeled and thinly sliced

3 garlic cloves, peeled and minced

4 TB. paprika, preferably Hungarian

6 skinless chicken thighs

1 (14.5-oz.) can diced tomatoes, undrained

½ cup chicken stock

½ cup dry white wine

1 TB. fresh thyme or 1 tsp. dried

2 TB. cornstarch

2 TB. cold water

⅓ cup sour cream

Salt and freshly ground black pepper

2 cups buttered egg noodles

Serves: 4 to 6
Prep time: 15 minutes
Minimum cook time: 3 hours in a medium slow cooker

1. Heat vegetable oil and butter in a large skillet over medium-high heat. Add onion and garlic, and cook, stirring frequently, for 3 minutes or until onion is translucent. Reduce the heat to low, and stir in paprika. Cook for 1 minute, stirring constantly. Scrape mixture into the slow cooker.

2. Rinse chicken and pat dry with paper towels. Arrange chicken in the slow cooker. Stir in tomatoes, stock, wine, and thyme. Cook on low for 6 to 8 hours or on high for 3 or 4 hours or until chicken is cooked through, tender, and no longer pink.

3. Mix cornstarch with water, and stir cornstarch mixture into the slow cooker. Cook for an additional 20 to 30 minutes or until juices are bubbling and slightly thickened.

4. If cooking on high, reduce the heat to low. Stir in sour cream and cook for 5 to 10 minutes or until sour cream is heated. *Do not let mixture come to a boil.* Season with salt and pepper, and serve with buttered egg noodles.

Variation: Veal is as good in this dish as chicken, and it cooks in the same amount of time.

 Cooker Caveats

Sour cream can curdle if it's allowed to boil, so always add it at the end of cooking a dish. Stir in the sour cream and allow the mixture to cook on low until the juices are once again hot. Then turn off the heat.

Curried Chicken with Dried Currants (Country Captain)

The light stock sauce for this historic dish is laced with a bit of dry sherry for additional character.

Serves: 4 to 6
Prep time: 20 minutes
Minimum cook time: 3 hours in a medium slow cooker

1 (3- to 4-lb.) chicken or 6 chicken pieces of your choice (breasts, thighs, legs) with bones

3 TB. unsalted butter

1 large onion, peeled and diced

3 garlic cloves, peeled and minced

1 red bell pepper, seeds and ribs removed, and diced

1 TB. curry powder

½ tsp. ground ginger

½ tsp. ground allspice

½ tsp. dried thyme

⅔ cup dried currants

1 (14.5-oz.) can diced tomatoes, undrained

⅔ cup chicken stock

⅓ cup dry sherry

2 TB. cornstarch

2 TB. cold water

Salt and freshly ground black pepper

2 cups cooked white or brown rice

1. Preheat the oven broiler, and line a broiler pan with heavy-duty aluminum foil.

2. If using a whole chicken, cut it into serving pieces. Rinse chicken and pat dry with paper towels. Arrange chicken on the foil, and broil for 3 to 5 minutes or until browned. Turn and brown the other side. Arrange chicken in the slow cooker.

3. Melt butter in a medium skillet over medium-high heat. Add onion, garlic, and red bell pepper. Cook, stirring frequently, for 3 to 5 minutes or until onion is translucent and pepper begins to soften. Add curry powder, ginger, allspice, and thyme to the pan. Cook for 1 minute, stirring constantly.

4. Scrape mixture into the slow cooker. Add currants, tomatoes, stock, and sherry. Stir well. Cook on low for 6 to 8 hours or on high for 3 or 4 hours or until chicken is cooked through, tender, and no longer pink.

5. If cooking on low, raise the heat to high. Mix cornstarch and cold water in a small cup. Stir mixture into the slow cooker, and cook for an additional 10 to 20 minutes or until liquid is bubbling and has slightly thickened. Season with salt and pepper and serve with hot rice.

Crock Tales

Country Captain is a chicken dish that dates to Colonial times. Some food historians say it originated in Savannah, Georgia, a major port for the spice trade. Other sources say a British captain brought the curry-flavored dish back from India.

Chicken Cacciatore

The tomato sauce is infused with many different herbs in this robust way to cook tender chicken breasts.

Serves: 4
Prep time: 15 minutes
Minimum cook time: 2 hours in a medium slow cooker

3 TB. olive oil

1 large onion, peeled and diced

3 garlic cloves, peeled and minced

½ green bell pepper, seeds and ribs removed, and finely chopped

4 (6-oz.) boneless, skinless chicken breast halves

1 (8-oz.) can tomato sauce

½ cup dry white wine

½ cup chicken stock

2 TB. fresh oregano or 2 tsp. dried

1 TB. fresh thyme or 1 tsp. dried

1 TB. fresh rosemary or 1 tsp. dried

1 bay leaf

Salt and freshly ground black pepper

2 cups cooked orzo or rice

Crock Tales

Cacciatore is Italian for "hunter's style." A number of dishes from chicken to beef to veal use cacciatore as a handle, but all it means is that the dish is cooked with tomatoes. The rest of the ingredients are up to the cook.

1. Heat olive oil in a medium skillet over medium-high heat. Add onion, garlic, and green bell pepper. Cook, stirring frequently, for 3 minutes or until onion is translucent. Scrape mixture into the slow cooker.

2. Rinse chicken and pat dry with paper towels. Arrange chicken on top of vegetables in the slow cooker.

3. Combine tomato sauce, wine, stock, oregano, thyme, rosemary, and bay leaf in a small bowl. Pour mixture over chicken. Cook on low for 4 to 6 hours or on high for 2 or 3 hours or until chicken is cooked through, tender, and no longer pink. Remove and discard bay leaf, and season with salt and pepper. Serve chicken with orzo or rice.

Chinese Red-Cooked Chicken

Simmering foods in aromatic stock is one of the oldest forms of Chinese cooking and is gaining popularity in this country.

1 (3- to 4-lb.) chicken or 6 chicken pieces of your choice (breasts, thighs, legs) with bones

2 TB. Asian sesame oil

4 scallions, rinsed, trimmed, and sliced

6 garlic cloves, peeled and minced

2 TB. grated fresh ginger

¾ cup *tamari*

¾ cup chicken stock

¼ cup dry sherry

¼ cup firmly packed dark brown sugar

1 tsp. Chinese five-spice powder

2 cups cooked white rice or fried rice

Serves: 4 to 6		
Prep time: 15 minutes		
Minimum cook time: 3 hours in a medium slow cooker		

1. Preheat the oven broiler, and line a broiler pan with heavy-duty aluminum foil.

2. If using a whole chicken, cut it into serving pieces. Rinse chicken and pat dry with paper towels. Arrange chicken on the foil, and broil for 3 to 5 minutes or until browned. Turn and brown the other side. Arrange chicken in the slow cooker.

3. Heat sesame oil in a small skillet over medium-high heat. Add scallions, garlic, and ginger. Cook, stirring frequently, for 2 minutes or until fragrant. Scrape mixture into a mixing bowl. Add tamari, stock, sherry, brown sugar, and Chinese five-spice powder. Stir well to dissolve sugar, and pour mixture over chicken. Cook on low for 6 to 8 hours or on high for 3 or 4 hours or until chicken is cooked through, tender, and no longer pink. Serve with white rice or fried rice.

Variation: This dish is also great served cold for a picnic. If serving it cold, use boneless, skinless breasts and/or thighs, and reduce the cooking time to 4 to 6 hours on low or 2 or 3 hours on high.

> **Slow Speak**
>
> Similar to soy sauce, **tamari** is a dark sauce made from soy beans. But unlike soy sauce, it has a distinctive and mellow flavor rather than being overwhelmingly salty. You can substitute a light Japanese-style soy sauce in a pinch.

Chicken Jambalaya

With its combination of chicken, sausage, and shrimp nestled in yellow rice, this is one of the prettiest dishes you'll bring to the table.

Serves: 6 to 8	
Prep time: 25 minutes	
Minimum cook time: 3½ hours in a medium slow cooker	

1 (3- to 4-lb.) chicken or 6 to 8 chicken pieces of your choice (breasts, thighs, legs) with bones

½ lb. kielbasa or other smoked sausage, cut into ½-in. slices

3 TB. olive oil

2 celery ribs, rinsed, trimmed, and chopped

1 large onion, peeled and diced

½ green bell pepper, seeds and ribs removed, and diced

4 garlic cloves, peeled and minced

1 (14.5-oz.) can diced tomatoes, drained

1½ cups chicken stock

1 TB. fresh thyme or 1 tsp. dried

1 bay leaf

2 (5-oz.) pkg. yellow rice

½ lb. extra-large (16 to 20 per lb.) raw shrimp, peeled and deveined

Salt and freshly ground black pepper

1. Preheat the oven broiler, and line a broiler pan with heavy-duty aluminum foil.

2. If using a whole chicken, cut it into serving pieces, with breasts cut into 2 sections. Rinse chicken and pat dry with paper towels. Arrange chicken on the foil, and broil for 3 or 4 minutes or until lightly browned. Turn chicken pieces with tongs, add sausage to the broiler pan, and broil for an additional 3 or 4 minutes. Set aside.

3. Heat olive oil in a medium skillet over medium-high heat. Add celery, onion, green bell pepper, and garlic. Cook, stirring frequently, for 3 minutes or until onion is translucent. Scrape mixture into the slow cooker, and stir in tomatoes, stock, thyme, and bay leaf.

4. Arrange chicken pieces and sausage in the slow cooker. Cook on low for 6 to 8 hours or on high for 3 or 4 hours or until chicken is cooked through, tender, and no longer pink.

5. If cooking on low, raise the heat to high. Stir in rice, and cook on high for 20 to 30 minutes or until rice is almost soft. Add shrimp, and cook on high for an additional 10 to 15 minutes or until shrimp are pink. Remove and discard bay leaf, and season with salt and pepper.

Crock Tales

Jambalaya is a staple of Louisiana cooking, where culinary traditions of France, Spain, Italy, and the New World, among others, blended. Jambalaya was the local adaptation of the Spanish rice dish paella and became a favorite among the Cajuns, French transplants who settled in the Louisiana bayous.

Mexican Chicken and Rice (Arroz con Pollo)

Green olives, peas, and tomatoes are all part of this slow cooked authentic Mexican dish.

Serves: 4 to 6	
Prep time: 20 minutes	
Minimum cook time: 4 hours in a medium slow cooker	

1 (3- to 4-lb.) chicken or 6 chicken pieces of your choice (breasts, thighs, legs) with bones

⅓ cup olive oil

1 large onion, peeled and diced

4 garlic cloves, peeled and minced

½ green or red bell pepper, seeds and ribs removed, and diced

1 TB. paprika

1 TB. chili powder or to taste

2 tsp. dried oregano

1 (14.5-oz.) can diced tomatoes

½ cup dry white wine

½ cup chicken stock

1 bay leaf

1 cup uncooked converted long-grain rice

½ cup sliced pimiento-stuffed green olives

1 cup frozen peas, thawed

Salt and freshly ground black pepper

1. Preheat the oven broiler, and line a broiler pan with heavy-duty aluminum foil.

2. If using a whole chicken, cut it into serving pieces, with breasts cut into 2 sections. Rinse chicken and pat dry with paper towels. Arrange chicken on the foil, and broil for 3 to 5 minutes or until browned. Turn and brown the other side. Arrange chicken in the slow cooker.

3. Heat 2 tablespoons olive oil in a medium skillet over medium-high heat. Add onion, garlic, and green bell pepper. Cook, stirring frequently, for 3 minutes or until onion is translucent. Reduce the heat to low. Add paprika, chili powder, and oregano. Cook for 1 minute, stirring constantly. Scrape mixture into the slow cooker.

4. Add tomatoes, wine, stock, and bay leaf to the slow cooker. Cook on low for 4 to 6 hours or on high for 2 or 3 hours or until chicken is cooked through.

5. While chicken is cooking, add remaining oil to the skillet. Cook rice for 3 or 4 minutes, stirring frequently, or until grains are opaque and lightly browned. Remove the pan from the heat and set aside.

6. If cooking on low, raise the heat to high. Add rice to the slow cooker. Cook for 1 hour or until rice is almost tender and chicken is no longer pink. Add olives and peas to the slow cooker, and cook for 10 to 15 minutes or until peas are hot. Remove and discard bay leaf, and season with salt and pepper.

Cooker Caveats

For the success of this dish and other dishes that include rice, it's important that you use long-grain converted rice. A shorter-grain rice will turn to mush. Converted white rice has undergone a steam-pressure process that makes the grains fluffier and keeps them separate when cooked.

Cranberry-Glazed Turkey Meatloaf

The slow cooker's low heat and its closed environment keep this lean, herbed turkey loaf very moist.

Serves: 4 to 6	
Prep time: 15 minutes	
Minimum cook time: 3 hours in a medium slow cooker	

4 TB. unsalted butter

2 onions, peeled and diced

2 garlic cloves, peeled and minced

1 celery rib, trimmed and chopped

1½ lb. ground turkey

2 large eggs, lightly beaten

½ cup plain breadcrumbs

1 TB. chopped fresh sage or 1 tsp. dried

1 TB. fresh thyme or 1 tsp. dried

Salt and freshly ground black pepper

½ cup Cranberry Chutney (recipe in Chapter 21) or canned whole berry cranberry sauce

3 cups stuffing or mashed potatoes

Slow Savvy

Store your dried herbs and spices in a cool, dark place to preserve their potency—not in pretty, clear jars over the stove. To test for freshness and potency, simply smell the contents. If there's no strong aroma, you need a new bottle.

1. Melt butter in a medium saucepan over medium-high heat. Add onions, garlic, and celery. Cook, stirring frequently, for 3 minutes or until onions are translucent. Scrape mixture into a mixing bowl. Add turkey, eggs, breadcrumbs, sage, thyme, salt, and pepper. Mix well to combine.

2. Fold a sheet of heavy-duty aluminum foil in half, and place it in the bottom of the slow cooker with the sides of the foil extending up the sides of the slow cooker.

3. Form meat mixture into an oval or round, depending on the shape of your cooker, and place it into the cooker on top of the foil. Spread Cranberry Chutney on top of meat. Cook meatloaf on low for 6 to 8 hours or on high for 3 or 4 hours or until an instant-read thermometer inserted into the center of meat reads 165°F.

4. Remove meat from the cooker by pulling up the sides of the foil. Drain off any grease from the foil, and slide meatloaf onto a serving platter. Serve meatloaf with stuffing or mashed potatoes.

Variation: Try this recipe with ground pork or a combination of pork and veal. The cooking time won't change.

Turkey Tonnato

This is one of my favorite summer entrées because cooking the turkey in the slow cooker means the kitchen doesn't get hot! And the chilled turkey with tuna sauce is a delicious combination.

1 (1½-lb.) boneless, skinless turkey breast	Salt and freshly ground black pepper
3 garlic cloves, peeled and cut into quarters	1 (6.5-oz.) can imported tuna packed in olive oil
1½ cups chicken stock	¼ cup freshly squeezed lemon juice
½ cup dry white wine	2 TB. anchovy paste
1 onion, peeled and sliced	¼ cup mayonnaise
1 carrot, peeled and sliced	2 TB. capers, drained and rinsed
4 sprigs fresh parsley	1½ lb. cold pasta salad or potato salad
2 sprigs fresh thyme or 1 tsp. dried	
1 bay leaf	

> *Serves: 4 to 6*
>
> **Prep time:** 20 minutes
> **Minimum cook time:**
> 3 hours in a medium slow cooker plus 8 hours to chill

1. Rinse turkey breast and pat dry with paper towels. Place turkey between two sheets of plastic wrap, and pound with the flat side of a meat mallet or bottom of a small saucepan until it's a uniform thickness. Roll turkey breast into a shape that will fit into your slow cooker, and tie with kitchen string. Make 12 slits around turkey breast, and insert a garlic sliver in each one. Place turkey breast in the slow cooker.

2. Add stock, wine, onion, carrot, parsley, thyme, bay leaf, salt, and pepper to the slow cooker. Cook on low for 6 to 8 hours or on high for 3 or 4 hours or until a thermometer inserted in the center of turkey reads 165°F. Remove turkey from the slow cooker and chill well.

3. Combine tuna, lemon juice, and anchovy paste in a food processor fitted with a steel blade or in a blender. Purée until smooth, and scrape mixture into a mixing bowl. Stir in mayonnaise and capers, and season with pepper.

4. To serve, remove and discard the string, and thinly slice turkey. Spoon some sauce on turkey slices, and pass the rest separately. Serve turkey with cold pasta salad or potato salad.

Variation: You can make the same sauce for poached veal loin. Cook the veal for the same amount of time.

 Slow Savvy

Save the braising liquid in this recipe. It's a richly flavored stock and it's a shame to throw it away. Freeze it and use it in place of chicken stock when cooking another recipe.

Duck Confit

There's no question that this is my favorite way to eat duck. The meat literally falls off the bone because it's so tender after gently cooking in fat.

Serves: 4

Prep time: 15 minutes

Minimum cook time:
7 hours in a medium slow cooker plus 24 hours to marinate

---

4 duck legs or 1 duck cut into quarters

6 garlic cloves, peeled and minced

2 bay leaves, broken into pieces

1 TB. dried thyme

2 TB. kosher salt

1 tsp. coarsely ground black pepper

2 cups duck fat, chicken fat, or vegetable oil

1 lb. oven-roasted potatoes

1. Rinse duck legs, and pat dry with paper towels.

2. Combine garlic, bay leaves, thyme, kosher salt, and pepper in a small bowl. Rub both sides of duck legs with seasoning mixture, and place duck in a heavy plastic bag. Marinate duck in the refrigerator for 24 hours.

3. If using duck or chicken fat, heat it in the slow cooker on high for 30 minutes or until it melts. If using vegetable oil, pour it into the slow cooker.

4. Remove duck legs from the refrigerator, and rinse under cold running water. Arrange duck legs in the slow cooker, skin side down. They should be almost submerged in fat. Cook on low for 7 to 9 hours or until duck is incredibly tender.

5. Remove duck from fat with a slotted spatula. If using duck in other dishes, remove meat from the bones when cool enough to handle and discard bones. Store duck meat refrigerated, covered with fat from the slow cooker. If serving duck legs as an entrée, place them under a preheated broiler for 4 or 5 minutes or until the skin is brown and crisp. Serve duck with oven-roasted potatoes.

Crock Tales

Confit is a gastronomic specialty of the Gascony region of France. It can be either duck or goose that's gently cooked in fat and then stored submerged in fat. This was one of the earliest methods of preserving meats, and it still produces a dish that's melt-in-your-mouth tender.

Chapter **16**

Beefing Up Dinner

In This Chapter

- ◆ Delicious ways to cook inexpensive cuts of beef
- ◆ Family-pleasing pot roast recipes from around the world
- ◆ International ground beef dishes

After women started working outside the home in large numbers, dishes like pot roast were reserved for weekends. Very few cooks felt comfortable leaving a pot unattended on a burner or in the oven all day while the house was empty. Today there's an alternative—the slow cooker. Pot roast can once again become a dish for any evening.

Slowly cooked beef dishes use less-expensive cuts of meat than those reserved for roasting. These succulent cuts, like short ribs and chuck, become meltingly tender after many hours of the slow cooker's gentle heat. In this chapter, you'll find a number of ways to cook large pieces of beef as well as ground beef.

The Daily Grind

Generally, ground beef is made from the less-tender and less-popular cuts of beef, although it sometimes includes trimmings from more tender cuts like steak. Grinding tenderizes the meat, and the fat on these bargain cuts reduces its dryness and improves flavor of hamburgers or any dish.

The price of ground beef is determined by the cut of meat it's from and the amount of fat incorporated into the mix. High-fat mixtures are less costly but shrink more when cooked. The least expensive product, made from the shank and brisket, is sold as ground beef and can contain up to 30 percent fat. Moderately priced ground chuck is the next category. Because it contains enough fat (about 15 to 20 percent) to give it flavor and make it juicy, yet not enough to cause excess shrinkage, ground chuck is a good choice for these recipes.

The Tiffany of hamburger, boasting 10 percent fat or less, are ground round and ground sirloin. Because these are extremely lean cuts, there's little fat to remove after browning the meat.

Sunday Pot Roast

This is the American classic. It's made with potatoes, mushrooms, and other vegetables in a lightly seasoned beef broth.

1 (2- to 2½-lb.) beef rump or chuck roast

3 TB. vegetable oil

1 onion, peeled and diced

3 garlic cloves, peeled and minced

½ lb. white mushrooms, rinsed, stemmed, and sliced

4 medium red-skinned potatoes, scrubbed and cut into ½-in. cubes

2 carrots, peeled and cut into ½-in. pieces

2 celery ribs, rinsed, trimmed, and cut into ½-in. slices

1 (14.5-oz.) can diced tomatoes, undrained

2 cups beef stock

1 TB. fresh thyme or 1 tsp. dried

1 bay leaf

1 TB. cornstarch

2 TB. cold water

Salt and freshly ground black pepper

Serves: 4 to 6
Prep time: 20 minutes
Minimum cook time: 5½ hours in a medium slow cooker

1. Preheat the oven broiler, and line a broiler pan with heavy-duty aluminum foil. Broil beef for 3 to 5 minutes per side or until browned. Set aside.

2. Heat vegetable oil in a large skillet over medium-high heat. Add onion, garlic, and mushrooms. Cook, stirring frequently, for 3 to 5 minutes or until onion is translucent and mushrooms are soft. Scrape mixture into the slow cooker.

3. Add potatoes, carrots, celery, tomatoes, stock, thyme, and bay leaf, and mix well. Add beef to the slow cooker, pushing it down into liquid. Cook for 10 to 12 hours on low or 5 or 6 hours on high or until beef and vegetables are very tender.

4. If cooking on low, raise the heat to high. Mix cornstarch with water, and stir cornstarch mixture into the slow cooker. Cook for an additional 15 to 20 minutes or until juices are bubbling and slightly thickened. Remove and discard bay leaf, and season pot roast with salt and pepper. (You can do this up to 3 days in advance and refrigerate tightly covered. Reheat covered in a 350°F oven for 20 to 30 minutes or until hot.)

Variation: You can use just about any root vegetable in a pot roast. Try some turnips, parsnips, fennel, or celery root as additions or substitutions.

Slow Savvy

Do you have some vegetables like carrots and celery ribs that have gotten a little limp in the refrigerator? Save them for stock. Wrap the vegetables and place them in the freezer, and thaw them before they go into the slow cooker to make the stock.

Short Ribs of Beef with Rosemary and Celery

This is one of my favorite beef dishes. The delicate celery and aromatic rosemary are the perfect foils for the hearty beef.

Serves: 4 to 6

Prep time: 15 minutes

Minimum cook time: 4 hours in a large slow cooker

---

5 lb. meaty short ribs with bones or 2½ lb. boneless short ribs

¼ cup vegetable oil

1 large onion, peeled and *diced*

4 garlic cloves, peeled and minced

2 cups beef stock

3 celery ribs, rinsed, trimmed, and sliced

3 TB. chopped fresh rosemary or 1 TB. dried

2 TB. cornstarch

2 TB. cold water

Salt and freshly ground black pepper

2 cups buttered egg noodles

Slow Speak

Dice means to cut food into squares of the same size. In some recipes the size is specified, while in others the word is open to personal interpretation because the size of the pieces doesn't matter for the success of a dish. In those cases, try not to make the pieces larger than ½ inch.

1. Preheat the oven broiler, and line a broiler pan with heavy-duty aluminum foil. Broil short ribs for 3 or 4 minutes per side or until browned. Arrange short ribs in the slow cooker, and pour in any juices that have collected in the pan.

2. Heat vegetable oil in a medium skillet over medium-high heat. Add onion and garlic, and cook, stirring frequently, for 3 minutes or until onion is translucent. Scrape mixture into the slow cooker. Add stock, celery, and rosemary to the slow cooker and stir well. Cook on low for 8 to 10 hours or on high for 4 or 5 hours or until short ribs are very tender.

3. Remove as much grease as possible from the slow cooker with a soup ladle.

4. If cooking on low, raise the heat to high. Mix cornstarch with water in a small cup. Stir cornstarch mixture into the slow cooker, and cook on high for 15 to 20 minutes or until juices are bubbling and slightly thickened. Season with salt and pepper, and serve with buttered egg noodles. (You can do this up to 3 days in advance and refrigerate tightly covered. Reheat covered in a 350°F oven for 20 to 30 minutes or until hot.)

Short Ribs with Beans and Barley (Cholent)

This is a hearty dish, by all means, but it's subtly seasoned and has a variety of textures and delicate flavors.

2 cups dried white beans

5 lb. meaty short ribs with bones, or 2½ lb. boneless short ribs

¼ cup vegetable oil

3 large onions, peeled and diced

2 garlic cloves, peeled and minced

3 TB. paprika, preferably Hungarian

1 cup pearl barley

1 lb. new potatoes, scrubbed and halved

4 cups beef stock

Salt and freshly ground black pepper

Serves: 6
Prep time: 25 minutes
Minimum cook time: 6 hours in a large slow cooker

1. Rinse beans in a colander, and place them in a mixing bowl covered with cold water. Allow beans to soak overnight. Or place beans into a saucepan and bring to a boil over high heat. Boil 1 minute. Turn off the heat, cover the pan, and soak beans for 1 hour. Drain, discard soaking water, and place beans into the slow cooker.

2. Preheat the oven broiler, and line a broiler pan with heavy-duty aluminum foil. Broil short ribs for 3 or 4 minutes per side or until browned. Arrange short ribs in the slow cooker, and pour in any juices that have collected in the pan.

3. Heat 2 tablespoons vegetable oil in a medium skillet over medium-high heat. Add onions and garlic, and cook, stirring frequently, for 10 minutes or until onions are browned. Scrape mixture into the slow cooker. Reduce the heat to low, stir in paprika, and cook for 1 minute, stirring constantly. Scrape mixture into the slow cooker.

4. Heat remaining vegetable oil in the skillet over medium heat. Add barley and cook, stirring constantly, for 5 minutes or until browned. Add barley to the slow cooker along with potatoes and stock. Cook on low for 12 to 14 hours or on high for 6 or 7 hours or until short ribs are very tender.

5. Remove as much grease as possible from the slow cooker with a soup ladle. Season with salt and pepper. (You can do this up to 3 days in advance and refrigerate tightly covered. Reheat covered in a 350°F oven for 45 to 50 minutes or until hot.)

Crock Tales

No cooking is allowed on Saturday, the Sabbath, in orthodox Jewish households, so this dish was developed to be started on Friday afternoon and then allowed to slowly cook overnight—which is why it's so perfect for the slow cooker.

Sauerbraten

The thickening for the gravy of this traditional German pot roast comes from crushed gingersnap cookies, which also reinforce the flavor.

Serves: 4 to 6
Prep time: 15 minutes
Minimum cook time: 5 hours in a medium slow cooker plus 1 day for marinating

1 cup dry red wine

1 cup beef stock

½ cup red wine vinegar

2 TB. tomato paste

2 TB. Worcestershire sauce

1 TB. Dijon mustard

½ tsp. salt

½ tsp. allspice

½ tsp. ground ginger

¼ cup firmly packed dark brown sugar

1 onion, peeled and thinly sliced

3 garlic cloves, peeled and thinly sliced

2 or 3 lb. rump or chuck roast

10 gingersnap cookies, crushed

Salt and freshly ground black pepper

3 cups buttered spaetzle or egg noodles

Cooker Caveats

In this recipe, because the marinade becomes the braising liquid and is subjected to high heat, there's no danger of contamination. As a general rule, never use a marinade raw. Either discard it or bring it to a boil for at least 5 minutes.

1. Combine wine, stock, vinegar, tomato paste, Worcestershire sauce, Dijon mustard, salt, allspice, ginger, and brown sugar in a heavy resealable plastic bag. Mix well, and add onion, garlic, and beef. Marinate in the refrigerator for 24 to 48 hours, turning the bag occasionally so meat marinates evenly.

2. Transfer beef and marinade to the slow cooker, and stir in gingersnap crumbs. Cook on low for 10 to 12 hours or on high for 5 or 6 hours or until beef is very tender. Season with salt and pepper.

3. Remove as much grease as possible from the slow cooker with a soup ladle. (You can do this up to 3 days in advance and refrigerate tightly covered. Reheat covered in a 350°F oven for 20 to 30 minutes or until hot.) Slice beef, spoon some gravy over it, and serve it with spaetzle or egg noodles.

Smoked Beef Brisket with Barbecue Sauce

I use the slow cooker in the summer as well as the winter, especially for long-cooked dishes like this succulent pot roast that would otherwise heat up the kitchen.

1 cup hickory or mesquite chips	Salt and freshly ground black pepper
2½ lb. beef brisket	2 cups beef stock
2 garlic cloves, peeled and crushed	1 cup My Favorite Barbecue Sauce (recipe in Chapter 21) or your favorite sauce

> *Serves: 4 to 6*
>
> **Prep time:** 15 minutes
> **Minimum cook time:**
> 5 hours in a medium slow cooker

1. Soak wood chips in cold water for 30 minutes, and light a charcoal grill. Drain the wood chips, and sprinkle chips on the hot coals.

2. Rub brisket with garlic, salt, and pepper. Place brisket on the grill rack, and close the grill's lid or cover it with a sheet of heavy heavy-duty aluminum foil. Smoke brisket for 10 minutes per side, turning it with tongs.

3. Place brisket into the slow cooker and add stock. Cook brisket for 10 to 12 hours on low or 5 or 6 hours on high or until meat is very tender. Season with salt and pepper.

4. Remove as much grease as possible from the slow cooker with a soup ladle. (You can do this up to 3 days in advance and refrigerate tightly covered. Reheat covered in a 350°F oven for 20 to 30 minutes or until hot.) Remove brisket from the slow cooker, and slice it against the grain into thin slices. Spoon some pan juices over meat, and pass barbecue sauce separately.

Variation: You can also use this recipe for a boneless pork shoulder. Reduce the cooking time to 8 to 10 hours on low or 4 or 5 hours on high.

 Slow Savvy

The best way to rid meat dishes of unwanted saturated fat is to chill the dish and then remove and discard the solid layer of fat that forms on the top. If you want to eat the dish the same day it's made, let the dish stand for 10 to 15 minutes, and use a shallow ladle to gather and discard the grease.

Beef Brisket in Red Wine Sauce

The "secret ingredient" that creates the rich, thick gravy in this feast fit for company is an envelope of gravy mix.

Serves: 4 to 6	
Prep time: 15 minutes	
Minimum cook time: 5 hours in a medium slow cooker	

1 (2- to 2½-lb.) beef brisket

1 (1.2-oz.) pkg. dehydrated brown gravy mix

2 garlic cloves, peeled and minced

1 TB. herbes de Provence, or 1 tsp. dried thyme, 1 tsp. dried oregano, and 1 tsp. dried rosemary

1 cup dry red wine

½ cup beef stock

Salt and freshly ground black pepper

2 cups cooked mashed potatoes or buttered egg noodles

Slow Savvy

If you have left-overs from this dish, turn them into barbecue sandwiches the next night. Chop up the meat, heat it in some of the juices, and mound it on buns with barbecue sauce.

1. Preheat the oven broiler, and line a broiler pan with heavy-duty aluminum foil. Broil brisket for 3 to 5 minutes per side or until browned. Set aside.

2. Pour gravy mix into the slow cooker, and stir in garlic, herbes de Provence, wine, and stock. Place brisket into the slow cooker. Cook on low for 10 to 12 hours or on high for 5 or 6 hours or until meat is tender.

3. Turn brisket over with tongs halfway through the cooking process. Season with salt and pepper. Remove as much grease as possible from the slow cooker with a soup ladle. (You can do this up to 3 days in advance and refrigerate tightly covered. Reheat covered in a 350°F oven for 20 to 30 minutes or until hot.)

4. Remove brisket from the slow cooker, and slice it against the grain into thin slices. Spoon some gravy over meat, and serve with mashed potatoes or buttered egg noodles.

Variation: For a fancier dish, use mushroom gravy mix and add some sautéed mushrooms to the slow cooker for the last hour of cooking.

Great American Meatloaf

To really make the family happy, serve this with macaroni and cheese as the side dish. The cheese in the meatloaf helps keep it moist.

2 TB. vegetable oil	½ cup grated mozzarella cheese
1 medium onion, peeled and diced	½ tsp. dried thyme
2 garlic cloves, peeled and minced	Salt and freshly ground black pepper
2 large eggs, lightly beaten	1½ lb. lean ground beef
¼ cup whole milk	½ cup ketchup
½ cup *Italian breadcrumbs*	3 cups mashed potatoes

> *Serves: 4 to 6*
>
> **Prep time:** 20 minutes
> **Minimum cook time:**
> 3 hours in a medium slow cooker

1. Heat vegetable oil in a small skillet over medium-high heat. Add onion and garlic, and cook, stirring frequently, for 3 minutes or until onion is translucent. Set aside.

2. Combine eggs, milk, breadcrumbs, cheese, thyme, salt, and pepper in a large mixing bowl, and stir well. Add meat and onion-garlic mixture, and mix well.

3. Fold a sheet of heavy-duty aluminum foil in half, and place it in the bottom of the slow cooker with the sides of the foil extending up the sides of the slow cooker. Form meat mixture into an oval or round, depending on the shape of your cooker, and place it into the cooker on top of the foil. Spread ketchup on top of meat.

4. Cook meatloaf on low for 6 to 8 hours or on high for 3 or 4 hours or until an instant-read thermometer inserted into center of loaf reads 165°F.

5. Remove meat from the cooker by pulling it up by the sides of the foil. (You can do this up to 3 days in advance and refrigerate tightly covered. Reheat covered in a 350°F oven for 20 to 30 minutes or until hot.) Drain off any grease from the foil, and slide meatloaf onto a serving platter. Serve meatloaf with mashed potatoes.

Variation: Tired of beef? Try this recipe with a combination of beef, veal, and pork for a lighter flavor and texture. It cooks in the same amount of time.

Slow Speak

Italian breadcrumbs are flavored with herbs and cheese. If all you have is plain breadcrumbs, add 1 tablespoon chopped parsley, 1 tablespoon grated Parmesan cheese, and ½ teaspoon dried oregano to the recipe.

Sweet and Sour Stuffed Cabbage

Ground beef, rice, and seasonings are cooked slowly with apples and raisins in a sweet and sour tomato sauce in this Austrian-influenced dish.

Serves: 4 to 6

Prep time: 25 minutes

Minimum cook time: 5 hours in a medium slow cooker

1 small head (about 1 lb.) green cabbage

1½ lb. lean ground beef

1 cup cooked white rice

1 small onion, peeled and grated

Salt and freshly ground black pepper

2 McIntosh or Rome apples, peeled, cored, and diced

½ cup raisins

1 (8-oz.) can tomato sauce

½ cup cider vinegar

½ cup firmly packed dark brown sugar

Slow Savvy

If you like cabbage but not the aroma in the house after it's cooked, add a few hunks of bread to the water in which you're blanching the leaves. The bread acts as a natural deodorizer.

1. Bring a 4-quart saucepan of water to a boil.

2. Remove core from cabbage by cutting around it with a sharp knife. Pull off 10 to 12 large leaves from outside and set aside. Cut remaining cabbage in ½, and cut off 2 cups thin shreds. Blanch leaves and shreds in the boiling water for 5 minutes and then drain.

3. Combine ground beef, rice, onion, salt, and pepper in a mixing bowl, and mix well.

4. Place ½ of drained cabbage shreds in the bottom of the slow cooker. Top with ½ of apples and ½ of raisins.

5. Place ½ cup beef mixture at the root end of 1 cabbage leaf. Tuck in sides, and roll up leaf into a cylinder. Repeat with remaining cabbage leaves and beef filling. Place rolls seam side down in the slow cooker in a single layer. Top with remaining cabbage shreds, apple, and raisins, and start a new layer of cabbage rolls, if necessary.

6. Mix tomato sauce, vinegar, and brown sugar in a mixing bowl, and stir well to dissolve sugar. Pour sauce over cabbage rolls. Cook on low for 10 to 12 hours or on high for 5 or 6 hours or until sauce is bubbly and an instant-read thermometer inserted into beef filling reads 165°F. Remove as much grease

as possible from the slow cooker with a soup ladle. (You can do this up to 3 days in advance and refrigerate tightly covered. Reheat covered in a 350°F oven for 40 to 50 minutes or until hot.)

Variation: For a lighter version, use ground turkey, pork, or veal for the dish. The cooking time remains the same because the cabbage takes so long to cook.

Spaghetti with Meat Sauce

This is a traditional Italian sauce, with herbs and mushrooms added as well. The slow cooking means it doesn't need constant stirring.

Serves: 6 to 8
Prep time: 20 minutes
Minimum cook time: 4 hours in a medium slow cooker

¼ cup olive oil

1 large onion, peeled and diced

6 garlic cloves, peeled and minced

½ lb. white mushrooms, rinsed, stemmed, and sliced

1½ lb. lean ground beef

2 TB. dried oregano

1 TB. dried basil

1 TB. granulated sugar

2 tsp. dried thyme

1 bay leaf

3 (14.5-oz.) cans diced tomatoes, undrained

1 (8-oz.) can tomato sauce

½ cup dry red wine

Salt and freshly ground black pepper or red pepper flakes

4 to 6 cups cooked spaghetti or other cooked pasta

Freshly grated Parmesan cheese

Slow Savvy

Markets today are drowning in olive oils. The expensive stuff is a condiment and is meant to be drizzled on salads. The cheap stuff is for frying foods before they're placed in the slow cooker.

1. Heat olive oil in a large skillet over medium-high heat. Add onion, garlic, and mushrooms. Cook, stirring frequently, for 3 to 5 minutes or until onion is translucent and mushrooms are soft. Scrape mixture into the slow cooker.

2. Add ground beef to the pan, breaking up any lumps with a fork. Brown beef for 3 to 5 minutes. Remove beef from the pan with a slotted spoon, and add to the slow cooker.

3. Add oregano, basil, sugar, thyme, bay leaf, tomatoes, tomato sauce, and wine to the slow cooker, and stir well.

4. Cook on low for 8 to 10 hours or on high for 4 or 5 hours. Remove and discard bay leaf, and season sauce with salt and pepper. Remove as much grease as possible from the slow cooker with a soup ladle. (You can do this up to 3 days in advance and refrigerate tightly covered. Reheat over low heat, stirring occasionally, until hot.) Serve sauce over cooked spaghetti, and pass sauce and cheese separately.

Variation: You can use a proportion of mild or hot Italian sausage in place of some of the ground beef. Or you can transform it into spaghetti with meatballs instead of meat sauce. Form meat into balls and brown them in a 500°F oven for 10 minutes. Then drop them into the liquid in the slow cooker.

Eastern European Beef and Carrots with Dried Fruits (*Tsimmis*)

The natural sweetness of both carrots and sweet potatoes are enhanced with dried fruit and apple cider in this easy-to-prepare dish.

2 lb. boneless short ribs or chuck roast, cut into 2-in. cubes	1 cup dried apricots
	1 cup pitted prunes
1½ lb. carrots, peeled and cut into ½-in. slices	1 cup apple cider
	1 cup beef stock
1½ lb. sweet potatoes, peeled and cut into 1-in. cubes	½ tsp. grated nutmeg
	½ to 1 tsp. ground cinnamon
1 large onion, peeled and diced	Salt and freshly ground black pepper

Serves: 6 to 8
Prep time: 15 minutes
Minimum cook time: 5 hours in a large slow cooker

1. Preheat the oven broiler, and line a broiler pan with heavy-duty aluminum foil. Brown short ribs for 3 to 5 minutes per side or until lightly browned. Transfer beef to the slow cooker.

2. Add carrots, sweet potatoes, onion, apricots, and prunes to the slow cooker. Combine cider, stock, nutmeg, and cinnamon in a mixing bowl, and pour into the slow cooker.

3. Cook on low for 10 to 12 hours or on high for 5 or 6 hours or until carrots and beef are very tender. Season with salt and pepper. (You can do this up to 3 days in advance and refrigerate tightly covered. Reheat covered in a 350°F oven for 20 to 30 minutes or until hot.)

Crock Tales

Tsimmis is a traditional dish served by Eastern European Jews. Its name also has slang meaning in Yiddish: "What's the big tsimmis" means "What's the big deal?"

Corned Beef and Cabbage

Here it is, all in one pot and cooking away all day while you're gone. This Irish dish couldn't be easier to make, and the vegetables absorb flavor from the broth.

Serves: 4 to 6
Prep time: 15 minutes
Minimum cook time: 5 hours in a medium slow cooker

1 (2½- to 3-lb.) corned beef brisket

1 onion, peeled and sliced

1 celery rib, sliced

1 carrot, peeled and sliced

4 garlic cloves, peeled and minced

1 bay leaf

½ small head green cabbage

1. Cut off as much fat as possible from top of corned beef. Rinse and set aside.

2. Place onion, celery, carrot, garlic, and bay leaf in the slow cooker. Place corned beef on top of vegetables. Add enough water to come halfway up sides of corned beef.

3. Cut cabbage in half. Cut core from one half, and slice into wedges. Arrange wedges on top of corned beef. Cook on low for 10 to 12 hours or on high for 5 or 6 hours or until corned beef is tender. Remove as much grease as possible from the slow cooker with a soup ladle. (You can do this up to 3 days in advance and refrigerate tightly covered. Reheat covered in a 350°F oven for 20 to 30 minutes or until hot.)

4. Remove and discard bay leaf, and thinly slice corned beef. Serve with cabbage and other vegetables.

Variation: You can easily turn this dish into one called New England Boiled Dinner. Instead of cooking in water, use half wine and half chicken stock. Voilà! You've got it. Then serve it with Dijon mustard on the side.

Cooker Caveats

Corned beef is cured in salt, so no additional salt should ever be added when cooking it. There's sufficient salt in the brisket to season all the vegetables in the slow cooker as well. As curing is not really necessary for preserving the meat anymore, many reduced-sodium brands of corned beef are available today. They're a good bet for any corned beef dish.

Chapter 17

Beyond Beef

In This Chapter

◆ Dishes for lamb and veal shanks

◆ Easy pork recipes for chops, roasts, and country ribs

◆ Hearty European casseroles

Although beef remains the nation's favorite red meat, the other four-legged creatures have their own sets of fans as well. The recipes in this chapter give you great-tasting ways to cook rosy, rich lamb and delicate pork. Veal is also included because, although it's technically beef, it's not cooked in the same way.

Shanks, the lower part of animals' legs, are perhaps one of the best meats to cook in the slow cooker because they really require hours of low-temperature cooking. You'll find that pork and veal don't take as much time to cook as lamb or beef, and their delicate flavor melds well with seasonings from myriad ethnic cuisines.

The Meat of Substitutions

Often you can change the meat without sacrificing the quality of a recipe as long as the change is in the same flavor and texture family. For example, beef and lamb are interchangeable in recipes because both are hearty meats. In the same way, pork and veal are similar, and both can be substituted for whole pieces of chicken without changing the timing. But do ask yourself is if it's a red meat or a white meat. Even though veal is a young cow, the flavor and texture are more similar to pork or chicken than beef.

Cooker Caveats

If you're substituting chicken or turkey for pork or veal it's important to use an instant-read thermometer to ensure that the poultry is cooked to the proper temperature of 165°F.

If you see a recipe that calls for a roast and all you have are chops, go ahead and use the recipe as written and just substitute the cut you've got on hand. Many times it's less expensive to buy a whole roast rather than having the butcher cut it into chops. Then you can cut the chops as thick as you like.

Braised Lamb Shanks with Winter Vegetables

Red wine and fresh herbs meld magically with the richness of lamb for this one-dish meal.

4 to 6 (12- to 14-oz.) meaty lamb shanks

3 TB. olive oil

1 large onion, peeled and diced

3 garlic cloves, peeled and minced

1 carrot, peeled and thinly sliced

1 celery rib, peeled and thinly sliced

1 cup dry red wine

½ cup water

1 (1.2-oz.) pkg. dehydrated brown gravy mix

2 TB. chopped fresh parsley

2 TB. chopped fresh rosemary or 2 tsp. dried

1 tsp. herbes de Provence or 1 tsp. dried thyme

1 bay leaf

Salt and freshly ground black pepper

2 cups buttered egg noodles or steamed potatoes

Serves: 4 to 6
Prep time: 15 minutes
Minimum cook time: 4 hours in a large slow cooker

1. Preheat the oven broiler, and line a broiler pan with heavy-duty aluminum foil. Broil lamb shanks for 3 to 5 minutes per side or until lightly browned. Arrange lamb shanks in the slow cooker, and pour in any juices that have accumulated in the pan.

2. Heat olive oil in a medium skillet over medium-high heat. Add onion, garlic, carrot, and celery, and cook, stirring frequently, for 3 minutes or until onion is translucent. Scrape mixture into the slow cooker.

3. Add wine, water, gravy mix, parsley, rosemary, herbes de Provence, and bay leaf to the slow cooker, and stir well. Cook lamb shanks on low for 8 to 10 hours or on high for 4 or 5 hours or until lamb is very tender.

4. Remove lamb shanks from the slow cooker, and keep warm by covering shanks with aluminum foil. Remove and discard bay leaf, and season sauce with salt and pepper. Serve shanks with buttered egg noodles or steamed potatoes.

Variation: Rather than browning the shanks in the broiler, smoke them on a charcoal grill, adding soaked mesquite chips to the coals. Then add ½ pound shiitake mushrooms to the slow cooker with the other vegetables.

 Slow Savvy

Frequently, lamb shanks have a membrane over the lower part of the bone. It's not really necessary to trim this off, as it becomes tender after the long hours of cooking.

Greek Lamb and Eggplant with Custard Topping (*Moussaka*)

There's a bit of cinnamon in the meat layer of this traditional dish, and the aromatic dill flavors the custard.

Serves: 4 to 6
Prep time: 25 minutes
Minimum cook time: 4 hours in a medium slow cooker

1 (1-lb.) eggplant, rinsed, trimmed, and cut into 1-in. cubes

Salt

⅓ cup olive oil

1 large onion, peeled and diced

2 garlic cloves, peeled and minced

1 lb. lean ground lamb

⅓ cup dry red wine

1 (8-oz.) can tomato sauce

2 TB. chopped fresh parsley

1 tsp. dried oregano

¼ tsp. ground cinnamon

2 TB. unsalted butter

2 TB. all-purpose flour

1 cup whole milk

2 large eggs, lightly beaten

¼ cup freshly grated Parmesan cheese

1 TB. chopped fresh dill or 1 tsp. dried

Freshly ground black pepper

1. Place eggplant in a colander, and sprinkle it liberally with salt. Place a plate on top of eggplant, and weight it with cans. Let eggplant sit for 30 minutes, rinse well, and squeeze eggplant it with paper towels.

2. Heat ½ of olive oil in a large skillet over medium heat. Add eggplant cubes, and cook, stirring frequently, for 5 minutes or until eggplant begins to soften. Transfer eggplant to the slow cooker.

3. Heat remaining olive oil in the skillet, and add onion and garlic. Cook, stirring frequently, for 3 minutes or until onion is translucent. Scrape mixture into the slow cooker. Add lamb to the skillet and brown for 3 to 5 minutes, breaking up any lumps with a fork. Transfer lamb to the slow cooker with a slotted spoon.

4. Add wine, tomato sauce, parsley, oregano, and cinnamon to the slow cooker, and stir well. Cook on low for 5 to 7 hours or on high for 2½ to 3 hours or until eggplant is tender.

5. While the mixture is cooking, prepare topping. Heat butter in a small saucepan over low heat. Stir in flour, and cook for 2 minutes, stirring constantly. Gradually add milk, whisking constantly. Bring mixture to a boil, and remove the pan from the heat. Stir in eggs, cheese, and dill. Stir well and season with salt and pepper.

6. When meat is cooked, if cooking on low, raise the heat to high. Level meat filling, and pour topping evenly over the top. Cook for 1 to 1½ hours or until custard is set.

Variation: Not a fan of lamb? Try this recipe with ground beef or ground turkey for a lighter dish.

Slow Savvy _____

Like tomatoes, eggplants are botanically classified as fruits, but we treat them as vegetables. Eggplants have male and female gender, and the males are preferable because they're less bitter and have fewer seeds. To tell a male from a female, look at the nonstem end. The male is rounded and has a more even hole; the female hole is indented.

Chinese Roast Pork

Serve this flavorful pork with some stir-fried vegetables for a textural contrast, and use any leftovers in fried rice.

Serves: 4 to 6

Prep time: 15 minutes

Minimum cook time: 3 hours in a medium slow cooker

2 TB. Asian sesame oil

2 TB. vegetable oil

2 lb. boneless pork loin, or 2 lb. boneless country ribs

6 scallions, rinsed, trimmed, and thinly sliced

2 TB. grated fresh ginger

4 garlic cloves, peeled and minced

½ cup hoisin sauce

¼ cup rice wine vinegar

¼ cup chicken stock

1 TB. soy sauce

1 TB. Chinese chili paste with garlic

2 or 3 cups cooked white rice or fried rice

 Cooker Caveats

The success of this recipe depends on the cut of pork having a bit of fat. Don't substitute lean pork tenderloin; it will be dry and stringy.

1. Heat sesame and vegetable oils in a medium skillet over medium-high heat. Remove any visible fat from pork, add pork to the skillet, and brown on all sides. Place pork in the slow cooker.

2. Reduce the heat to medium, and add scallions, ginger, and garlic to the skillet. Cook, stirring constantly, for 2 minutes or until fragrant. Scrape mixture into the slow cooker.

3. Combine hoisin sauce, vinegar, stock, soy sauce, and chili paste in a small bowl. Stir well and pour over meat in the slow cooker. Cook on low for 6 to 8 hours or on high for 3 or 4 hours or until an instant-read thermometer inserted into the center of meat reads 155°F. If using a pork loin, turn meat upside down halfway through the cooking time if one part of meat is out of the liquid. Serve pork with white or fried rice.

Variation: Not in a meat mood? Try this with a boneless turkey breast tied into a cylinder, and cook it to an internal temperature of 165°F.

Pork Loin with Mushroom Stuffing

The long, slow cooking process produces a roast that's meltingly tender and delicious. The stuffing completes the meal.

½ lb. white mushrooms

3 TB. unsalted butter

1 large onion, peeled and diced

1 celery rib, rinsed, trimmed, and thinly sliced

3 cups dried herb stuffing

¼ cup chicken stock

3 garlic cloves, peeled and crushed

1 TB. dried sage

1 tsp. dried thyme

Salt and freshly ground black pepper

2 lb. boneless pork loin roast

Serves: 4 to 6
Prep time: 15 minutes
Minimum cook time: 6 hours in a medium slow cooker

1. Grease the inside of the slow cooker liberally with vegetable oil spray.

2. Wipe mushrooms with a damp paper towel. Discard stems and slice mushrooms thinly.

3. Heat butter in a medium skillet over medium-high heat. Add onion, celery, and mushrooms, and cook, stirring frequently, for 3 to 5 minutes or until onion is translucent and mushrooms are soft. Remove the pan from the heat, and stir in herb stuffing and stock. Scrape mixture into the slow cooker.

4. Combine garlic, sage, thyme, salt, and pepper in a small bowl. Rub seasoning onto pork roast, and place roast on top of stuffing. Cook on low for 6 to 8 hours or until an instant-read thermometer inserted into center of meat reads 155°F.

Slow Savvy _____

This stuffing will seem dry when you put it in the slow cooker, but don't worry. Both the juices that escape from the meat as it cooks and the steam that forms from the heat of the slow cooker moisten it sufficiently.

Norman Pork Chops with Apples and Cream

Many delicate dishes such as this native to the Normandy region of France join apples and the region's famed apple brandy with cream.

Serves: 4
Prep time: 20 minutes
Minimum cook time: 3 hours in a medium slow cooker

4 (8-oz.) pork chops

2 Granny Smith apples

1 cup chicken stock

¼ cup dry white wine

2 TB. *Calvados*

2 TB. firmly packed light brown sugar

1 TB. fresh chopped sage or 1 tsp. dried

2 TB. cornstarch

½ cup heavy cream

Salt and freshly ground black pepper

2 cups cooked white or brown rice

Slow Speak

The apple brandy **Calvados** is one of Normandy's culinary claims to fame. It's frequently bottled with a small apple in the bottom. Although it's expensive, it's well worth the money, even for cooking.

1. Preheat the oven broiler, and line a broiler pan with heavy-duty aluminum foil. Brown chops for 3 to 5 minutes per side or until lightly browned. Transfer chops to the slow cooker, and pour in any juices that accumulated in the pan.

2. Peel and core apples. Cut each apple into 6 pieces. Place apples around pork chops in the slow cooker.

3. Combine stock, wine, Calvados, brown sugar, and sage in a mixing bowl, and stir well to dissolve sugar. Pour mixture over pork chops and apples. Cook on low for 6 to 8 hours or on high for 3 or 4 hours or until pork chops are tender.

4. If cooking on low, raise the heat to high. Stir cornstarch into cream, and stir cornstarch mixture into the slow cooker. Cook for an additional 15 to 20 minutes or until juices are bubbling and slightly thickened. Season with salt and pepper, and serve with white or brown rice.

Variation: Use chicken pieces on the bone—either white or dark—in place of the pork chops.

Cuban Pork Chops

The sunny flavor of these chops comes from a combination of heady rum, ginger, and brown sugar.

4 (8-oz.) boneless pork chops, or 1½ lb. boneless country pork ribs

3 TB. vegetable oil

2 large onions, peeled and thinly sliced

3 garlic cloves, peeled and minced

3 TB. grated fresh ginger

¾ cup chicken stock

⅓ cup cider vinegar

⅓ cup dark rum

⅓ cup firmly packed dark brown sugar

Salt and freshly ground black pepper

2 TB. cornstarch

2 TB. cold water

2 cups cooked white or brown rice

Serves: 4
Prep time: 15 minutes
Minimum cook time: 3½ hours in a medium slow cooker

1. Preheat the oven broiler, and line a broiler pan with heavy-duty aluminum foil. Brown chops for 3 to 5 minutes per side or until lightly browned. Transfer chops to the slow cooker, and pour in any juices that accumulated in the pan.

2. Heat vegetable oil in a large skillet over medium-high heat. Add onions, garlic, and ginger to the skillet. Cook, stirring frequently, for 3 minutes or until onions are translucent. Arrange mixture on top of pork chops.

3. Combine stock, vinegar, rum, and brown sugar in a small bowl, and stir well to dissolve sugar. Pour liquid into the slow cooker. Cook on low for 6 to 8 hours or on high for 3 or 4 hours or until chops are tender.

4. If cooking on low, raise the heat to high. Season with salt and pepper. Mix cornstarch with water in a small cup, and stir cornstarch mixture into juices in the slow cooker. Cook for an additional 15 to 20 minutes or until juices are bubbling and slightly thickened. Serve chops with white or brown rice.

Variation: Use chicken pieces on the bone—either white or dark—in place of the pork chops.

 Slow Savvy

To soften rock-hard brown sugar, add a few slices of apple, and close the bag securely for a day or so. If you need to use some immediately, chip off some of the hard sugar and dissolve it in water or some of the liquid specified in a recipe.

Spicy Chinese Pork Ribs

This is a hearty dish. Don't be put off by the amount of garlic; it becomes very mellow when cooked this way.

Serves: 4 to 6
Prep time: 10 minutes
Minimum cook time: 3 hours in a medium slow cooker

2 lb. boneless country pork ribs, cut into 1-in. segments

1 cup water

5 TB. Chinese fermented black beans, coarsely chopped

10 garlic cloves, peeled and minced

2 TB. soy sauce

2 TB. Asian sesame oil

1 TB. firmly packed dark brown sugar

2 TB. cornstarch

2 TB. cold water

½ to 1 tsp. red pepper flakes

2 cups steamed white rice

1 bunch scallions, rinsed, trimmed, and thinly sliced

1. Arrange pork ribs in the slow cooker.

2. Combine water, black beans, garlic, soy sauce, sesame oil, and brown sugar in a small bowl, and stir well. Pour mixture over ribs. Cook on low for 6 to 8 hours or on high for 3 or 4 hours or until meat is tender.

3. If cooking on low, raise the heat to high. Mix cornstarch with cold water in a small cup, and stir cornstarch mixture into the slow cooker along with red pepper flakes. Cook for an additional 15 to 20 minutes or until sauce is bubbling and slightly thickened. Serve over white rice, and sprinkle each serving with scallions.

Slow Savvy

For a dish like this one, there's no need to take the time to brown the pork. It will absorb excellent color from the sauce ingredients. If cooking pork in a light-colored sauce, it's more visually appealing to brown it first.

Swedish Meatballs

Aromatic dill adds its delicate flavor to this traditional dish, which also makes a great party hors d'oeuvre.

2 TB. unsalted butter	¼ tsp. freshly grated nutmeg
1 small onion, peeled and finely chopped	Salt and freshly ground black pepper
2 garlic cloves, peeled and minced	1 (12-oz.) can evaporated milk
1 lb. ground pork	½ cup chicken stock
1 lb. ground veal, or an additional 1 lb. ground pork	¼ cup chopped fresh dill or 2 TB. dried
2 large eggs, lightly beaten	1 TB. cornstarch
¼ cup milk	1 TB. cold water
½ cup breadcrumbs	2 cups buttered egg noodles

> *Serves: 4 to 6*
>
> **Prep time:** 20 minutes
> **Minimum cook time:** 2 hours in a medium slow cooker

1. Preheat the oven to 500°F, line a baking sheet with heavy-duty aluminum foil, and spray the foil with vegetable oil spray.

2. Melt butter in a small skillet over medium-high heat. Add onion and garlic, and cook, stirring frequently, for 3 minutes or until onion is translucent. Scrape mixture into a mixing bowl. Add pork, veal, eggs, milk, breadcrumbs, nutmeg, salt, and pepper, and mix well.

3. Form heaping tablespoons of mixture into meatballs. Place meatballs on the baking sheet, and brown in the oven for 10 minutes or until lightly browned.

4. While meatballs are baking, combine evaporated milk, stock, and dill in the slow cooker and stir well. Transfer meatballs to the slow cooker with a slotted spoon. Cook on low for 4 to 6 hours or on high for 2 or 3 hours or until meatballs are cooked through.

5. If cooking on low, raise the heat to high. Combine cornstarch and cold water in a small cup, and stir cornstarch mixture into the slow cooker. Cook for 10 to 15 minutes or until the liquid is bubbling and slightly thickened. Serve meatballs over buttered noodles.

Variation: This dish is also delicious made with ground turkey. The cooking time remains the same.

 Slow Savvy

Oven-browning meatballs is a great trick. One of the pitfalls of meatballs is that they tend to fall apart when browned in a skillet, and this oven-browning method retains their shape. Plus, you don't have a messy skillet to wash later.

Italian Ham Steaks

This lean cut of meat is braised with herbs, onions, garlic, and bell peppers in a tomato sauce.

Serves: 4 to 6

Prep time: 15 minutes

Minimum cook time: 3 hours in a medium slow cooker

3 TB. olive oil

2 large onions, peeled and thinly sliced

3 garlic cloves, peeled and minced

1 green bell pepper, seeds and ribs removed, and thinly sliced

1 TB. *Italian seasoning* or herbes de Provence

1 (1½-lb.) ham steak, cut into serving pieces

1 (14.5-oz.) can crushed tomatoes in tomato purée

2 TB. chopped fresh parsley

1 bay leaf

Salt and freshly ground black pepper

2 cups cooked small pasta, such as penne or shells

1. Heat olive oil in a medium skillet over medium-high heat. Add onions, garlic, and bell pepper, and cook, stirring frequently, for 3 minutes or until onions are translucent. Stir in Italian seasoning, and cook for 1 minute, stirring constantly. Scrape mixture into the slow cooker.

2. Arrange ham slices over vegetables, and add tomatoes, parsley, and bay leaf.

3. Cook on low for 6 to 8 hours or on high for 3 or 4 hours or until vegetables are tender. Remove and discard bay leaf, and season steaks with salt and pepper. Serve ham steaks and vegetables with cooked pasta.

Slow Speak

Italian seasoning is a premixed herb blend available in almost every market. It's a blend of marjoram, thyme, rosemary, savory, sage, oregano, and basil. If you don't have any, see what you've got from this list and make your own blend.

Alsatian Sauerkraut and Meats (Choucroute Garnie)

Even if you shy away from sauerkraut in general, you'll love this dish. The sauerkraut is soaked and then braised to render it sweet and silky.

3 lb. sauerkraut

2 TB. unsalted butter

1 large onion, peeled and thinly sliced

1 carrot, peeled and thinly sliced

1 cup dry white wine

¼ cup gin, or 10 whole juniper berries

1 cup chicken stock

1 bay leaf

1½ lb. smoked pork butt, cut into 1-in. cubes

½ lb. kielbasa or other smoked sausage, cut into ½-in. slices

Salt and freshly ground black pepper

Serves: 6 to 8	
Prep time: 25 minutes	
Minimum cook time: 4 hours in a large slow cooker	

1. Drain sauerkraut in a colander. Place sauerkraut in a large mixing bowl of cold water for 10 minutes. Drain and repeat the soaking. Press out as much water as possible from sauerkraut, and place sauerkraut in the slow cooker.

2. Heat butter in a large skillet over medium-high heat. Add onion and carrot, and cook, stirring frequently, for 3 minutes or until onion is translucent. Scrape mixture into the slow cooker, and add wine, gin, stock, and bay leaf. Mix well. Add pork and kielbasa. Press meats down into sauerkraut.

3. Cook on low for 8 to 10 hours or on high for 4 or 5 hours or until meats are very tender. Remove and discard bay leaf, and season dish with salt and pepper. Serve immediately.

Cooker Caveats

Don't bypass soaking the sauerkraut. After it's been soaked, the pickled cabbage retains some lip-pursing flavor, but it's quite mild. If you don't soak it, your dish will taste like a pickle that's been heated.

French Mixed Meats and Beans (*Cassoulet*)

There's no question that this is a hearty dish, with lamb, sausage, and duck mingling with stewed beans.

Serves: 6 to 8
Prep time: 30 minutes
Minimum cook time: 5½ hours in a large slow cooker

1 lb. flageolet or other small beans such as navy beans

2 TB. olive oil

2 large onions, peeled and diced

5 garlic cloves, peeled and minced

2 cups chicken stock

1 cup dry white wine

1 (14.5-oz.) can diced tomatoes, undrained

3 TB. tomato paste

1 TB. herbes de Provence, or 1 tsp. dried thyme, 1 tsp. dried rosemary, and 1 tsp. dried oregano

1 bay leaf

1½ lb. stewing lamb, cut into 1-in. cubes

1 lb. kielbasa or other smoked pork sausage, cut into ½-in. slices

2 duck legs from Duck Confit (recipe in Chapter 15), skinned, boned, and diced, or ½ lb. roasted duck, boned and diced

Salt and freshly ground black pepper

1. Rinse beans in a colander, and place them in a mixing bowl covered with cold water. Allow beans to soak overnight. Or place beans in a saucepan and bring to a boil over high heat. Boil 1 minute. Turn off the heat, cover the pan, and soak beans for 1 hour. Drain beans, discard soaking water, and place beans into the slow cooker.

2. Heat oil in a medium skillet over medium-high heat. Add onions and garlic, and cook, stirring frequently, for 3 minutes or until onions are translucent. Scrape mixture into the slow cooker.

3. Add stock, wine, tomatoes, tomato paste, herbes de Provence, and bay leaf to the slow cooker. Cook bean mixture for 4 hours on low or 2 hours on high.

4. Preheat the oven broiler, and line a broiler pan with heavy-duty aluminum foil. Broil lamb and kielbasa for 3 minutes per side or until browned. Stir meats into the slow cooker along with any juices that have accumulated in the pan. Cook for 5 to 7 hours on low or 3 or 4 hours on high or until lamb is tender.

5. Stir duck meat into the slow cooker. Cook for an additional 15 to 20 minutes or until duck is hot. Remove and discard bay leaf, and season cassoulet with salt and pepper.

Milanese-Style Veal Shanks (Osso Buco alla Milanese)

These veal rounds are cooked in an herbed tomato sauce with vegetables for both flavor and texture.

½ cup olive oil or as needed

4 to 6 meaty veal shanks, about 2 in. thick

All-purpose flour for dredging

4 TB. unsalted butter

4 large onions, peeled and diced

4 garlic cloves, peeled and minced

2 carrots, peeled and diced

2 celery ribs, rinsed, trimmed, and diced

½ cup dry white wine

1 (14.5-oz.) can crushed tomatoes in tomato purée

1 cup chicken stock

1 TB. herbes de Provence, or 1 tsp. dried thyme, 1 tsp. dried oregano, and 1 tsp. dried rosemary

1 bay leaf

Salt and freshly ground black pepper

5 TB. chopped fresh parsley

2 TB. finely minced garlic

2 TB. grated lemon zest

1 TB. grated orange zest

2 or 3 cups cooked orzo

Serves: 4 to 6

Prep time: 25 minutes

Minimum cook time: 3 hours in a medium slow cooker

1. Heat ¼ cup oil in a large skillet over medium-high heat. Rub veal shanks with flour, shaking off any extra over the sink or a plate. Add as many veal shanks to the skillet as will fit in a single layer, and brown for 3 or 4 minutes per side or until lightly browned. Work in batches if necessary. Place shanks into the slow cooker.

2. Add remaining ¼ cup olive oil and butter to the skillet. Add onions, 4 cloves garlic, carrots, and celery. Cook, stirring frequently, 3 minutes or until onions are translucent. Scrape mixture into the slow cooker. Stir in wine, tomatoes, stock, herbes de Provence, and bay leaf.

3. Cook on low for 7 or 8 hours or on high for 3 or 4 hours or until meat is very tender. Remove as much fat as possible from the surface of the slow cooker with a soup ladle. Remove and discard bay leaf, and season dish with salt and pepper.

4. While shanks are cooking, prepare topping. Combine parsley, 2 tablespoons finely minced garlic, lemon zest, and orange zest in a small mixing bowl. Serve veal shanks over orzo with a sprinkling of topping.

Crock Tales

Osso buco has become synonymous with *veal shank* in this country as well as in Italy. Unlike lamb shanks, which are almost always braised whole, veal shanks are cut into crosswise slices. *Osso buco* means "pierced bone," and the marrow from the bone is considered such a delicacy that special marrow spoons are served with the dish.

Part 6

The Side Show

In Part 6, the supporting characters are given starring roles. You'll find in these chapters a treasure trove of side dish recipes that are perfect to serve with simple main courses. One chapter focuses on long cooked vegetables like beets and cabbage, while there's another devoted to the way beans are cooked around the world. Grains and other carbohydrates are featured in their own chapter, too.

Part 6 ends with a chapter of little dishes like sauces and chutneys that can be used in myriad ways. And don't overlook the recipes for slow cooked nuts. They're spectacular.

"Momma always said, 'Slow and steady wins the rice'."

Chapter 18

Very Good Vegetables

In This Chapter

- ◆ Great summer and winter squash recipes
- ◆ Dishes that spruce up root vegetables
- ◆ International vegetable medleys

If you're cooking an elaborate entrée, probably the best side dish to serve is a simply prepared steamed vegetable to add contrasting color and texture as well as its nutrition to the plate. But if your entrée is a simple grilled or broiled dish, the vegetable and other side dishes can be a bit more elaborate. This chapter presents some of those vegetable dishes that are meant to be dazzlers.

Successful Veggie Shopping

Shopping for vegetables is much easier than shopping for fruit. Vegetables should be eaten as soon as possible after they're picked. It's best to buy vegetables at least two or three times a week, and always try to use up what's in the refrigerator before replenishing them.

Always rinse produce just before cooking it. Water can cause any leafy vegetable or herb to rot or mold more quickly than if it's stored dry.

Asian Butternut Squash

Asian seasonings give this squash dish a complex flavor that blends with any poultry or pork.

Serves: 6 to 8
Prep time: 20 minutes
Minimum cook time: 3 hours in a medium slow cooker

2½ lb. butternut squash, peeled and cut into ½-in. cubes

½ cup hoisin sauce

¼ cup freshly squeezed orange juice

3 TB. unsalted butter, melted

1 tsp. grated orange zest

½ tsp. Chinese five-spice powder

Salt and freshly ground black pepper

1. Place squash in the slow cooker. Combine hoisin sauce, orange juice, melted butter, orange zest, and Chinese five-spice powder in a small mixing bowl. Stir well, and pour mixture over squash.

2. Cook on low for 6 to 8 hours or on high for 3 or 4 hours or until squash is tender. For chunky squash, mash cubes with a potato masher right in the slow cooker. For smooth squash, spoon the contents of the slow cooker into a food processor fitted with a steel blade. Purée until smooth. Season with salt and pepper. Serve immediately.

Variation: Can't find butternut squash? Acorn, turban, Hubbard, or any winter squash tastes similar.

 Slow Savvy

One of the greatest advances of civilization is already-peeled butternut squash in the supermarket's produce section, especially during the fall and winter. If you buy it, the prep time for this or any other winter squash recipe is mere minutes.

Baked Acorn Squash

The slow cooker is a great way to make this classic fall side dish because the bottom of the squash doesn't burn.

1 (1½-lb.) acorn squash

2 TB. unsalted butter, melted

¼ cup firmly packed dark brown sugar

¼ tsp. ground cinnamon

Pinch of salt

Serves: 4
Prep time: 10 minutes
Minimum cook time: 3 hours in a medium slow cooker

1. Cut squash into quarters with a sharp knife. Scrape out and discard seeds. Place squash in the slow cooker, skin side down, so hollow in flesh faces upward.

2. Combine butter, brown sugar, cinnamon, and salt. Spoon ¼ of mixture into each squash piece hollow.

3. Cook on low for 5 to 7 hours or on high for 3 or 4 hours or until squash is tender when pierced with the tip of a knife. Serve immediately.

Slow Savvy _____

When making a recipe such as this one, the slow cooker is being used as a low-temperature oven, so it's not necessary that it be half full. That rule applies to dishes that contain liquid like soups, stews, and roasts.

Sweet and Sour Red Cabbage

This Austrian recipe is my favorite side dish for hearty meat dishes in the winter. The cabbage is slightly sweet from the apple and red currant jelly.

Serves: 6 to 8	
Prep time: 15 minutes	
Minimum cook time: 3 hours in a medium slow cooker	

Slow Savvy

It's important to sprinkle the red cabbage with the vinegar because that's what keeps it red while it cooks. Otherwise, the cabbage will turn purple.

1 (2-lb.) red cabbage, cored and shredded	½ cup dry red wine
2 TB. red wine vinegar	½ cup vegetable stock or chicken stock
2 TB. granulated sugar	1 cinnamon stick
3 TB. unsalted butter	1 bay leaf
1 medium onion, peeled and chopped	⅓ cup red currant jelly
1 apple, peeled and chopped	Salt and freshly ground black pepper

1. Rinse cabbage and cut it into quarters. Discard core from each quarter and shred cabbage. Place cabbage in the slow cooker, sprinkle with vinegar and sugar, and toss.

2. Heat 2 tablespoons butter in a medium skillet over medium heat. Add onion and apple, and cook, stirring frequently, for 3 minutes or until onion is translucent. Scrape mixture into the slow cooker.

3. Stir wine, stock, cinnamon stick, and bay leaf into the slow cooker. Cook on low for 6 to 8 hours or on high for 3 or 4 hours or until cabbage is almost tender.

4. If cooking on low, raise the heat to high. Remove and discard cinnamon stick and bay leaf, and stir jelly and remaining 1 tablespoon butter into cabbage. Cook on high for an additional 30 to 40 minutes or until cabbage is tender and glazed. Season with salt and pepper, and serve immediately.

Maple-Glazed Beets

The natural sweetness of vibrantly colored beets is enhanced with a touch of maple syrup in this easy dish.

6 to 8 small beets	**2 TB. unsalted butter, melted**
⅓ cup balsamic vinegar	**2 TB. chopped fresh parsley**
¼ cup pure maple syrup	**Salt and freshly ground black pepper**

> *Serves: 4 to 6*
>
> **Prep time:** 15 minutes
>
> **Minimum cook time:** 3 hours in a medium slow cooker

1. Discard beet greens. Scrub, peel, and cut beets into ¼-inch slices. Arrange beet slices in the slow cooker.

2. Combine vinegar, maple syrup, and melted butter in a small mixing bowl. Pour mixture over beets. Cook on low for 6 to 8 hours or on high for 3 or 4 hours or until beets are tender. Sprinkle beets with parsley, and season with salt and pepper. Serve immediately.

Slow Savvy

A good way to judge the freshness of beets is by their fresh, lively beet greens. But remember to cut off those greens as soon as you come home. They leech moisture from the beets and make them dry and bitter.

Ginger-Glazed Carrots

Orange, ginger, and brown sugar are the flavoring in this family-pleasing vegetable dish.

Serves: 6 to 8
Prep time: 20 minutes
Minimum cook time: 2 hours in a medium slow cooker

1½ lb. carrots

½ cup freshly squeezed orange juice

3 TB. unsalted butter, melted

3 TB. firmly packed dark brown sugar

2 TB. grated fresh ginger

1 tsp. grated orange zest

2 scallions, rinsed, trimmed, and finely chopped

Salt and freshly ground black pepper

1. Peel, trim, and slice carrots into ¼-inch slices. Arrange carrots in the slow cooker.

2. Combine orange juice, butter, brown sugar, ginger, and orange zest in a small mixing bowl. Pour liquid over carrots.

3. Cook on low for 4 to 6 hours or on high for 2 or 3 hours or until carrots are tender. Sprinkle carrots with chopped scallions, and season with salt and pepper. Serve immediately.

Slow Savvy

If you're peeling one carrot, a vegetable peeler is probably the quickest way. When you're doing a whole bunch, however, there's an easier method: boil the carrots for 2 minutes and then plunge them into a bowl of ice water. The peels will slip off when you rub the carrots with your fingers.

Braised Radicchio

Even when cooked, radicchio retains its vibrant red color and bitter flavor, making it a great addition to any plate.

1½ lb. *radicchio* (4 to 6 heads, depending on size)

4 TB. unsalted butter, melted

¾ cup vegetable or chicken stock

2 TB. chopped fresh parsley

1 TB. fresh thyme or 1 tsp. dried

Salt and freshly ground black pepper

Serves: 4 to 6
Prep time: 10 minutes
Minimum cook time: 3 hours in a medium slow cooker

1. Rinse radicchio and discard outer leaves. Cut in half, discard core, and cut into 1-inch slices. Place radicchio in the slow cooker.

2. Add butter, stock, parsley, and thyme to the slow cooker, and toss well. Cook on low for 6 to 8 hours or on high for 3 or 4 hours or until radicchio is very soft. Season with salt and pepper. Serve immediately.

Slow Speak

Radicchio (*rah-DEE-key-oh*) is a bright burgundy-colored lettuce with strong white ribs that's related to the chicory family. Native to Italy, radicchio comes in two types. *Radicchio di Verona* is what we find in American markets and grows in small, round heads. *Radicchio di Treviso* has tapered heads and grows in looser bunches.

Braised Fennel

Fennel's licorice flavor mellows when it cooks, and the texture becomes silky and rich.

Serves: 4 to 6
Prep time: 10 minutes
Minimum cook time: 2 hours in a medium slow cooker

2 (1-lb.) medium fennel bulbs

2 TB. unsalted butter

½ small onion, peeled and thinly sliced

1 garlic clove, peeled and minced

1 cup vegetable stock or chicken stock

½ tsp. dried thyme

Salt and freshly ground black pepper

1. Cut stalks off fennel bulb, and cut bulb in half through the root. Trim out root, slice fennel thinly across the bulb, and place slices in the slow cooker. Repeat with second bulb.

2. Heat butter in a small skillet over medium heat. Add onion and garlic, and cook, stirring frequently, for 3 minutes or until onion is translucent. Scrape mixture into the slow cooker.

3. Add stock and thyme to the slow cooker. Cook on low for 4 to 6 hours or on high for 2 or 3 hours or until fennel is tender. Season with salt and pepper. Serve immediately.

Slow Savvy

Although the celerylike stalks are trimmed off the fennel bulb for this dish, don't throw them out. They add a wonderful anise flavor as well as a crisp texture and can be used in place of celery in salads and other raw dishes.

Stewed Collard Greens

Long-stewed collards are rich and robust in flavor, and in this dish, they're enhanced with some sweet and sour seasonings.

2½ lb. collard greens

1 cup vegetable or chicken stock

2 garlic cloves, peeled and minced

¼ cup cider vinegar

¼ cup granulated sugar

½ tsp. dried thyme

1 bay leaf

Salt and red pepper flakes

Serves: 4 to 6
Prep time: 15 minutes
Minimum cook time: 2 hours in a medium slow cooker

1. Rinse collard greens well, rubbing leaves to remove all grit and sand. Discard stems and cut leaves crosswise into ½-inch-wide strips.

2. Bring stock, garlic, vinegar, sugar, and thyme to a boil in a large saucepan. Add as many greens as will fit into the pan by pushing greens into boiling liquid. Add more greens as those in the pan wilt. When all greens are wilted, pour greens into the slow cooker, and add bay leaf.

3. Cook on low for 4 to 6 hours or on high for 2 or 3 hours or until greens are very tender. Remove and discard bay leaf, and season greens with salt and red pepper flakes. Serve immediately.

Variation: Want a green that's less bitter? Try kale or Swiss chard in this recipe, and you'll be able to cut back the cooking time by 30 minutes, too.

Slow Savvy

Greens were a mainstay of the poor Southern diet, and although the nutritional profile might not have been known at the time, it is certainly impressive. One serving of greens provides more than your daily requirement of vitamins C and A. Greens have a substantial amount of iron, calcium, fiber, and minerals. And they are one of the few good nondairy sources of calcium.

Deviled Leeks

This is an elegant vegetable dish that conveys the subtle flavor of this mild member of the onion family.

Serves: 6
Prep time: 15 minutes
Minimum cook time: 2 hours in a medium slow cooker

12 to 18 small leeks

2 TB. unsalted butter, melted

⅓ cup vegetable or chicken stock

¼ cup dry white wine

2 TB. chopped fresh *marjoram* or 1 tsp. dried

Salt and freshly ground black pepper

3 TB. Dijon mustard

½ cup Italian breadcrumbs

½ cup freshly grated Parmesan cheese

1. Trim root end off leeks and discard all but 1 inch of green tops. Split leeks lengthwise, and rinse well under cold running water, rubbing with your fingers to dislodge all grit. Arrange leeks in the slow cooker.

2. Add butter, stock, wine, and marjoram to the slow cooker. Cook on low for 4 or 5 hours or on high for 2 to 2½ hours or until leeks are tender.

3. Preheat the oven to 400°F. Remove leeks from the slow cooker with a slotted spatula and arrange them in a 9×13-inch pan. Season with salt and pepper. Spread leeks with Dijon mustard and then sprinkle with breadcrumbs and Parmesan cheese.

4. Bake leeks for 15 minutes or until top is browned. Serve immediately.

Slow Speak

Marjoram (*MAHR-jur-umm*) is a member of the mint family. The flavor from the long, pale-green leaves is similar to that of oregano but sweeter. If you can't find marjoram, use oregano, but only use half as much as you would marjoram.

Balsamic Onions

This flavorful dish made with aromatic heady Italian vinegar is a snap to assemble because it uses frozen onions.

1 lb. pkg. frozen pearl onions, thawed and drained

3 TB. unsalted butter, cut into small pieces

¼ cup *balsamic vinegar*

¼ cup vegetable or chicken stock

2 TB. granulated sugar

2 tsp. fresh thyme or ½ tsp. dried

Salt and freshly ground black pepper

Serves: 4 to 6
Prep time: 10 minutes
Minimum cook time: 1½ hours in a medium slow cooker

1. Put onions in the slow cooker, and dot with butter pieces.

2. Combine vinegar, stock, sugar, and thyme in a small bowl, and stir to dissolve sugar. Pour mixture over onions.

3. Cook on low for 3 to 5 hours or on high for 1½ to 2 hours or until onions are tender. Stir onions a few times after liquid starts to simmer. Season with salt and pepper. Serve immediately.

Slow Speak

Balsamic vinegar comes from the Modena region of Italy, where it's called *aceto balsamico*. It's made by reducing trebbiano and lambrusco grape juice and then aging the vinegar in wooden barrels for several years. It's quite dark in color and is sweet as well. If you don't have any balsamic vinegar, cider vinegar with a bit of sugar or molasses is the best substitution.

Italian Eggplant Relish (*Caponata*)

This Italian dish is a mélange of eggplant, celery, and onions in a rich tomato sauce dotted with olives and capers.

Serves: 6 to 8
Prep time: 25 minutes
Minimum cook time: 2½ hours in a medium slow cooker

1 (1-lb.) eggplant

Salt

⅓ cup olive oil

2 celery ribs, rinsed, trimmed, and diced

1 large onion, peeled and diced

4 garlic cloves, peeled and minced

¼ cup red wine vinegar

1 tsp. granulated sugar

1 (14.5-oz.) can diced tomatoes, undrained

1 TB. tomato paste

¼ cup sliced green olives

2 TB. small capers, drained and rinsed

2 TB. anchovy paste (optional)

Salt and freshly ground black pepper

Crock Tales

Caponata is a Sicilian vegetable dish that always has eggplant, although some of the other ingredients can vary. The name probably comes from the Latin word *caupo,* or "tavern," because this is the sort of robust food that men would eat in taverns.

1. Rinse and trim eggplant, and cut into ½-inch cubes. Put eggplant in a colander and sprinkle liberally with salt. Place a plate on top of eggplant cubes, and weight the plate with cans. Place the colander in the sink or on a plate, and allow eggplant to drain for 30 minutes. Rinse eggplant cubes, and wring them dry with paper towels.

2. Heat half of olive oil in a medium skillet over medium-high heat. Add celery, onion, and garlic, and cook, stirring frequently, for 3 minutes or until onion is translucent. Remove vegetables from the pan with a slotted spoon, and place them in the slow cooker.

3. Pour remaining olive oil into the skillet, and add eggplant cubes. Cook, stirring frequently, for 5 minutes or until eggplant is lightly browned. Spoon eggplant into the slow cooker.

4. Add vinegar, sugar, tomatoes, tomato paste, olives, capers, and anchovy paste (if using), and stir well. Cook on low for 5 or 6 hours or on high for 2½ to 3 hours or until vegetables are soft. Season with salt and pepper. Allow mixture to reach room temperature and serve either at room temperature or chilled.

Summer Squash au Gratin

Sharp cheddar cheese is the perfect foil to the innate sweetness of summer squash.

2 lb. yellow summer squash, rinsed, trimmed, and cut into ½-in. slices

Salt

3 TB. unsalted butter

1 large onion, peeled and thinly sliced

¾ cup evaporated milk

½ tsp. dried thyme

1 cup grated sharp cheddar cheese

Freshly ground black pepper

Serves: 4 to 6
Prep time: 15 minutes
Minimum cook time: 2 hours in a medium slow cooker

1. Place squash slices in a colander and sprinkle liberally with salt. Place the colander in the sink or on a plate, and allow squash to drain for 30 minutes. Rinse squash, and set aside.

2. Heat butter in a medium skillet over medium heat. Add onion, and cook, stirring frequently, for 3 minutes or until onion is translucent. Layer onion and squash in the slow cooker.

3. Add evaporated milk and thyme to the slow cooker. Cook on low for 4 to 6 hours or on high for 2 or 3 hours or until squash is tender. Stir halfway through the cooking time.

4. If cooking on low, raise the heat to high. Add cheese and season with salt and pepper. Cook for an additional 10 to 20 minutes or until cheese melts. Serve immediately.

Variation: Make this a green-veggie casserole by using zucchini instead of summer squash.

 Slow Savvy

When selecting yellow squash (or zucchini), choose small ones. They are sweeter, and the seeds aren't hard. Salting these tender squash allows them to hold their shape better after they're cooked.

Fall Tomato Gratin

When evenings are a bit colder but tomatoes are still local and lovely, this is a great side dish, and the bread absorbs the tomato flavor as well.

Serves: 4 to 6
Prep time: 15 minutes
Minimum cook time: 2 hours in a medium slow cooker

3 lb. ripe tomatoes

⅓ cup olive oil

4 garlic cloves, peeled and minced

¼ loaf French or Italian bread, cut into ½-in. cubes (about 3 cups)

2 tsp. chopped fresh oregano or ½ tsp. dried

1 tsp. thyme or ¼ tsp. dried

⅓ cup heavy cream

¼ cup freshly grated Parmesan cheese

Salt and freshly ground black pepper

Slow Speak

Gratin is any dish that's topped with cheese. Like many French cooking terms, this one comes from the name of the gratin pan. It's shallow so there's a larger top surface area for the topping.

1. Grease the inside of the slow cooker liberally with vegetable oil spray.

2. Rinse tomatoes and discard cores. Squeeze tomatoes to discard seeds, and cut tomatoes into ½-inch dice. Set aside.

3. Heat olive oil in a large skillet over medium heat. Add garlic and cook, stirring constantly, for 2 minutes. Add bread cubes, and cook for 3 or 4 minutes, stirring frequently, until cubes are lightly browned. Scrape mixture into the slow cooker.

4. Add tomatoes, oregano, thyme, cream, Parmesan cheese, salt, and pepper to the slow cooker. Toss to combine, and spread mixture evenly, patting it down with the back of a spoon. Cook on low for 3 or 4 hours or on high for 2 or 3 hours or until tomatoes are soft. Serve *gratin* immediately.

Chapter **19**

Where Have You *Bean?*

In This Chapter

- ◆ Nutritious vegetarian bean dishes
- ◆ A variety of beans—and a variety of bean-y dishes
- ◆ Cold bean salads

The world has changed its attitude toward what it once regarded as the lowly bean. Beans are now praised for their nutritional value as well as their flavor. Beans are high in fiber and protein and low in fat, and they contain no cholesterol. They are also a good source of B vitamins, especially B_6. And they're the stars of the recipes you'll be cooking in this chapter.

Not only are beans good food, but they're also easy to cook in the slow cooker. In fact, before we had a slow cooker, the same shape of cooking device was called a bean pot. That shows you how perfect this machine is for cooking beans. And with a slow cooker, you don't have to worry about beans on the bottom of the pan scorching, even set on high—a pitfall of bean dishes cooked on the stove.

Beans also work well in cold salads, and you'll find some recipes for those here, too.

Completing Proteins

Beans are paired with rice or other grains in dishes around the world for more reasons than the flavor. What generations before us knew instinctively, we now know scientifically: the protein in beans is "incomplete." To deliver its best nutritional content—to "complete" the protein—beans need to be paired with carbohydrate-rich grains such as rice or corn. When beans and grains are eaten together, they supply a quality of protein that's as good as that from eggs or beef.

If you're serving any of these dishes as a vegetarian entrée rather than as a side dish, be sure to serve it on top of some rice or polenta.

Boston Baked Beans

This is as luscious as a baked bean can be, with cheese added at the end of the cooking for extra richness.

1 lb. dried navy beans or any small white bean

2 TB. vegetable oil or bacon fat

1 red onion, peeled and diced

2½ cups water

½ cup firmly packed dark brown sugar

½ cup cider vinegar

6 slices cooked bacon, drained and crumbled (optional)

½ cup prepared barbecue sauce

1 TB. prepared mustard

½ cup grated Monterey Jack cheese

Salt and freshly ground black pepper

Serves: 6 to 8
Prep time: 15 minutes
Minimum cook time: 4 hours in a medium slow cooker

1. Rinse beans in a colander, place them in a mixing bowl, and cover with cold water. Allow beans to soak overnight. Or place beans in a saucepan and bring to a boil over high heat. Boil 1 minute. Turn off the heat, cover the pan, and soak beans for 1 hour. Drain, and discard soaking water. Place beans in the slow cooker.

2. Heat vegetable oil in a small skillet over medium-high heat. Add onion, and cook, stirring frequently, for 3 minutes or until onion is translucent. Add onion to the slow cooker.

3. Add water, brown sugar, vinegar, bacon (if using), barbecue sauce, and mustard to the slow cooker. Cook on low for 8 to 10 hours or on high for 4 or 5 hours or until beans are tender. Stir in cheese, and season with salt and pepper. Cook for an additional 5 to 10 minutes until cheese melts.

Variation: For an even prettier dish, use a combination of types of beans. Look at the bean cooking times table in Chapter 2 and pick any and all that take the same amount of time to cook.

Crock Tales

Boston baked beans are so interwoven into the city's history that it's still known as "Beantown." During the Colonial era, Puritans baked beans on Saturday and served them for dinner that night and for lunch on Sunday because cooking wasn't allowed on the Sabbath.

Savory Lentils with Black-Eyed Peas

This combination of legumes is so pretty, and the Middle Eastern seasonings meld well with the earthy beans.

Serves: 4 to 6
Prep time: 15 minutes
Minimum cook time: 4 hours in a medium slow cooker

1½ cups dried red *lentils*

1 medium onion, peeled and finely chopped

3 garlic cloves, peeled and minced

1½ cups vegetable or chicken stock

1 (14.5-oz.) can crushed tomatoes

2 tsp. ground cumin

1 tsp. ground coriander

1 (15-oz.) can black-eyed peas, drained and rinsed

Salt and freshly ground black pepper

1. Place lentils, onion, garlic, stock, tomatoes, cumin, and coriander in the slow cooker. Cook on low for 8 to 10 hours or on high for 4 or 5 hours or until lentils are tender.

2. If cooking on low, raise the heat to high. Stir in black-eyed peas, and season with salt and pepper. Cook for an additional 15 to 20 minutes until black-eyed peas are hot.

Slow Speak

Lentils are one member of the legume family with the greatest geographic spread. The tiny, lens-shaped pulse has been used as a protein source from France to India and all through the Middle East. The lentils we find most often are the common brown ones, but there are also red and yellow lentils. They all cook the same way.

Kidney Bean and Roasted Garlic Purée

Sweet and mellow roasted garlic—also made in the slow cooker—flavors this rosy purée of healthful beans.

1½ **cups dried kidney beans**

5 **cups water**

1 **medium onion, peeled and halved**

3 **garlic cloves, peeled and minced**

1 **bay leaf**

Salt and freshly ground black pepper

4 **heads Roasted Garlic (recipe in Chapter 2)**

¼ **cup olive oil**

Serves: 4 to 6
Prep time: 20 minutes
Minimum cook time: 3 hours in a medium slow cooker

1. Rinse beans in a colander, place them in a mixing bowl, and cover with cold water. Allow beans to soak overnight. Or place beans in a saucepan and bring to a boil over high heat. Boil 1 minute. Turn off the heat, cover the pan, and soak beans for 1 hour. Drain, and discard soaking water. Place beans in the slow cooker.

2. Add water, onion, garlic, and bay leaf to the slow cooker. Cook on low for 6 to 8 hours or on high for 3 or 4 hours or until beans are tender. Add salt and pepper prior to the last hour of cooking time. Remove and discard onion and bay leaf.

3. Drain beans, reserving 1 cup cooking liquid. Remove pulp from roasted garlic and discard skins. Combine garlic with ½ cup cooking liquid in a food processor fitted with a steel blade or a blender. Purée until smooth. Add beans and purée until smooth, adding more cooking liquid if necessary. Drizzle olive oil through the feed tube. Season with salt and pepper, and serve immediately.

Variation: I like the color of the red beans, but feel free to use white beans or garbanzo beans for this recipe. And for a more spicy dish, add 1 or 2 chipotle peppers in adobo sauce to the roasted garlic purée.

Slow Savvy

Roasted garlic freezes very well, so fill up the slow cooker and make a large batch. I add it to everything from mashed potatoes to scrambled eggs.

Refried Beans

When you see how easy it is to make this Mexican favorite, you'll never turn to a can again!

Serves: 6 to 8
Prep time: 20 minutes
Minimum cook time: 4½ hours in a medium slow cooker

1 lb. dried red kidney beans, rinsed

6 cups water

½ cup vegetable oil or bacon fat

2 large red onions, peeled and diced

6 garlic cloves, peeled and minced

½ (4-oz.) can diced mild green chiles, drained

½ cup refrigerated commercial tomato salsa

Salt and cayenne

> **Slow Savvy**
>
> This dish can be started up to 2 days ahead of when you want to serve it. Cook the beans and then refrigerate them, tightly covered. You can do the frying and mashing when the beans are cold. It just takes a few more minutes to get them hot.

1. Rinse beans in a colander, place them in a mixing bowl, and cover with cold water. Allow beans to soak overnight. Or place beans in a saucepan and bring to a boil over high heat. Boil 1 minute. Turn off the heat, cover the pan, and soak beans for 1 hour. Drain, and discard soaking water. Place beans in the slow cooker.

2. Add water to the slow cooker, and cook on low for 8 to 10 hours or on high for 4 or 5 hours or until beans are very tender and beginning to fall apart. Remove beans from the slow cooker with a slotted spoon, and reserve ½ cup cooking liquid.

3. Heat vegetable oil in a large skillet over medium-high heat. Add onions and garlic, and cook, stirring frequently, for 4 or 5 minutes or until onions are soft. Stir in beans, chiles, reserved bean cooking liquid, and salsa. Mash beans with a potato masher or the back of a heavy spoon until beans are soft but some beans still remain whole. Season with salt and cayenne.

Hoppin' John

Black-eyed peas flavored with smoky ham and herbs is an American classic, and after you try it, you'll know why.

1 cup dried black-eyed peas	**½ tsp. dried thyme**
½ lb. smoked pork butt or ham, cut into ½-in. cubes	**1 bay leaf**
2 cups chicken or ham stock	**Salt and freshly ground black pepper**

Serves: 4 to 6
Prep time: 15 minutes
Minimum cook time: 3 hours in a medium slow cooker

1. Rinse black-eyed peas in a colander, place them in a mixing bowl, and cover with cold water. Allow black-eyed peas to soak overnight. Or place black-eyed peas in a saucepan and bring to a boil over high heat. Boil 1 minute. Turn off the heat, cover the pan, and soak black-eyed peas for 1 hour. Drain, and discard soaking water. Place black-eyed peas in the slow cooker.

2. Add pork butt or ham, stock, thyme, and bay leaf to the slow cooker. Cook on low for 6 to 8 hours or on high for 3 or 4 hours or until black-eyed peas are tender. Remove and discard bay leaf, and season with salt and pepper. Serve immediately.

Variation: To make this a vegetarian dish, use vegetable stock, omit the ham, and add 1 or 2 finely chopped chipotle peppers to the slow cooker for some heat and smoky flavor.

Crock Tales

No self-respecting southerner would start the New Year without eating a bowl of Hoppin' John, the regional good luck charm. The dish probably came from Africa, and it's mentioned in literature long before the Civil War. Some food authorities say the name comes from children hopping around the table on New Year's Day as a prelude to eating the dish.

Black-Eyed Peas with Ginger

Black-eyed peas are a part of Middle Eastern cooking, and that's the inspiration for this zesty dish with fresh ginger finished with yogurt.

Serves: 4 to 6
Prep time: 20 minutes
Minimum cook time: 3 hours in a medium slow cooker

1 cup dried black-eyed peas

¼ cup olive oil

1 large onion, peeled and minced

3 garlic cloves, peeled and minced

1 tsp. ground cumin

1 tsp. ground coriander

2 cups water

4 TB. grated fresh ginger

1 (14.5-oz.) can petite diced tomatoes, drained

Salt and freshly ground black pepper

¼ cup plain low-fat yogurt

Hot red pepper sauce

2 TB. chopped fresh cilantro

Crock Tales

Coriander, a member of the parsley family, is native to both the Mediterranean and Asia. There's mention of its pungent seeds in early Sanskrit writings, while the seeds themselves have been found in Egyptian tombs.

1. Rinse black-eyed peas in a colander, place them in a mixing bowl, and cover with cold water. Allow black-eyed peas to soak overnight. Or place black-eyed peas in a saucepan and bring to a boil over high heat. Boil 1 minute. Turn off the heat, cover the pan, and soak black-eyed peas for 1 hour. Drain, and discard soaking water. Place black-eyed peas in the slow cooker.

2. Heat olive oil in a medium skillet over medium-high heat. Add onion and garlic, and cook, stirring frequently, for 3 minutes or until onion is translucent. Add cumin and coriander, and reduce the heat to low. Cook, stirring constantly, for 1 minute. Scrape mixture into the slow cooker.

3. Add water and ginger to the slow cooker. Cook on low for 6 to 8 hours or on high for 3 or 4 hours or until beans are tender. Add tomatoes, salt, and pepper prior to the last hour of cooking time.

4. Stir in yogurt, and add hot red pepper sauce. Stir in cilantro, and serve immediately.

Italian Cannellini Beans

This great bean dish with vegetables and cheeses is like a side dish of pizza.

1 lb. dried cannellini beans or other small white beans

2 TB. olive oil

1 medium onion, peeled and diced

3 garlic cloves, peeled and minced

½ green or red bell pepper, seeds and ribs removed, and finely chopped

2 cups tomato juice

1 (14.5-oz.) can diced tomatoes

1 TB. Italian seasoning

½ cup grated mozzarella cheese

¼ cup freshly grated Parmesan cheese

Salt and freshly ground black pepper

Serves: 6 to 8	
Prep time: 15 minutes	
Minimum cook time: 5 hours in a medium slow cooker	

1. Rinse beans in a colander, place them in a mixing bowl, and cover with cold water. Allow beans to soak overnight. Or place beans in a saucepan and bring to a boil over high heat. Boil 1 minute. Turn off the heat, cover the pan, and soak beans for 1 hour. Drain, and discard soaking water. Place beans in the slow cooker.

2. Heat olive oil in a medium skillet over medium-high heat. Add onion, garlic, and green bell pepper. Cook, stirring frequently, for 3 minutes or until onion is translucent. Scrape mixture into the slow cooker. Add tomato juice, tomatoes, and Italian seasoning, and stir well. Cook on low for 10 to 12 hours or on high for 5 or 6 hours or until beans are tender.

3. If cooking on low, raise the heat to high. Stir mozzarella and Parmesan cheeses into beans, and season with salt and pepper. Cook for 10 to 15 minutes or until cheeses melt. Serve immediately.

Cooker Caveats

Most cheeses, especially ones like Parmesan and feta, have a natural salt content. When cooking with these cheeses, add them before you add the salt. Then taste and season accordingly.

Black Bean and Papaya Salad

Cinnamon and garlic flavor the beans in this colorful salad, and jicama adds its crunchy texture.

Serves: 4 to 6

Prep time: 20 minutes

Minimum cook time: 2 hours in a medium slow cooker plus at least 1 hour to chill

½ lb. dried black beans

1 cinnamon stick

4 garlic cloves, peeled and minced

Salt

1 ripe papaya, peeled, seeded, and cut into ½-in. dice

1 medium jicama, peeled and cut into ½-in. dice

3 shallots, peeled and chopped

½ tsp. ground cumin

⅓ cup freshly squeezed orange juice

3 TB. balsamic vinegar

2 TB. freshly squeezed lime juice

Salt and cayenne

3 TB. olive oil

Slow Savvy

Papaya contains papain, an enzyme that naturally tenderizes meats and poultry. Save the skin when peeling the papaya and add it to a marinade.

1. Rinse beans in a colander, place them in a mixing bowl, and cover with cold water. Allow beans to soak overnight. Or place beans in a saucepan and bring to a boil over high heat. Boil 1 minute. Turn off the heat, cover the pan, and soak beans for 1 hour. Drain, and discard soaking water. Place beans in the slow cooker.

2. Pour in enough water to cover beans by 2 inches, and add cinnamon stick and 2 garlic cloves. Cook on low for 4 to 6 hours or on high for 2 or 3 hours or until beans are tender but still slightly chewy. Add salt prior to the last hour of cooking time. Drain beans, discard cinnamon stick, and chill well.

3. Combine chilled beans with papaya and jicama in a mixing bowl.

4. For dressing, combine shallots, remaining 2 garlic cloves, cumin, orange juice, vinegar, lime juice, salt, and cayenne in a jar with a tight-fitting lid. Shake well, add oil, and shake well again. Pour over salad and toss. Serve immediately.

Variation: No papaya ripe in your market? Feel free to use mango or pineapple; both deliver the same tropical sweetness.

White Bean Salad

Lemon juice and scallions in the dressing give this salad a fresh flavor and lovely aroma.

2 cups dried white navy beans

2 garlic cloves, peeled and minced

Salt

⅓ cup finely chopped fresh parsley

4 scallions, rinsed, trimmed, and chopped

3 TB. freshly squeezed lemon juice

Freshly ground black pepper

⅓ cup olive oil

Serves: 4 to 6
Prep time: 15 minutes
Minimum cook time: 2 hours in a medium slow cooker plus at least 2 hours to chill

1. Rinse beans in a colander, place them in a mixing bowl, and cover with cold water. Allow beans to soak overnight. Or place beans in a saucepan and bring to a boil over high heat. Boil 1 minute. Turn off the heat, cover the pan, and soak beans for 1 hour. Drain, and discard soaking water. Place beans into the slow cooker.

2. Pour in enough water to cover beans by 2 inches and add garlic. Cook on low for 4 to 6 hours or on high for 2 or 3 hours or until beans are tender. Add salt prior to the last hour of cooking time. Drain beans and chill well.

3. Combine parsley and scallions in a mixing bowl, and stir in lemon juice, salt, and pepper. Mix well, add oil, and mix well again. Gently stir dressing into beans, season dish with salt and pepper, and serve chilled.

Variation: To make this salad into an entrée, add 2 (6.5-ounce) cans imported tuna packed in olive oil. Break the tuna into chunks, and use the oil from the cans as part of the oil in the dressing.

Slow Savvy

This might be viewed as heresy when writing a book on slow cooking, but you can make any of these bean salads very quickly by using canned beans. But look at what seasonings the beans are cooked with and add them to the dressing.

Mexican Pinto Bean Salad

Tomatoes and corn join the beans in this salad and all are tossed in a spicy mayonnaise dressing.

Serves: 4 to 6
Prep time: 20 minutes
Minimum cook time: 3 hours in a medium slow cooker plus at least 2 hours to chill

1 cup dried pinto beans

4 cups water

1 small onion, peeled and diced

3 garlic cloves, peeled and minced

1 jalapeño chile, seeds and ribs removed, and finely chopped

Salt and freshly ground black pepper

3 ripe plum tomatoes

1 cup cooked corn

¼ cup chopped fresh cilantro

¼ small red onion, peeled and diced

⅓ cup mayonnaise

1 chipotle chile in adobo sauce

2 tsp. ground cumin

 Slow Savvy

Here's a trick I learned as a caterer for making salads in advance: you can certainly cut up the vegetables and make the dressing, but don't toss the salad until a few hours before serving so it doesn't seem "tired."

1. Rinse beans in a colander, place them in a mixing bowl, and cover with cold water. Allow beans to soak overnight. Or place beans in a saucepan and bring to a boil over high heat. Boil 1 minute. Turn off the heat, cover the pan, and soak beans for 1 hour. Drain, and discard soaking water. Place beans in the slow cooker.

2. Add water, onion, garlic, and jalapeño to the slow cooker. Cook on low for 6 to 8 hours or on high for 3 or 4 hours or until beans are tender. Add salt and pepper prior to the last hour of cooking time. Remove and discard onion, drain beans, and chill for at least 2 hours.

3. While beans are cooking rinse, core, and halve tomatoes. Squeeze tomatoes to remove seeds, and cut into ½-inch dice. Add tomatoes, corn, cilantro, and red onion to beans.

4. Combine mayonnaise, chipotle chile, and cumin in a blender or food processor fitted with a steel blade. Purée until smooth. Season with salt and pepper, and stir dressing into salad. Refrigerate until cold, and serve.

Garbanzo Bean Salad Provençale

All the sunny flavors of Provence—including olives and orange zest—are part of this healthful salad made with chopped bright red radicchio.

1 cup dried garbanzo beans	2 tsp. fresh thyme or ½ tsp. dried
5 cups water	2 tsp. chopped fresh oregano or ½ tsp. dried
5 garlic cloves, peeled and minced	1 tsp. grated orange zest
1 TB. herbes de Provence	⅓ cup olive oil
1 bay leaf	¾ cup pitted Niçoise or other oil-cured black olives, chopped
Salt and freshly ground black pepper	5 scallions, rinsed, peeled, and chopped
¼ cup red wine vinegar	1 small head radicchio, rinsed, cored, and chopped
¼ cup freshly squeezed orange juice	
3 TB. chopped fresh parsley	
1 TB. chopped fresh rosemary or 1 tsp. dried	

> *Serves: 4 to 6*
>
> **Prep time:** 20 minutes
> **Minimum cook time:**
> 3 hours in a medium slow cooker plus at least 2 hours for chilling

1. Rinse beans in a colander, place them in a mixing bowl, and cover with cold water. Allow beans to soak overnight. Or place beans in a saucepan and bring to a boil over high heat. Boil 1 minute. Turn off the heat, cover the pan, and soak beans for 1 hour. Drain, and discard soaking water. Place beans in the slow cooker.

2. Add water, 2 garlic cloves, herbes de Provence, and bay leaf to the slow cooker. Cook on low for 6 to 8 hours or on high for 3 or 4 hours or until beans are tender. Add salt and pepper prior to the last hour of cooking time. Remove and discard bay leaf, drain beans, and chill for at least 2 hours.

3. Combine vinegar, orange juice, parsley, rosemary, thyme, oregano, and orange zest in a jar with a tight-fitting lid. Shake well. Add olive oil, and shake well again.

4. Add olives, scallions, and radicchio to bowl with beans. Toss with dressing, and season with salt and pepper. Serve immediately.

 Cooker Caveats

Salt and pepper are usually added to a salad dressing along with other seasonings, but when a dish contains a food like olives that are already salty, it's best to try the salad to see if additional salt is needed.

Chapter 20

Celebrating Spuds and Grains

In This Chapter

◆ Dishes showcasing both white and sweet potatoes

◆ Grain-glorifying recipes

◆ Old-fashioned corn puddings

Potatoes, sweet potatoes, and grains are all complex carbohydrates that are increasingly important in maintaining a healthy body. These foods are also versatile, as you'll see when cooking the recipes in this chapter. Each food has its own inherent texture and mild flavor, so they take to a wide variety of seasonings.

All grains, including rice, are the fruit produced by grasses. Many nonrice grains like barley and buckwheat—with their interesting textures, innately sweet and nutty flavors, and high nutrient and fiber content—are now vying in popularity with rice.

Size Specifics

Rice is classified by the length of individual grains. Perhaps the most popular is long-grain rice. The length of the grain is four or five times the size of the width. When cooked, it produces light, dry grains that separate easily.

Along with basic white rice, other species are popular, including *basmati* and *jasmine rice*, which are both long-grain varieties from Asia and produce an aromatic fragrance when cooked. The aroma is created by a high concentration of acetyl pyroline, a compound naturally found in all rice.

Brown rice is the entire grain with only the inedible outer husk removed. The nutritious, high-fiber bran coating gives it a light tan color, nutlike flavor, and chewy texture. The presence of the bran means brown rice is subject to rancidity, which limits its shelf life to only about 6 months. It also takes slightly longer to cook than regular white long-grain rice (up to 50 minutes total).

Slow Savvy

The 7,000-plus varieties of rice are grown in one of two ways. Aquatic (or paddy-grown) rice is cultivated in flooded fields. The lower-yielding, lower-quality hill-grown rice can be grown on almost any tropical or subtropical terrain.

Arborio rice, almost all of which is imported from Italy, is a medium-grain rice (a softer rice that is two to three times as long as it is wide). Arborio rice has a high starch content. This natural carbohydrate is released as the rice is stirred to create a creamy texture in risotto dishes.

Potato Pointers

Potatoes are tubers, which are the swellings of the root of the plant, which is why they're so nutritious. It's in the roots that the valuable nutrients of the plant are stored.

Broadly speaking, potatoes are divided into "bakers," "boilers," and "all-purpose." Baking potatoes have more starch so they're light and fluffy when cooked. In addition to baking, they're wonderful for mashing and French fries. Boilers have less starch, but more moisture. That's why they're the ones to use for potato salads and also for sautéed potatoes. They have thin skin, yet hold their shape quite well when sliced. All-purpose potatoes can be either baked or boiled and are generally white or red.

Potatoes Provençal

The cheese and herbs in this dish make it the star when served with a simple grilled or baked entrée.

2½ lb. red-skinned potatoes, scrubbed and thinly sliced

2 medium onions, peeled and thinly sliced

2 garlic cloves, peeled and minced

3 TB. unsalted butter, cut into small pieces

2 TB. chopped fresh parsley

1 TB. herbes de Provence, or 1 tsp. dried thyme, 1 tsp. dried oregano, and 1 tsp. dried rosemary

1½ cups vegetable or chicken stock

1 cup grated Swiss or Gruyère cheese

Salt and freshly ground black pepper

Serves: 6 to 8
Prep time: 15 minutes
Minimum cook time: 3 hours in a medium slow cooker

1. Spray the inside of the slow cooker with vegetable oil spray.

2. Combine potatoes, onions, garlic, butter, parsley, and herbes de Provence in the slow cooker. Pack it down evenly. Pour stock over potatoes.

3. Cook on low for 6 to 8 hours or on high for 3 or 4 hours or until potatoes are tender.

4. If cooking on low, raise the heat to high. Stir in cheese, and season with salt and pepper. Cook for an additional 10 to 15 minutes or until cheese melts. Serve immediately.

Variation: For a more all-American flavor, omit the herbs and substitute sharp cheddar cheese.

Cooker Caveats

If you're cooking potatoes in a slow cooker on low, they might discolor. To avoid this, before cooking the potatoes, submerge them in a bowl of water to which lemon juice has been added. The lemon won't be detectable after the dish is cooked, and it will keep the spuds snowy white.

Leek and Potato Purée

Leeks are the most delicate member of the onion family, and their flavor melds beautifully with creamy potatoes.

Serves: 4 to 6
Prep time: 20 minutes
Minimum cook time: 3 hours in a medium slow cooker

6 leeks, white part only

6 TB. unsalted butter

2 garlic cloves, peeled and minced

3 large russet potatoes, peeled and cut into ½-in. dice

1 cup evaporated milk

Salt and freshly ground black pepper

1. Trim leeks, split lengthwise, and slice thinly. Place slices in a colander and rinse well under cold running water, rubbing with your fingers to dislodge all dirt. Shake leeks in the colander.

2. Heat butter in a medium skillet over low heat. Add leeks and garlic, toss to coat leeks with butter, and cover the pan. Cook, stirring occasionally, for 10 minutes or until leeks are soft. Scrape leeks into the slow cooker, and add potatoes and evaporated milk.

3. Cook on low for 6 to 8 hours or on high for 3 or 4 hours or until potatoes are tender. Put mixture through a food mill, or purée it in a food processor fitted with a steel blade using on-and-off pulsing. Don't overprocess, or potatoes will become gluey. Season with salt and pepper, and serve immediately.

Cooker Caveats

I'm all in favor of using red-skinned potatoes whenever possible and don't mind bits of healthful skin in mashed potatoes. But don't use them when the spuds are to be puréed. The skin makes the dish visually unappealing.

Hot German Potato Salad

Onion cooks with the potatoes to make this a zesty salad that's perfect with grilled meats.

4 medium red-skinned potatoes, scrubbed and thinly sliced

1 large onion, peeled and chopped

⅓ cup water

¼ cup distilled white vinegar

2 TB. granulated sugar

1 TB. prepared mustard

Salt and freshly ground black pepper

¼ cup bacon grease or vegetable oil

3 TB. chopped fresh parsley

6 slices bacon, cooked until crisp, drained, and crumbled (optional)

Serves: 4 to 6
Prep time: 15 minutes
Minimum cook time: 4 hours in a medium slow cooker

1. Arrange ½ of potato slices in the slow cooker, and top with ½ of onion. Repeat with remaining potatoes and onion.

2. Combine water, vinegar, sugar, mustard, salt, and pepper in a jar with a tight-fitting lid. Shake well. Add bacon grease, and shake well again. Pour mixture over potatoes.

3. Cook on low for 8 to 10 hours or on high for 4 or 5 hours or until potatoes are tender. Stir in parsley and bacon (if using). Serve immediately.

Slow Savvy

If you see a greenish-tinged potato, it means it was exposed to light. Cut away that portion of the potato because the green flesh can be toxic. Store potatoes in a cool, dry place—but not with onions. Onions give off a natural gas that can cause potatoes to rot more quickly.

Sweet Potatoes and Apples

Maple syrup and cinnamon add their innate flavors to this splendid dish made with applesauce as well as apples.

Serves: 6 to 8
Prep time: 20 minutes
Minimum cook time: 3 hours in a medium slow cooker

3 large sweet potatoes or yams (about 3 lb.), peeled and thinly sliced

2 Granny Smith apples, peeled, cored, and thinly sliced

1 cup chunky applesauce

½ cup pure maple syrup

6 TB. unsalted butter, melted

¾ tsp. ground cinnamon

Pinch of salt

1. Grease the inside of the slow cooker liberally with vegetable oil spray.

2. Arrange ½ of sweet potatoes and apples in the slow cooker.

3. Combine applesauce, maple syrup, melted butter, cinnamon, and salt in a mixing bowl. Pour ½ of mixture over sweet potatoes and apples, and repeat with remaining sweet potatoes, apples, and applesauce mixture.

4. Cook on low for 6 to 8 hours or on high for 3 or 4 hours or until sweet potatoes are tender.

Variation: Give this dish some Asian spice by using hoisin sauce instead of maple syrup and Chinese five-spice powder instead of cinnamon.

Slow Savvy

Although sweet potatoes and yams are used interchangeably in recipes, they are different tubers. Yams are native to Africa and have a flesh lighter in color but sweeter than sweet potatoes. Yams also have a higher moisture content, so cut back slightly on liquids if you're using an authentic yam in a dish.

Citrus-Glazed Yams

Slices of orange and lemon add interest to this traditional dish made with butter and brown sugar.

3 navel oranges

2 lemons

1 stick (¼ lb.) unsalted butter, melted

1½ cups firmly packed dark brown sugar

3 large yams or sweet potatoes (about 3 lb.), peeled and thinly sliced

Serves: 6 to 8
Prep time: 20 minutes
Minimum cook time: 3½ hours in a medium slow cooker

1. Grease the inside of the slow cooker liberally with vegetable oil spray or butter.

2. Trim peel and white pith from oranges and lemons. Thinly slice oranges and lemons, saving any juices. Remove and discard lemon seeds.

3. Mix melted butter with brown sugar in a small bowl.

4. Layer ½ of yams in the slow cooker. Arrange ½ of orange and lemon slices on top of yams, and dot surface of fruit layer with ½ of butter mixture. Repeat with remaining yams, fruit, and butter mixture.

5. Cook on low for 6 to 8 hours or on high for 3 or 4 hours or until potatoes are tender.

6. If cooking on low, raise the heat to high. Remove the lid from the slow cooker and cook for 30 minutes to reduce juices. Serve immediately.

Slow Savvy

Here's an easy way to peel citrus fruits: cut off a slice from the top and bottom so the fruit sits firmly on a counter. With a paring knife or flexible-blade fruit knife, cut down the sides beneath the peel so the flesh is exposed. Turn the fruit over and do the same on the other side. This is quicker and easier than peeling the fruit and then cutting off the white pith.

Fontina Polenta

Polenta is the famous Italian version of cornmeal pudding, and it's frequently used as an alternative to pasta and topped with sauce.

Serves: 4 to 6
Prep time: 10 minutes
Minimum cook time: 3 hours in a medium slow cooker

5 cups chicken stock

1 cup half-and-half

1 cup polenta or yellow cornmeal

1 TB. fresh thyme or 1 tsp. dried

3 TB. unsalted butter, cut into small pieces

1 cup grated fontina cheese

Salt and freshly ground black pepper

1. Grease the inside of the slow cooker liberally with vegetable oil spray.

2. Combine stock, half-and-half, polenta, and thyme in the slow cooker. Whisk well, and cook on high for 1½ hours or until mixture begins to boil.

3. Whisk well again, and cook on high for an additional 1½ hours or on low for 3 hours or until polenta is very thick.

4. Stir in butter and cheese, and season with salt and pepper. Serve immediately as a side dish or topped with sauce. (Polenta can remain on low or warm for up to 4 hours.)

Variation: Fontina is an Italian cheese, but this dish is also great with cheddar cheese or jalapeño Jack. And for a less creamy texture, add 1 cup fresh or frozen corn kernels to the mixture before reducing the heat to low.

Slow Savvy

Polenta is a very versatile dish. An alternative way to serve it is to pack the hot polenta into a well-oiled loaf pan and chill it well. When it's chilled, you can cut it into ¾-inch slices and either grill them or sauté them in butter or olive oil.

Southwest Spoon Bread

While it's called a bread, the texture of this egg-rich dish is more like a pudding.

4 large eggs

1⅓ cups whole milk

1 (15-oz.) can creamed corn

4 TB. unsalted butter, melted

⅓ cup all-purpose flour

⅓ cup cornmeal

2 tsp. baking powder

Salt and freshly ground black pepper

1 cup fresh corn kernels or 1 cup frozen corn, thawed

1 cup grated Monterey Jack cheese

1 (4-oz.) can chopped green chiles, drained

Serves: 6 to 8
Prep time: 15 minutes
Minimum cook time: 3 hours in a medium slow cooker

1. Spray the inside of the slow cooker liberally with vegetable oil spray.

2. Place eggs in a large mixing bowl and whisk well. Add milk, creamed corn, butter, flour, cornmeal, baking powder, salt, and pepper, and whisk well again. Stir corn kernels, cheese, and chiles into mixing bowl. Scrape mixture into the slow cooker.

3. Cook on high for 3 to 3½ hours or until spoon bread is puffed and a toothpick inserted into the center comes out clean. Serve immediately.

Variation: Feel free to play with the flavors in this recipe. Use cheddar cheese, omit the green chiles, and add ½ cup chopped ham or crumbled cooked bacon. Or omit both the cheese and the chiles and add ½ cup pure maple syrup.

Crock Tales _____

Spoon bread, a form of corn pudding, is one of the oldest American dishes. The Native Americans who greeted the Pilgrims taught them how to dry and grind corn into cornmeal. Spoon breads are the next generation from "corn pone"—the Native American bread served at the first Thanksgiving.

Thai Rice Salad

Aromatic jasmine rice is combined with crunchy vegetables in a sweet and sour dressing for this refreshing salad.

Serves: 6 to 8	

Prep time: 25 minutes

Minimum cook time: 1¼ hours in a medium slow cooker plus at least 2 hours for chilling

1½ cups jasmine rice

6 TB. vegetable oil

4 garlic cloves, peeled and minced

1 large shallot, peeled and minced

2½ cups water

Salt and freshly ground black pepper

½ cup rice wine vinegar

¼ cup firmly packed dark brown sugar

2 TB. fish sauce (nam pla)

1 or 2 tsp. Chinese chili paste with garlic

1 large carrot, peeled and shredded

1 red bell pepper, seeds and ribs removed, and finely chopped

6 scallions, rinsed, trimmed, and finely chopped

Cooker Caveats

It's important to use jasmine rice for this recipe because the innate fragrance and flavor are necessary for the salad to be successful. It's now very easy to find, even at supermarkets.

1. Rinse rice in a sieve under cold running water and place in the slow cooker.

2. Heat 2 tablespoons vegetable oil in a small skillet over medium-high heat. Add garlic and shallot, and cook, stirring frequently, for 3 minutes or until shallot is translucent. Scrape mixture into the slow cooker. Add water, salt, and pepper to the slow cooker, and stir well.

3. Cook on high for 1¼ hours or until rice is soft and liquid is absorbed. Turn off the slow cooker and allow rice to sit undisturbed for 10 minutes. Remove the lid, and fluff rice with a fork.

4. While rice is cooking, combine vinegar, brown sugar, fish sauce, and chili paste in a jar with a tight-fitting lid. Shake well until sugar dissolves. Add remaining 4 tablespoons oil, and shake well again.

5. Place rice in a mixing bowl or serving dish. Pour dressing over hot rice. Add carrot, red pepper, and scallions, and mix well to combine. Refrigerate salad for at least 2 hours or until chilled, tightly covered with plastic wrap. (Salad can be made up to 2 days in advance.)

Variation: Try slices of raw celery or cooked asparagus instead of or in addition to the carrot and red bell pepper.

Risotto-Style Rice

The creamy texture of this rice dish comes from the high starch content of the rice, and it goes well with any Italian dish.

3 TB. unsalted butter

1 medium onion, peeled and finely chopped

1 cup arborio rice

½ cup dry white wine

2½ cups vegetable or chicken stock

½ cup freshly grated Parmesan cheese

Salt and freshly ground black pepper

Serves: 4 to 6
Prep time: 15 minutes
Minimum cook time: 2 hours in a medium slow cooker

1. Heat butter in a medium saucepan over medium-high heat. Add onion and cook, stirring frequently, for 3 minutes or until onion is translucent. Add rice and stir to coat grains. Increase the heat to high and add wine. Stir for 2 minutes or until wine is almost evaporated. Scrape mixture into the slow cooker.

2. Add stock to the slow cooker and stir well. Cook on high for 2 hours or until rice is soft and liquid is absorbed. Stir in cheese, and season with salt and pepper. Serve immediately.

Variation: You can add ½ pound sautéed mushrooms or a combination of white and wild mushrooms. Or try this with either fresh asparagus or broccoli cut into ½-inch pieces.

Crock Tales

Risotto is one of Milan's contributions to Italian cuisine, and according to legend, it originated in the sixteenth century. True risotto *alla milanese* is made with saffron, which perfumes the rice and creates a pale yellow dish. Today, almost any creamy rice dish with cheese added is called a risotto, but the authentic dish is made with arborio rice, which, when cooked, releases a starch and creates its own sauce. The traditional dish requires constant stirring—a step happily unnecessary with the slow cooker version.

Wild Rice Pilaf

Wild rice has an inherently nutty flavor, and when it's cooked properly, its texture is light and fluffy.

Serves: 4 to 6	
Prep time: 15 minutes	
Minimum cook time: 3 hours in a medium slow cooker	

3 TB. unsalted butter

1 large onion, peeled and finely chopped

1 carrot, peeled and finely chopped

1 cup wild rice, rinsed

¼ cup dried currants

3 cups vegetable or chicken stock

Salt and freshly ground black pepper

1. Melt butter in a small skillet over medium-high heat. Add onion and carrot, and cook, stirring frequently, for 3 minutes or until onion is translucent. Scrape mixture into the slow cooker.

2. Add wild rice, currants, and stock to the slow cooker. Stir well. Cook on low for 7 or 8 hours or on high for 3 or 4 hours or until rice is fluffed and tender and stock is absorbed. Season *pilaf* with salt and pepper, and serve immediately.

Slow Speak

Pilaf (*PEE-laf*) is used in our culture for almost any grain dish that includes other ingredients, such as the vegetables and dried currants in this dish. Pilaf originated in the Middle East, where it was always made with rice or bulgur wheat, which were browned before any liquid was added.

Toasted Barley with Mushrooms

Barley has a sweet flavor similar to that of an almond, and the delicate mushrooms in this dish enhance its natural flavor and color.

1 cup pearl barley

3 TB. unsalted butter

1 TB. olive oil

1 shallot, peeled and minced

½ lb. white mushrooms, rinsed, trimmed, and sliced

2 cups vegetable or chicken stock

Salt and freshly ground black pepper

Serves: 4 to 6
Prep time: 15 minutes
Minimum cook time: 2 hours in a medium slow cooker

1. In a medium skillet over medium-high heat, add barley and cook, stirring frequently, for 3 to 5 minutes or until barley is lightly toasted. Transfer barley to the slow cooker.

2. Add butter and olive oil to the skillet. When butter melts, add shallot and mushrooms. Cook, stirring frequently, for 3 to 5 minutes or until mushrooms begin to soften. Scrape mixture into the slow cooker.

3. Add stock to the slow cooker, and cook on low for 4 to 6 hours or on high for 2 or 3 hours or until barley is soft. Season with salt and pepper, and serve immediately.

Slow Savvy

Toasting grains is an additional step for many recipes, but the results are worth it. Toasting cooks the starch on the exterior of the grain so the dish doesn't become gummy from too much starch when it cooks. Although barley is best toasted dry, any species of rice can be toasted in butter or oil. With rice, the grains just need to become opaque. They don't even have to brown.

Bulgur with Fennel

The mild licorice flavor of fresh fennel adds interest to this healthful grain dish.

Serves: 4 to 6
Prep time: 15 minutes
Minimum cook time: 2 hours in a medium slow cooker

3 TB. unsalted butter

½ small onion, peeled and finely chopped

½ fennel bulb, cored and thinly sliced

½ carrot, peeled and finely chopped

1 cup medium or coarse *bulgur*

1½ cups vegetable or chicken stock

½ tsp. dried thyme

Salt and freshly ground black pepper

1. Melt butter in a medium skillet over medium-high heat. Add onion, fennel, and carrot. Cook, stirring frequently, for 3 minutes or until onion is translucent. Add bulgur and cook for 2 minutes to coat grains. Scrape mixture into the slow cooker.

2. Add stock and thyme to the slow cooker. Cook on low for 4 to 6 hours or on high for 2 or 3 hours or until liquid is absorbed. Season with salt and pepper, and serve immediately.

Slow Speak

Bulgur (*BULL-gurr*) is a wheat kernel that's been steamed, dried, and crushed. It's similar to cracked wheat and can be used in the same way. It has a chewy texture and comes both coarse and fine. Fine bulgur is best known in this country as the basis for Middle Eastern tabbouleh.

Creole Farro

A cornucopia of vegetables make this grain dish visually stunning and lend their flavors, too.

3 TB. olive oil	2½ cups vegetable stock
1 medium onion, peeled and chopped	1 (14.5-oz.) can diced tomatoes, undrained
1 red bell pepper, seeds and ribs removed, and chopped	1 TB. fresh thyme or 1 tsp. dried
1 celery rib, rinsed, trimmed, and chopped	1 bay leaf
3 garlic cloves, peeled and minced	Salt and freshly ground black pepper
1½ cups *farro*, rinsed	3 TB. chopped fresh parsley

> *Serves: 4 to 6*
>
> **Prep time:** 20 minutes
>
> **Minimum cook time:** 2½ hours in a medium slow cooker

1. Heat olive oil in a large skillet over medium-high heat. Add onion, red bell pepper, celery, and garlic. Cook, stirring frequently, for 3 minutes or until onion is translucent. Scrape mixture into the slow cooker.

2. Add farro, stock, tomatoes, thyme, and bay leaf to the slow cooker, and stir well. Cook on low for 5 to 7 hours or on high for 2½ to 3 hours or until farro is plump and tender and liquid is absorbed.

3. Remove and discard bay leaf. Season with salt and pepper, and stir in parsley. Serve immediately.

Variation: Can't find farro? You can use coarse bulgur or wheat-berries for this recipe. The cooking time is the same.

 Slow Speak

Farro, sometimes called *spelt*, is an ancient grain native to southern Europe. It has a mellow, nutty flavor and is easily digestible. It contains more protein than wheat, and it's sometimes ground into flour, too.

Chapter 21

Enticing Extras

In This Chapter

- ◆ Nuts to nibble
- ◆ Sauces for all occasions
- ◆ Chutneys and conserves for you or to give as gifts

Sometimes it's the little touches that make a meal memorable. It could be a homemade jam to spread on toast at breakfast or a unique and sensational sauce for topping or dipping. Those are the recipes you'll find in this chapter because the slow cooker creates these foods easily. There's no constant stirring; you just follow the recipe and let the slow cooker do the work. Once you've discovered how easy it is to make condiments for yourself—and how the homemade taste is so special—you'll make it part of your cooking routine.

In addition, many of these recipes are candidates for canning so you can have a batch to enjoy for months to come or present a homemade gift from your kitchen to your friends.

Glazed Walnuts

In addition to being an addictive nibble, these nuts are great chopped on top of a tossed salad or added to a chicken salad.

Yield: 1 pound
Prep time: 15 minutes
Minimum cook time: 2½ hours in a medium slow cooker

1 lb. walnut halves   **¼ cup granulated sugar**

2 TB. walnut oil   **1 TB. kosher salt**

1. Bring a large pot of water to a boil over high heat. Stir in walnuts, and remove the pan from the stove. Let nuts soak for 1 hour, drain, and pat dry with paper towels.

2. While nuts are soaking, preheat the oven to 350°F. Spread walnuts on a large baking sheet, and bake them in the oven for 45 minutes or until they're dry.

3. Place walnuts in the slow cooker, drizzle with walnut oil, and stir to coat nuts evenly. Sprinkle with sugar and kosher salt. Cook on low for 2 or 3 hours or until nuts are glazed. Raise the heat to high, and cook an additional 30 minutes uncovered. Once nuts have cooled, store them in an airtight container.

 Slow Savvy

Soaking walnuts this way is an ancient Chinese method. The soaking takes all the bitterness out of the walnuts. Don't believe me? Just taste the soaking water before you throw it out!

Chili Pecans

These sweet and hot nuts are flavored with a combination of lusty Latin and subtle European seasonings.

2 TB. vegetable oil

1 lb. pecan halves

¼ cup granulated sugar

2 TB. chili powder

1 TB. herbes de Provence

1 TB. *kosher salt*

Yield: 1 pound
Prep time: 15 minutes
Minimum cook time: 2½ hours in a medium slow cooker

1. Place vegetable oil and pecans in the slow cooker, and stir to coat.

2. Combine sugar, chili powder, herbes de Provence, and kosher salt in a small bowl. Sprinkle mixture over nuts, and stir well.

3. Cook on low for 2 or 3 hours or until sugar is melted. Uncover the pan, and cook on high for an additional 30 minutes or until nuts are crisp. Serve warm or cold.

Slow Speak

Kosher salt is a coarse-grained salt that's made without any additives or iodine. Religious Jews use it in the rituals of preparing meats, and many cooks like using it because it doesn't have any chemical flavor. It's used for dishes such as this nut dish because it's granular. If you're using table salt instead, use ⅓ the amount.

Herbed Tomato Sauce

Use this easy sauce to top grilled or broiled foods, or mix it with some browned chopped meat or Italian sausage for a quickie pasta sauce.

Yield: 2 pints
Prep time: 20 minutes
Minimum cook time: 4 hours in a medium slow cooker

3 TB. olive oil

1 large onion, peeled and chopped

½ red bell pepper, seeds and ribs removed, and chopped

2 garlic cloves, peeled and minced

1 (28-oz.) can crushed tomatoes

1 (6-oz.) can tomato paste

½ cup dry white wine

½ cup water

2 TB. chopped fresh oregano or 2 tsp. dried

2 TB. chopped fresh basil or 2 tsp. dried

1 TB. chopped fresh rosemary or 1 tsp. dried

1 bay leaf

Salt and freshly ground black pepper

1. Heat olive oil in a medium skillet over medium-high heat. Add onion, red bell pepper, and garlic. Cook, stirring frequently, for 3 minutes or until onion is translucent. Scrape the mixture into the slow cooker.

2. Add tomatoes, tomato paste, wine, water, oregano, basil, rosemary, and bay leaf. Stir well. Cook on low for 6 to 8 hours or on high for 3 or 4 hours or until vegetables are tender.

3. If cooking on low, increase the heat to high. Cook sauce, uncovered, for 1 hour, stirring occasionally until slightly thickened. Remove and discard bay leaf, and season with salt and pepper.

Slow Savvy

For many recipes, you only need a few tablespoons or a partial cup of tomato sauce. Try this tip: freeze a batch in different-size containers; then you'll know the ½-pint container is 1 cup and a pint is 2 cups.

My Favorite Barbecue Sauce

The "secret ingredient" that adds sparkle to this sauce is fresh ginger, which you simmer along with fresh lemon.

1 (20-oz.) bottle ketchup

1 cup cider vinegar

½ cup firmly packed dark brown sugar

5 TB. Worcestershire sauce

¼ cup vegetable oil

2 TB. dry mustard

2 garlic cloves, peeled and minced

1 TB. grated fresh ginger

1 lemon, washed and thinly sliced

½ to 1 tsp. hot red pepper sauce or to taste

Yield: 2 pints
Prep time: 10 minutes
Minimum cook time: 2 hours in a medium slow cooker

1. Combine ketchup, vinegar, brown sugar, Worcestershire sauce, vegetable oil, mustard, garlic, ginger, and lemon in the slow cooker. Stir well. Cook on low for 4 to 6 hours or on high for 2 to 3 hours or until sauce is bubbly. Add hot red pepper sauce.

2. Ladle sauce through a strainer, pressing with the back of a spoon to extract as much liquid as possible. Discard solids. Ladle sauce into containers, cover tightly, and refrigerate.

Cooker Caveats

Even though citrus fruits might look pristine, you should still wash the fruits with mild soap and water before using them. You won't taste the soap, and it doesn't remove any of the essential oils from the skin.

Pineapple Chile Sauce

Use this sauce as a topping for grilled or baked poultry or fish or as a dipping sauce for corn fritters.

Yield: 3 cups
Prep time: 15 minutes
Minimum cook time: 2 hours in a medium slow cooker

1 ripe pineapple

1 jalapeño or serrano chile, seeds and ribs removed, and finely chopped

½ cup firmly packed light brown sugar

2 TB. chopped fresh cilantro

2 TB. freshly squeezed lime juice

1. Cut top and bottom off pineapple and cut off peel. Use a paring knife to remove the woody eyes. Slice pineapple in half, and cut out tough core from each half. Cut pineapple into 2-inch chunks and then chop flesh in a food processor fitted with a steel blade using the on-and-off pulsing action or by hand.

2. Combine pineapple, jalapeño, and brown sugar in the slow cooker. Cook on low 4 to 6 hours or on high for 2 or 3 hours or until pineapple is tender. Scrape sauce into an airtight container and refrigerate until cold. Stir in cilantro and lime juice just before serving.

Slow Savvy

Fresh pineapple is really best, but you can save time if you use crushed pineapple packed in pineapple juice. You should have about 3 cups, drained. Don't use the pineapple packed in heavy syrup, though. It'll make the sauce too sweet.

Applesauce

The liqueur gives this sauce a fruity flavor as well as luscious pink color. Try it as a nonfat option for a cake topping as well as a side dish.

**3 lb. McIntosh apples, peeled,   ½ cup crème de cassis
cored, and sliced**

Yield: 2 pints
Prep time: 15 minutes
Minimum cook time: 2 hours in a medium slow cooker

1. Place apples into the slow cooker, and pour crème de cassis over them. Cook on low for 5 to 6 hours or on high for 2 to 3 hours or until apples are very tender.

2. For a chunky sauce, mash apples with a potato masher. For a smooth sauce, purée mixture in a food processor fitted with a steel blade or in a blender. Chill, tightly covered, until ready to serve.

Slow Savvy

While traditional slicing methods call for quartering and coring apples to slice them, these steps are unnecessary. After your apple is peeled, start shaving off slices from the outside with a paring knife, turning the apple in quarter turns. Continue slicing until you reach the core, and then discard the core.

Apple Butter

The flavor of this healthful spread is so rich, you won't believe it doesn't contain any fat.

Yield: 2 pints

Prep time: 15 minutes

Minimum cook time: 8 hours in a medium slow cooker

2 lb. McIntosh apples, unpeeled, cored, and sliced

1 cup firmly packed dark brown sugar

⅔ cup water

⅓ cup rum or additional water

1 tsp. ground cinnamon

***Pinch* ground allspice**

1. Combine apples, brown sugar, water, rum, cinnamon, and allspice in the slow cooker. Cook on high for 3 hours or until apples are tender. Stir and reduce the heat to low. Cook for an additional 5 or 6 hours, stirring occasionally, until mixture is very thick and dark brown.

2. Ladle apple butter into containers, cover tightly, and refrigerate.

Variation: Want to try this method with other fruits? Both pears and apricots work beautifully, and you don't have to peel them because the skins are so tender.

Slow Speak

Pinch is a term used for the amount of a dry ingredient you can hold between the tips of your thumb and forefinger of one hand. The smallest standard measuring spoon is ¼ teaspoon; a pinch is far less.

Candied Tangerine Peel

Tangerines are ideal citrus fruit for candied peel because the peel comes right off without any flesh attached. Chop them up for baking or as a sprinkling for hot breakfast cereal.

8 tangerines, washed with   **4 cups granulated sugar**
soap and water

Yield: 3 cups
Prep time: 15 minutes
Minimum cook time: 2 hours in a medium slow cooker

1. Bring a medium saucepan of water to a boil over high heat.

2. Wash tangerines with soap and water, and peel. Cut peel into strips 2 inches long and ½ inch wide. Add peel strips to the saucepan and boil for 5 minutes. Drain, and place them in the slow cooker.

3. Add 3 cups sugar, and stir well to coat strips. Cook on high for 2 or 3 hours or until peel strips are tender. Turn off the slow cooker and allow strips to cool for 45 minutes.

4. Remove strips from the slow cooker with a slotted spoon and spread them out on a baking sheet covered with heavy-duty aluminum foil. Sprinkle remaining 1 cup sugar over strips, rolling them around to coat strips evenly. Store strips for up to 2 weeks at room temperature in an airtight container.

Variation: You can use the same method for candied grapefruit peel or orange peel; the cooking time will be the same. Just be sure no flesh is attached to the rind.

Cooker Caveats

I use organic produce, so all I have to do is rinse the tangerines. If you're using conventional tangerines or other citrus fruits, they may have been waxed. If that's the case, pour boiling water over them to melt off the wax before starting the recipe.

Apple-Orange Conserve

This is such a pretty way to top cake or iced cream, with crunchy nuts, succulent apples, and zesty oranges in the same bowl.

Yield: 3 pints

Prep time: 20 minutes

Minimum cook time: 3½ hours in a medium slow cooker

½ cup chopped walnuts

4 Granny Smith apples, peeled, cored, and cut into ¾-in. dice

3 navel oranges, washed and cut into ¾-in. dice

1½ cups granulated sugar

½ cup dried cherries or raisins

1. Preheat the oven to 350°F.

2. Place walnuts on a baking sheet, and bake for 5 to 7 minutes or until lightly browned. Set aside.

3. Combine apples, oranges, sugar, and cherries in the slow cooker. Cook on high for 2 hours or until orange peel is almost tender.

4. Uncover the slow cooker, and cook on high for an additional 1½ to 2 hours or until mixture is very thick. Stir in walnuts. Ladle *conserve* into jars, cover tightly, and refrigerate.

Slow Speak

Conserve is one of the many families of preserves. A conserve always includes at least two different fruits, as well as nuts. It's kept fairly chunky, so you can appreciate the different ingredients.

Cranberry Chutney

Once you've served this spicy and complexly flavored chutney at Thanksgiving dinner, you'll never go back to cranberry sauce!

1 lb. fresh cranberries	**2 TB. molasses**
1½ cups granulated sugar	**2 TB. grated fresh ginger**
1 cup golden raisins	**1 TB. curry powder**
½ cup red wine vinegar	**1 TB. Worcestershire sauce**
½ cup red wine	**½ to 1 tsp. hot red pepper sauce**

Yield: 2 pints
Prep time: 10 minutes
Minimum cook time: 4 hours in a medium slow cooker

1. Rinse cranberries, picking out any shriveled ones or twigs. Place cranberries in the slow cooker. Stir in sugar, raisins, vinegar, wine, molasses, ginger, curry powder, and Worcestershire sauce. Cook on high for 3 or 4 hours or until cranberries have all "popped."

2. Uncover the slow cooker, add hot red pepper sauce, and cook on high for an additional 1 or 2 hours or until mixture has thickened. Ladle *chutney* into containers, cover tightly, and refrigerate.

Slow Speak _____

Chutneys are spicy combinations that are unified by a hot, sweet, or sour flavor profile. They can contain fruits or vegetables. Traditionally, chutney was one of the classic condiments to accompany Indian curry dishes. Today, chutneys are eaten with many foods in place of spreads like ketchup. Chutneys were introduced to the United States in Colonial times.

Smoked Apple Chutney

The apples and onions in this condiment absorb flavor from some time on the grill, which makes it perfect for cold meats and poultry.

Yield: 2 pints
Prep time: 30 minutes
Minimum cook time: 4 hours in a medium slow cooker

1 cup hickory or apple wood chips

6 large tomatoes, cut in half

1 large onion, cut in half

4 garlic cloves, peeled

2 apples, peeled, cored, and quartered

1 cup granulated sugar

¾ cup cider vinegar

¼ cup golden raisins

¼ cup dried currants

2 TB. grated fresh ginger

Salt and cayenne

> ### Slow Speak
>
> **Smoking** is a technique of both flavoring and preserving food by penetrating it with the chemicals in wood smoke. In this recipe, the smoking is for flavor; the cooking and canning or refrigeration is what actually preserves the food.

1. Light a charcoal or gas grill. Soak wood chips in cold water for 30 minutes. Drain wood chips, and place them on the fire. Cover the grill with a small-holed fish grill, and place tomatoes, onion, garlic, and apples on the grill. Close the grill lid, or cover the grill with a sheet of heavy-duty aluminum foil. *Smoke* vegetables and apples for 10 minutes.

2. Remove vegetables and apples from the grill. Peel, core, and seed tomatoes, and place them in the slow cooker. Peel and finely dice onion, and add it to the slow cooker along with garlic, apples, sugar, vinegar, raisins, currants, and ginger. Cook on high for 3 or 4 hours or until mixture is thick. Stir after mixture comes to a boil.

3. Uncover the slow cooker and cook for an additional 1 hour uncovered. Season with salt and cayenne. Ladle chutney into containers, cover tightly, and refrigerate.

Dried Fruit Chutney

Dried fruits are available all year, and this spicy chutney is a great pairing with roasts in winter or cold poultry in the summer.

½ lb. dried peaches, chopped	½ cup water
½ lb. dried apricots, chopped	1 cup granulated sugar
½ lb. dried pineapple, chopped	2 tsp. curry powder or to taste
½ lb. pitted prunes, chopped	1 tsp. ground ginger
½ lb. pitted dates, chopped	½ tsp. salt
1½ cups cider vinegar	Hot red pepper sauce

Yield: 3 pints
Prep time: 20 minutes
Minimum cook time: 4 hours in a medium slow cooker

1. Combine peaches, apricots, pineapple, prunes, dates, vinegar, water, sugar, curry powder, ginger, and salt in the slow cooker. Stir well. Cook on high for 3 or 4 hours or until fruit is soft.

2. Uncover the slow cooker, and cook on high for 1 or 2 hours more or until chutney has thickened. Season with hot red pepper sauce. Ladle chutney into containers, cover tightly, and refrigerate.

Slow Savvy

Most of today's dried fruit is moist and pliable, which is why you don't soak the dried fruits in this recipe before cooking. If your dried fruit is hard and brittle, soak it in very hot tap water for 30 minutes before placing it in the slow cooker.

Part 7

Grand Finales

If you look at the dessert menu in a restaurant before deciding what will come first, chances are you're looking at this part of the book first. If so, I'm right with you.

Puddings—ranging from rich bread puddings to light steamed puddings—are synonymous with slow-cooked desserts, so there's a chapter devoted to them. And because I feel the first duty of any dessert is to be luscious, I've included a whole chapter of decadent delights, from pudding cakes to dessert fondues.

And then there are those times that the meal is rather heavy so you want a lighter dessert. I've included a barrel of apple favorites, plus other fabulous ways to treat fruit. From start to finish, your slow cooker can do it all.

"Toil and trouble all you want, ladies—it still needs more chocolate."

Chapter 22

Perfect Puddings

In This Chapter

- ◆ Rich and moist bread puddings
- ◆ Creamy rice puddings
- ◆ English steamed puddings

Old-fashioned desserts are always in style. Foods such as a rich bread pudding or a creamy rice pudding are the definition of sweet comfort foods. And, with the variations, you'll find more than a baker's dozen of ways to make them in this chapter.

You probably won't be surprised (by now) to hear that the slow cooker can create a wide variety of delicious desserts that border on the decadent. The recipes in this chapter don't rely on seasonal fruits, so they are easy to make at any time of the year.

The Bread Basket

Bread puddings were seen as a way to use up stale bread in frugal households. They exist in many cuisines, but they're associated most with the Creole traditions of Louisiana.

As long as you stay with neutral or sweet breads, feel free to experiment with different types of bread than the ones listed in the recipes here. Just don't go for the olive or herb bread; the results could be disastrous!

Steamy Treats

Steamed puddings, part of the British culinary tradition, conjure images of Charles Dickens's London. The secret to their light texture is using breadcrumbs in place of or in addition to flour in the batter.

These puddings must be steamed in a closed environment, and metal pudding steamers with lids that snap firmly into place are available from kitchen specialty stores and catalogs. But there's no need to buy one for the occasional pudding. Any bundt pan or rounded metal or ceramic mixing bowl that fits into your slow cooker can be made into a steamer.

If using a bundt pan, it's necessary to plug the opening with crushed aluminum foil and then overwrap the entire pan with aluminum foil to keep the foil from falling out of the tube. If using a mixing bowl, use a few layers of foil on top and crimp it closed firmly on the edges of the bowl. As a safety precaution, I also tie the foil shut with kitchen string (but no rubber bands, please).

Classic Creole Bread Pudding with Caramel Sauce

Pecans and raisins dot this rich, cinnamon-scented pudding from New Orleans's tradition.

3 large eggs

1 cup granulated sugar

1¾ cups whole milk

6 TB. unsalted butter, melted

1½ tsp. pure vanilla extract

1 tsp. ground cinnamon

Pinch salt

5 cups cubed French bread

½ cup golden raisins

½ cup chopped pecans

½ cup (1 stick) unsalted butter

1½ cups firmly packed dark brown sugar

½ cup heavy cream

Serves: 6 to 8	
Prep time: 25 minutes	
Minimum cook time: 3 hours in a medium slow cooker	

1. Grease the inside of the slow cooker liberally with vegetable oil spray or butter.

2. Whisk eggs in a large mixing bowl with sugar until thick and lemon-colored. Whisk in milk, melted butter, vanilla extract, cinnamon, and salt. Add bread cubes, and press down with the back of a spoon so they absorb egg mixture. Stir in raisins and pecans.

3. Spoon mixture into the slow cooker. Cook on high for 1 hour and then reduce the heat to low and cook for 2 or 3 hours or until a toothpick inserted into the center comes out clean and an instant-read thermometer inserted into the center of the pudding reads 165°F.

4. While pudding is cooking, make sauce. Melt ½ cup butter in a small saucepan over medium heat. Add brown sugar, and cook, stirring frequently, for 3 minutes or until sugar melts. Whisk in cream and stir until smooth, about 2 minutes. To serve, reheat sauce, if necessary, and spoon over servings of bread pudding.

Crock Tales

Because it's a way to use up stale bread, bread pudding was a "peasant dish" until the twentieth century.

Maple Walnut Bread Pudding

Maple and walnuts are a classic New England flavor combination, and they're super in this pudding.

Serves: 6 to 8
Prep time: 15 minutes
Minimum cook time: 2½ hours in a medium slow cooker

1 cup chopped walnuts

3 large eggs

1¾ cups whole milk

¾ cup pure maple syrup

6 TB. unsalted butter, melted

1½ tsp. pure vanilla extract

½ tsp. ground cinnamon

Pinch salt

5 cups cubed brioche, challah, or other egg bread

Vanilla ice cream or whipped cream (optional)

1. Preheat the oven to 350°F. Grease the inside of the slow cooker liberally with vegetable oil spray or butter.

2. Place walnuts on a baking sheet and bake for 5 to 7 minutes or until browned. Remove nuts from the oven, and set aside.

3. Whisk eggs, milk, and maple syrup together in a large mixing bowl. Beat in melted butter, vanilla extract, cinnamon, and salt. Add bread cubes, and press down with the back of a spoon so they absorb egg mixture.

4. Spoon mixture into the slow cooker. Cook on high for 2 or 3 hours or until a toothpick inserted into the center comes out clean and an instant-read thermometer inserted into the center of pudding reads 165°F. Serve immediately, garnished with ice cream or whipped cream (if using).

Variation: For a dessert with a bit more kick to it, add 3 tablespoons brandy or rum to the recipe.

Slow Savvy

You might think it doesn't make any sense to take the time to toast nuts when they're going into a wet mixture. But do it anyway. The toasting keeps them crisper as they cook, and it also brings out the oils that deliver the flavor.

White Chocolate Bread Pudding

This dessert is my idea of perfection: aromatic orange zest and zesty dried cranberries dot a pudding flavored with heavenly white chocolate.

3 large eggs

2 cups whole milk

1½ cups chopped white chocolate, melted

6 TB. unsalted butter, melted

1 TB. grated orange zest

½ tsp. pure vanilla extract

Pinch salt

6 cups cubed French bread

½ cup dried cranberries

Vanilla ice cream or whipped cream (optional)

Serves: 6 to 8	
Prep time: 15 minutes	
Minimum cook time: 2 hours in a medium slow cooker	

1. Grease the inside of the slow cooker liberally with vegetable oil spray or butter.

2. Whisk eggs and milk together in a large mixing bowl. Beat in melted white chocolate, melted butter, orange zest, vanilla extract, and salt. Add bread cubes and dried cranberries, and press down with the back of a spoon so they absorb egg mixture.

3. Spoon mixture into the slow cooker. Cook on high for 2 to 3 hours or until a toothpick inserted into the center comes out clean and an instant-read thermometer inserted into the center of pudding reads 165°F. Serve immediately, garnished with ice cream or whipped cream (if using).

Variation: For a real chocolate hit, use bittersweet chocolate and chocolate milk in this recipe. Then omit the orange zest and add chocolate chips instead of dried cranberries.

Cooker Caveats

Be careful when selecting white chocolate. You don't want the ones called "baking pieces" because they're artificial and don't melt well.

Thanksgiving Bread Pudding

This pudding has all the flavors you'd expect from pumpkin pie, including the pumpkin!

Serves: 6 to 8

Prep time: 15 minutes

Minimum cook time:
3 hours in a medium slow cooker

---

2 cups solid-pack canned pumpkin

2 large eggs, lightly beaten

1 (12-oz.) can evaporated milk

1 (14-oz.) can sweetened condensed milk

4 TB. unsalted butter, melted

2 tsp. pumpkin pie spice or 1 tsp. ground cinnamon, ½ tsp. ground allspice, and ½ tsp. grated nutmeg

Pinch salt

6 cups cubed French bread

½ cup raisins

Vanilla ice cream or whipped cream (optional)

🔥 Cooker Caveats

There are two similar forms of canned pumpkin, and you want to be sure what you're buying is just pumpkin and not pumpkin pie filling. The filling is sweetened and already contains spices.

---

1. Grease the inside of the slow cooker liberally with vegetable oil spray or butter.

2. Combine pumpkin, eggs, evaporated milk, sweetened condensed milk, melted butter, pumpkin pie spice, and salt in a mixing bowl. Whisk until smooth. Add bread cubes, and press down with the back of a spoon so they absorb egg mixture. Stir in raisins.

3. Spoon mixture into the slow cooker. Cook on high for 1 hour, reduce the heat to low, and cook for 2 or 3 hours or until a toothpick inserted into the center comes out clean and an instant-read thermometer inserted into the center of pudding reads 165°F. Serve warm, topped with ice cream or whipped cream (if using).

Orange-Cranberry Rice Pudding

Thick and rich marmalade gives this creamy pudding its orange flavor, and the cranberries are a great foil.

1 cup converted long-grain rice	**1½ cups whole milk**
3 cups water	**½ cup orange marmalade**
1 cup granulated sugar	**2 large eggs, lightly beaten**
Pinch salt	**½ cup dried cranberries**
	1 cup heavy cream

Serves: 4 to 6

Prep time: 30 minutes
Minimum cook time:
2 hours in a medium slow cooker

1. Grease the inside of the slow cooker liberally with vegetable oil spray or butter.

2. Place rice in a sieve, and rinse it well under cold water. Place rice in a 2-quart saucepan with water, ½ cup sugar, and salt. Bring to a boil over high heat, and boil for 15 minutes or until rice is tender. Drain rice, and spoon into the slow cooker.

3. Combine milk, remaining ½ cup sugar, orange marmalade, and eggs in a mixing bowl, and whisk well. Stir mixture into rice, and add cranberries. Cook on low for 4 or 5 hours or on high for 2 or 3 hours or until custard is set. Remove pudding from the slow cooker and chill well.

4. When rice is chilled, place cream in a chilled mixing bowl. Whip cream with an electric mixer on medium speed until it thickens, increase the speed to high, and whip cream until stiff peaks form. *Fold* whipped cream into rice. Serve immediately or refrigerate for up to 1 day, tightly covered with plastic wrap.

Variation: For a change of pace, try lime or lemon marmalade in this recipe. Any dried fruit works well, too.

Slow Speak

Fold is the term used for combining a light mixture, such as whipped cream or beaten egg whites, with a denser mixture—in this case, the rice pudding. The light mixture goes on top, and you insert a rubber spatula into the center of the bowl and push it across the bottom of the bowl. This brings up the dense mixture. Then, turn the bowl a quarter turn and repeat the motion. The object is to combine the two mixtures without deflating the lighter one.

Gingered Rice Pudding

The rice is cooked in coconut milk and then topped with fresh fruit for this pudding that can be served at any temperature.

Serves: 6 to 8

Prep time: 15 minutes

Minimum cook time: 2½ hours in a medium slow cooker

1 cup arborio rice

1 (14-oz.) can unsweetened coconut milk

1 (14-oz.) can sweetened condensed milk

2 cups half-and-half

2 tsp. ground ginger

½ tsp. ground cinnamon

½ tsp. salt

½ cup heavy cream

3 or 4 cups chopped fresh mango or pineapple (optional)

1. Grease the inside of the slow cooker liberally with vegetable oil spray or butter.

2. Combine rice, coconut milk, sweetened condensed milk, half-and-half, ginger, cinnamon, and salt in the slow cooker. Stir well. Cook on low for 5 to 7 hours or on high for 2½ to 3 hours or until rice is soft and liquid is thick.

3. Stir in heavy cream. Serve hot, warm, or chilled, topped with chopped fruit (if using).

Cooker Caveats

Frequently, coconut milk separates in the can with the liquid on the bottom and a thick layer of coconut on top. Whisk it briskly until the lumps are gone because they won't break up well in the slow cooker and you might end up with islands of hard coconut in your soft pudding.

Mexican Chocolate Rice Pudding

Aromatic cinnamon, coffee liqueur, and crunchy almonds are the flavor and texture accents in this creamy pudding.

1 cup slivered almonds

1 cup arborio rice

3 cups half-and-half

1 (14-oz.) can sweetened condensed milk

¼ cup Kahlúa or other coffee-flavored liqueur

6 oz. good-quality bittersweet chocolate, chopped

½ tsp. ground cinnamon

Pinch salt

½ cup heavy cream

Vanilla ice cream or sweetened whipped cream (optional)

Serves: 4 to 6
Prep time: 15 minutes
Minimum cook time: 2½ hours in a medium slow cooker

1. Preheat the oven to 350°F. Grease the inside of the slow cooker liberally with vegetable oil spray or butter.

2. Place almonds on a baking sheet and bake for 5 to 7 minutes or until browned. Remove nuts from the oven, chop coarsely, and set aside.

3. Combine rice, half-and-half, sweetened condensed milk, Kahlúa, chocolate, cinnamon, and salt in the slow cooker. Stir well. Cook on low for 5 to 7 hours or on high for 2½ to 3 hours or until rice is soft and the liquid is thick.

4. Stir in heavy cream. Serve hot, warm, or chilled, topped with ice cream or whipped cream (if using).

Variation: Try this with white chocolate and substitute kirsch for the coffee liqueur. Omit the cinnamon, and add ½ cup dried cherries.

Crock Tales

The type of chocolate most popular in Mexico is a grainy block used to make hot chocolate. The most famous brand is Ibarra, and all Mexican chocolate contains both ground almonds and cinnamon, so they're the additions to this pudding.

Indian Pudding

This is a more flavorful version of the classic Native American dish because it's made with crystallized ginger.

> *Serves: 6 to 8*
>
> **Prep time:** 30 minutes
>
> **Minimum cook time:** 3 hours in a medium slow cooker

5 cups whole milk

¾ cup firmly packed dark brown sugar

½ cup pure maple syrup

¾ cup yellow cornmeal

6 TB. unsalted butter, cut into small pieces

½ tsp. pure vanilla extract

3 TB. finely chopped crystallized ginger

½ tsp. salt

Vanilla ice cream or sweetened whipped cream (optional)

1. Grease the inside of the slow cooker liberally with vegetable oil spray or butter.

2. Combine milk, brown sugar, and maple syrup in a 2-quart saucepan, and stir well. Heat over medium heat, stirring occasionally, until mixture comes to a boil. Whisk in cornmeal and simmer mixture, whisking frequently, for 10 minutes or until very thick.

3. Stir in butter and vanilla extract. Whisk until butter melts. Remove the pan from the heat, and stir in crystallized ginger and salt. Scrape mixture into the slow cooker. Cook on low for 3 to 5 hours or until the edges have darkened slightly and the center of pudding is set. Serve warm with vanilla ice cream or whipped cream (if using).

Crock Tales

Because Native Americans introduced corn to the Pilgrims, anything made with corn had "Indian" as a prefix at one time or another. Indian Pudding is sometimes called Hasty Pudding, and the Hasty Pudding Club at Harvard University was named for the dessert. Recipes for Indian or Hasty Pudding go back to the early eighteenth century.

Steamed Chocolate Pudding

This rich pudding has a light texture and a fabulous aroma when it's brought to the table.

1 TB. unsalted butter, softened

½ cup granulated sugar

¼ lb. good-quality bittersweet chocolate, chopped

¼ cup heavy cream

1 TB. rum or liqueur

3 large eggs, separated

1 tsp. pure vanilla extract

¼ tsp. cream of tartar

2 cups water

½ cup plain breadcrumbs

Ice cream (flavor of your choice) or sweetened whipped cream (optional)

Serves: 6 to 8
Prep time: 20 minutes
Minimum cook time: 3 hours in a medium slow cooker

1. Generously grease a pudding steamer or mold that will fit inside your slow cooker with butter. Sprinkle the inside of the mold with 1 tablespoon sugar and set aside.

2. Combine chocolate, cream, and rum in a microwave-safe dish. Microwave on medium (50 percent) power for 1 minute. Stir and repeat, if necessary, until chocolate is melted (this can also be done in a small saucepan over low heat). Whisk egg yolks, and stir into chocolate mixture along with vanilla extract.

3. Place egg whites in a mixing bowl and beat with an electric mixer at medium speed until frothy. Add cream of tartar, increase the speed to high, and beat until stiff peaks form, gradually adding remaining sugar. Fold chocolate into egg whites and then fold in breadcrumbs. Scrape batter into the prepared mold. Cover the mold with its lid or a double layer of aluminum foil, and crimp the edges of the foil to seal it tightly.

4. Place the sealed pudding steamer into the slow cooker, and add 2 cups water to the slow cooker. Steam pudding on low for 6 to 8 hours or on high for 3 or 4 hours or until a toothpick inserted into the center comes out clean. Remove pudding from the slow cooker and allow it to sit for at least 30 minutes. Unmold pudding onto a serving tray. Serve slices topped with ice cream or whipped cream (if using).

Variation: Want to make it mocha? Omit the rum and add 1 tablespoon instant coffee crystals mixed with 2 tablespoons hot water to the batter.

 Slow Savvy

Dark chocolate is like fine wine. If stored under the right conditions, its flavor improves with age. Store chocolate in a cool place and tightly wrapped because it does absorb flavors from foods around it. Use milk chocolate and white chocolate within a few months because the milk solids can spoil.

English Christmas Pudding

This is the grandmother of all steamed puddings, with myriad dried fruits and spices in the mix.

Serves: 6 to 8

Prep time: 20 minutes

Minimum cook time: 4 hours in a medium slow cooker

¼ lb. (1 stick) plus 5 TB. unsalted butter, softened to room temperature

1 TB. granulated sugar

½ cup chopped prunes

½ cup chopped dried figs

½ cup golden raisins

¼ cup dried currants

¼ cup chopped candied fruits

1 medium apple, peeled, cored, and finely chopped

¼ cup chopped walnuts

1 cup plus 2 TB. brandy

2 large eggs, lightly beaten

½ cup firmly packed dark brown sugar

½ cup plain breadcrumbs

¼ cup all-purpose flour

1 tsp. ground cinnamon

½ tsp. grated nutmeg

½ tsp. baking powder

¼ tsp. salt

1 lb. confectioners' sugar

¼ tsp. pure vanilla extract

1. Generously grease a 1½-quart pudding steamer or mold that will fit inside your slow cooker with 1 tablespoon butter. Sprinkle the inside of the mold with granulated sugar and set aside.

2. Melt 4 tablespoons butter in a small saucepan or in the microwave.

3. Combine prunes, figs, raisins, currants, candied fruits, apple, walnuts, and ½ cup brandy in a mixing bowl. Stir to combine. Stir in melted butter, eggs, brown sugar, breadcrumbs, flour, cinnamon, nutmeg, baking powder, and salt. Stir well and pack mixture into the prepared mold. Cover the mold with its lid or a double layer of aluminum foil, and crimp the edges of the foil to seal it tightly.

4. Place the sealed pudding steamer into the slow cooker, and add 2 cups water to the slow cooker. Steam pudding on low for 8 to 10 hours or on high for 4 or 5 hours or until a toothpick inserted into the center comes out clean. Remove pudding from the slow cooker, and allow it to sit for at least 30 minutes. Remove the cover, and place a sheet of aluminum foil on the top. Using oven mitts if necessary, place one hand on top of

the foil and flip the pudding steamer over with the other hand so it sits on the foil. Pour ½ cup brandy over hot pudding, and cover it with the foil to keep warm.

5. To make hard sauce, combine remaining ¼ pound butter, confectioners' sugar, remaining 2 tablespoons brandy, and vanilla extract in a food processor fitted with a steel blade. Process until smooth, scraping down the sides of the bowl. Alternately, combine ingredients in a mixing bowl and beat with an electric mixer at slow speed until smooth. Pass hard sauce separately.

Cooker Caveats

If you don't have a traditional copper or ceramic pudding steamer, you can make steamed puddings in any mold that will fit into your slow cooker. Do *not* use coffee cans or canned vegetable cans. Most of these contain lead and are painted with or sealed with materials that can release toxic gasses when heated.

Chapter 23

Sweet Sensations

In This Chapter

- ◆ Saucy pudding cakes
- ◆ Homey slow cooked cakes
- ◆ Gooey fondues

If you thought the various puddings in Chapter 22 comprised your slow cooker dessert options, just wait until you try the recipes in this chapter! Here you learn how versatile your slow cooker really can be when it comes to ending meals on a sweet note. "Pudding cakes" are slow cooker classics—and they're a mystery. You start with thick batter on the bottom and pour a boiling liquid over it, but by the end of the cooking time you've got a cake on top of a thick sauce. It's magic!

Many recipes in this chapter are made with chocolate—truly the "food of the gods" for many people, including me. The slow cooker's low heat generated makes it perfect for chocolate because scorching is the way most chocolate desserts fail. You'll see how easy making chocolate fondue in the slow cooker is, and you can prepare the foods to dip while it cooks.

Mysterious Cakes

The slow cooker cannot produce what pastry chefs define as an authentic cake. Cakes need the dry heat of an oven, and they need a higher temperature than a slow cooker can generate, even one set on high. But you can create delicious dishes that are technically baked puddings but have the dry texture of a cake.

The batters for the cake recipes in this chapter are much thicker than those for conventional cakes because batters baking in a hot oven release moisture into the oven as they bake; they need to "dry out." But the reverse is true for slow cooker cakes. The steam generated by the cooking process becomes part of the cake and moistens it as it cooks.

> **Slow Savvy**
>
> The shape of the slow cooker for savory dishes doesn't matter, but I've found that round slow cookers produce better cakes. In an oval machine, the center of the cake tends to remain underdone while the narrow edges are overdone.

Mocha Pecan Pudding Cake

Crunchy nuts dot this delicate chocolate and coffee flavored cake topped with a rich, hot syrup.

1 cup granulated sugar

1 cup all-purpose flour

1 cup chopped pecans

3 TB. plus ¼ cup *unsweetened cocoa powder*

1 TB. instant coffee granules

2 tsp. baking powder

½ cup whole milk

3 TB. unsalted butter, melted

½ tsp. pure vanilla extract

¾ cup firmly packed dark brown sugar

1¾ cups boiling water

Coffee, vanilla, or butter pecan ice cream (optional)

Serves: 6
Prep time: 15 minutes
Minimum cook time: 2 hours in a medium slow cooker

1. Grease the inside of the slow cooker liberally with vegetable oil spray or butter.

2. Combine granulated sugar, flour, pecans, 3 tablespoons cocoa powder, coffee, and baking powder in a mixing bowl. Stir in milk, melted butter, and vanilla extract. Stir until a stiff batter forms, and spread batter in the slow cooker.

3. Sprinkle brown sugar and remaining ¼ cup cocoa powder over batter. Pour boiling water over batter. Cook on high for 2 to 2¼ hours or until a toothpick inserted into the top cake layer comes out clean. Allow cake to sit for 15 minutes with the slow cooker turned off before serving. Serve cake hot, at room temperature, or chilled, topped with ice cream (if using).

Variation: You can omit the coffee granules and add 2 tablespoons of any liqueur or liquor to the cake. Also try butterscotch or peanut butter baking chips instead of the chocolate chips.

Slow Speak

Unsweetened cocoa powder is powdered chocolate that has had a portion of the cocoa butter removed. Dutch process cocoa powder is a type of cocoa powder that's formulated with reduced acidity and gives foods a more mellow flavor. Cocoa keeps almost indefinitely when stored at room temperature.

Chocolate Peanut Pudding Cake

If chocolate and peanuts are a favorite combination, this easy-to-make luscious dessert is for you!

Serves: 6
Prep time: 15 minutes
Minimum cook time: 2 hours in a medium slow cooker

1 cup all-purpose flour

⅓ cup unsweetened cocoa powder

1 cup granulated sugar

1½ tsp. baking powder

½ cup whole milk

3 TB. unsalted butter, melted

1 tsp. pure vanilla extract

¾ cup chunky peanut butter

½ cup chopped roasted peanuts

⅔ cup bittersweet chocolate chips

1¾ cups boiling water

Vanilla ice cream or sweetened whipped cream (optional)

1. Grease the inside of the slow cooker liberally with vegetable oil spray or butter.

2. Combine flour, 3 tablespoons cocoa powder, ⅓ cup sugar, and baking powder in a mixing bowl. Stir in milk, melted butter, and vanilla extract. Stir until a stiff batter forms and then stir in peanut butter, chopped peanuts, and chocolate chips. Spread batter in the slow cooker.

3. Pour boiling water into the mixing bowl, and stir in remaining cocoa powder and sugar. Pour mixture over batter. Cook on high for 2 to 2¼ hours or until a toothpick inserted into the top cake layer comes out clean. Allow cake to sit for 15 minutes with the slow cooker turned off before serving. Serve cake hot, at room temperature, or chilled, topped with ice cream or whipped cream (if using).

Variation: Afraid a guest might be allergic to peanuts? Try cashew butter or almond butter and their appropriate nuts instead. If the nut butter isn't sweetened, add an additional ¼ cup granulated sugar to the batter.

Crock Tales

Ancient Peruvians knew the nutritional value of peanuts; that's why they buried pots of this beneficial legume with their kings. But peanut butter is an American invention. It was developed in the 1890s and was touted as a health food at the 1904 St. Louis World's Fair.

Apple Pudding Cake

This cake has the texture of a cobbler, and the sauce is subtly seasoned.

2 cups apple cider or apple juice

2 Granny Smith apples

1 cup all-purpose flour

⅓ cup granulated sugar

1 tsp. baking powder

½ tsp. *apple pie spice*

Pinch salt

½ cup whole milk

4 TB. unsalted butter, melted

¼ tsp. pure vanilla extract

⅓ cup finely chopped dried apples

½ cup firmly packed dark brown sugar

Vanilla ice cream or sweetened whipped cream (optional)

Serves: 6	
Prep time: 20 minutes	
Minimum cook time: 2 hours in a medium slow cooker	

1. Grease the inside of the slow cooker liberally with vegetable oil spray or butter.

2. Bring apple cider to a boil in a small saucepan over high heat. Cook until cider is reduced by ½. Set aside.

3. While cider is boiling, peel and core apples, and chop apples finely in a food processor fitted with a steel blade using on-and-off pulsing.

4. Combine flour, granulated sugar, baking powder, apple pie spice, and salt in a mixing bowl. Stir in milk, melted butter, and vanilla extract. Stir until a stiff batter forms and then stir in apples and dried apples. Spread batter in the slow cooker.

5. Bring cider back to a boil, and stir in brown sugar. Pour mixture over batter. Cook on high for 2 to 2¼ hours or until a toothpick inserted into the top cake layer comes out clean. Turn off the slow cooker and remove the lid. Allow cake to sit for 15 minutes before serving. Served cake hot, at room temperature, or chilled, topped with ice cream or whipped cream (if using).

Variation: Feel more in the mood for apricots than apples? Use 8 fresh apricots, dried apricots, and apricot nectar for the various forms of apple in this recipe. Then omit the apple pie spice and add ½ teaspoon ground ginger to the batter.

Slow Speak

Apple pie spice is a combination of fragrant spices. You can make your own by combining ½ teaspoon cinnamon, ¼ teaspoon each nutmeg, and ground cloves, and ⅛ teaspoon each allspice, ground cardamom. In a pinch, substitute cinnamon with a dash of any of the other spices you might have on hand.

Greek Walnut and Fig Cake

This rich and dense cake filled with crunchy nuts and sweet figs is moistened with a lemony syrup.

Serves: 6

Prep time: 20 minutes

Minimum cook time:
2½ hours in a medium slow cooker

1½ cups chopped walnuts

¾ cup chopped dried figs, stems discarded if necessary

¼ cup brandy

1½ cups all-purpose flour

2 cups granulated sugar

1¾ tsp. baking powder

½ tsp. ground cinnamon

Pinch salt

3 large eggs

6 TB. unsalted butter, melted

1 cup water

2 cinnamon sticks

2 (3-in.) strips lemon zest

1. Preheat the oven to 350°F. Using the bottom of the slow cooker as a guide, cut out a circle of parchment paper. Grease the inside of the slow cooker liberally with vegetable oil spray or butter. Place the parchment paper into the bottom, and grease it liberally as well.

2. Spread nuts in a single layer on a baking sheet and toast for 5 to 7 minutes or until lightly browned. Set aside.

3. Place figs in a small mixing bowl and sprinkle with brandy. Set aside.

4. Combine flour, ½ cup sugar, baking powder, cinnamon, and salt in a mixing bowl.

5. Whisk eggs in another bowl, and add melted butter. Add egg mixture to dry ingredients, and stir well. Add toasted nuts and figs. Stir well again, and scrape batter into prepared slow cooker. Even the top with a rubber spatula. Cook cake on high for 2½ hours or until a toothpick inserted in the center comes out clean. Turn off the slow cooker, remove the lid, and allow cake to cool for 15 minutes. Run a spatula around the edge of the slow cooker, and invert cake onto a serving platter.

6. While cake is cooking, combine water, remaining 1½ cups sugar, cinnamon sticks, and lemon zest in a small saucepan. Bring to a boil over medium-high heat, stirring occasionally. Reduce the heat to low, and cook syrup for 10 minutes, stirring occasionally. Remove and discard cinnamon sticks and lemon

zest. To serve, cut cake into slices and *drizzle* syrup over each slice. Serve cake hot or at room temperature.

Variation: This recipe works just as well with toasted almonds, and chopped dried apricots or chopped dates can be used in place of the figs.

> **Slow Speak** _____
>
> **Drizzle** is a fancy term for pouring a small amount of liquid slowly over a large area rather than pouring it all in one place. You can drizzle with a measuring cup, but the liquid is more likely to scatter over more territory if you use a spoon.

Carrot Cake with Cream Cheese Topping

This dense cake contains all the ingredients of a traditional carrot cake, and the cream cheese topping is like a traditional creamy frosting.

½ cup chopped walnuts

3 or 4 medium carrots

12 TB. unsalted butter

1 (8-oz.) can crushed pineapple in pineapple juice

1½ cups all-purpose flour

½ cup granulated sugar

⅓ cup shredded coconut

1¾ tsp. baking powder

¾ tsp. ground cinnamon

¼ tsp. ground ginger

Pinch salt

2 large eggs

¾ tsp. pure vanilla extract

1 (3-oz.) pkg. cream cheese, softened

1½ cups confectioners' sugar

Serves: 6
Prep time: 20 minutes
Minimum cook time: 2½ hours in a medium slow cooker

1. Preheat the oven to 350°F. Using the bottom of the slow cooker as a guide, cut out a circle of parchment paper. Grease the inside of the slow cooker liberally with vegetable oil spray or butter. Place the parchment paper into the bottom, and grease it liberally as well.

2. Spread nuts in a single layer on a baking sheet and toast for 5 to 7 minutes or until lightly browned. Set aside.

3. Peel and grate carrots. You should have 1½ cups firmly packed grated carrots. Set aside.

4. Melt 8 tablespoons butter and set aside. Allow remaining butter to soften at room temperature.

5. Drain pineapple, reserving 3 tablespoons juice. Measure out ¼ cup pineapple, and set aside remaining ½ cup for garnish (optional).

6. Combine flour, granulated sugar, coconut, baking powder, cinnamon, ginger, and salt in a mixing bowl.

7. Whisk eggs in another bowl, and add melted butter, ½ teaspoon vanilla extract, and reserved pineapple juice. Add egg mixture to dry ingredients and stir well. Add carrots, ¼ cup pineapple, and toasted nuts. Stir well again, and scrape batter into the prepared slow cooker. Even the top with a rubber spatula. Cook cake on high for 2½ hours or until a toothpick inserted in the center comes out clean. Turn off the slow cooker, remove the lid, and allow cake to cool for 15 minutes.

8. While cake is cooking, combine remaining butter, cream cheese, remaining vanilla extract, and confectioners' sugar in a mixing bowl. Beat at slow speed with an electric mixer to combine. Increase the speed to medium and beat for 1 or 2 minutes or until mixture is light and fluffy.

9. To serve, run a spatula around the edge of the slow cooker, and invert cake onto a serving platter. Cut cake into servings, and top each with cream cheese topping and remaining crushed pineapple (if using). Serve cake hot or at room temperature.

Slow Savvy

If you need to peel a large number of carrots that will be cooked, save time by pouring boiling water over them. After 5 minutes, plunge them into ice water and the skins will slip right off.

Toffee Pecan Cake

This cake is like a warm praline, with caramel and pecan flavors blending.

1 cup chopped pecans

1½ cups all-purpose flour

¾ cup firmly packed dark brown sugar

1½ tsp. baking powder

Pinch salt

3 large eggs

5 TB. unsalted butter, melted

3 TB. whole milk

½ tsp. pure vanilla extract

1½ cups *toffee* chips

Confectioners' sugar for dusting (optional)

Serves: 6
Prep time: 15 minutes
Minimum cook time: 2½ hours in a medium slow cooker

1. Preheat the oven to 350°F. Using the bottom of the slow cooker as a guide, cut out a circle of parchment paper. Grease the inside of the slow cooker liberally with vegetable oil spray or butter. Place the parchment paper into the bottom, and grease it liberally as well.

2. Spread nuts in a single layer on a baking sheet and toast for 5 to 7 minutes or until lightly browned. Set aside.

3. Combine flour, brown sugar, baking powder, and salt in a mixing bowl.

4. Whisk eggs in another bowl, and add melted butter, milk, and vanilla extract. Add egg mixture to dry ingredients, and stir well. Add nuts and toffee chips. Stir well again, and scrape batter into prepared slow cooker. Even the top with a rubber spatula. Cook cake on high for 2½ hours or until a toothpick inserted in the center comes out clean. Turn off the slow cooker, remove the lid, and allow cake to cool for 15 minutes. To serve, run a spatula around the edge of the slow cooker, and invert cake onto a serving platter. Dust cake with confectioners' sugar (if using). Serve cake warm or at room temperature.

Variation: You can substitute chocolate, butterscotch, or peanut butter chips for the toffee, and the nuts can be changed to walnuts or omitted entirely if you prefer.

Slow Speak

Toffee is a candy made by cooking sugar with water and usually butter until it's browned. On a candy thermometer, the temperature should reach between 260°F and 300°F.

Chocolate Fondue

My dream as a chocoholic is to have a vat of this bubbly treat at every meal. You can personalize it in myriad ways.

Serves: 6

Prep time: 10 minutes

Minimum cook time: 45 minutes in a small slow cooker

¾ **lb. good-quality bittersweet chocolate, chopped**

½ **cup heavy cream**

3 TB. **liqueur or liquor (your favorite: rum, bourbon, tequila, cognac, brandy, triple sec, Grand Marnier, Chambord, kirsch, amaretto, Frangelico, crème de cacao, crème de banana, Irish cream liqueur, Kahlúa)**

1. Combine chocolate, cream, and liqueur in the slow cooker. Cook on low for 45 to 60 minutes or until chocolate melts. Stir gently toward the end of the cooking time.

2. Serve directly from the slow cooker with hulled strawberries (halved if large), banana chunks, clementine segments, apple slices, donut holes, waffle squares, butter cookies, angel food cake cubes, brownie cubes, biscotti, or sugar cookies.

Variation: If you're serving the fondue to children or adults who cannot tolerate alcohol, substitute ¼ to ½ teaspoon pure extract for the liqueur or liquor.

Cooker Caveats

It's a widely held misconception that the cooking process evaporates alcohol from a dish. While most of the alcohol is no longer present, some residual alcohol is still present, regardless of how long a dish cooks. Keep this in mind if you're adding alcohol to a dish children or adults who avoid alcohol could eat.

Bittersweet Chocolate Coconut Cream Fondue

If you're a fan of Mounds candy bars, you'll love this dessert. Sweet coconut laced with a bit of rum add ancillary flavors to the chocolate.

9 oz. bittersweet chocolate, chopped

1 oz. unsweetened chocolate, chopped

1 cup sweetened cream of coconut (such as Coco López)

½ cup heavy cream

¼ cup dark rum

¼ tsp. pure coconut extract

Serves: 6
Prep time: 10 minutes
Minimum cook time: 45 minutes in a small slow cooker

1. Combine bittersweet chocolate, unsweetened chocolate, cream of coconut, cream, rum, and coconut extract in the slow cooker. Cook on low for 45 to 60 minutes or until chocolate melts. Stir gently toward the end of the cooking time.

2. Serve directly from the slow cooker with hulled strawberries (halved if large), banana chunks, clementine segments, crystallized ginger slices, donut holes, waffle squares, butter cookies, angel food cake cubes, coconut macaroons, brownie cubes, biscotti, or sugar cookies.

Cooker Caveats

Be sure you only use pure extracts in cooking. They might cost a bit more, but you only use them in minute quantities and they last for up to 2 years after they're opened. The flavor of extracts is intense, and the chemical taste from artificial extracts is unpleasant.

Easy Mexican *Dulce de Leche* Fondue

Does luscious fondue get any easier than this? The milk becomes a delicious caramel as it simmers in the slow cooker.

Serves: 6
Prep time: 5 minutes
Minimum cook time: 4½ hours in medium slow cooker

3 (14-oz.) cans sweetened condensed milk

¼ cup dark rum

1 tsp. pure vanilla extract, preferably Mexican

1. Remove the labels from the cans, stand the cans in a medium or large slow cooker, and fill the slow cooker with very hot tap water; cans should be fully covered. Cook on high for 4½ hours. *It is imperative that the cans are covered with water at all times or they could explode.*

2. Remove the cans from the water with tongs and allow them to cool. Remove and carefully pour off water from the slow cooker. Pour the cans' contents back into the slow cooker, and whisk in rum and vanilla extract.

3. Reduce the heat to low, and serve directly from the slow cooker with hulled strawberries (halved if large), banana chunks, apple slices, dried coconut slices, dried apricots, crystallized ginger, donut holes, waffle squares, butter cookies, pound cake cubes, brownie cubes, coconut macaroons, or sugar cookies.

Variation: You can use pure almond extract in place of the vanilla for a different taste. You can also add chopped toasted almonds to the fondue along with the extract.

Crock Tales

Dulce de leche means "sweet milk" in Spanish, and it's popular in all Hispanic countries. It's sometimes called *cajeta*, and it's used as a spread, dip, or topping. This easy method is how it's made in the Yucatan province of Mexico.

Chapter 24

Fruity Favorites

In This Chapter

- ◆ Year-round apple desserts
- ◆ Homey American classics
- ◆ Winter treats with dried fruit

Fruit desserts enable you to satisfy your sweet tooth while also eating a nutritionally necessary helping of fruits. Most great fruit desserts let the fruit shine as the star, and you'll find that's true of the recipes in this chapter.

Apples are harvested in the fall, but thanks to cold storage techniques, we can enjoy them year-round. In this chapter, you'll find many options to enjoy them. Other fruits are more closely associated with summer, when they are local and at their lowest cost. But if you want to enjoy blueberries in January, modern transportation has made it possible to find them—it's the new definition of "airline food."

All About Apples

With a selection of more than 300 varieties of apples grown in North America, Americans consume about 20 pounds of apples per capita, and apples are right up there in the top 5 fruits we eat. But not all apples are created equal. Some are better for munching raw, and others are better for cooking. Some, such as McIntosh, are good cooking apples for applesauce because they fall apart so well. But that wouldn't be an advantage in a pie or tart. For these recipes, unless otherwise notes, all apples can be used interchangeably with any other.

Cooker Caveats

Keep apples away from foods with strong odors such as cabbage or onions to prevent flavor transfer. As an alternative, store apples in a dark cabinet with lots of circulating air. However, do not store apples near potatoes. Apples give off ethylene gas, which causes potatoes to sprout.

Apple Crumble

Cinnamon-flavored oats are the topping on this easy dessert.

¼ lb. (1 stick) unsalted butter

2 lb. apples, cored and thinly sliced (and peeled, if desired)

2 TB. freshly squeezed lemon juice

¼ cup granulated sugar

2 TB. all-purpose flour

1 tsp. ground cinnamon

¾ cup quick oats (not instant or old-fashioned)

½ cup firmly packed dark brown sugar

Vanilla ice cream or sweetened whipped cream (optional)

Serves: 4 to 6
Prep time: 15 minutes
Minimum cook time: 1½ hours in a medium slow cooker

1. Cut 2 tablespoons butter into small bits and set aside. Melt remaining 6 tablespoons butter and set aside.

2. Place apples in the slow cooker and toss with lemon juice. Mix granulated sugar, flour, and ½ teaspoon cinnamon in a small bowl. Toss apples with sugar mixture, and spread apples in an even layer. Dot top of apples with butter bits.

3. Mix oats with brown sugar, remaining cinnamon, and melted butter in a small mixing bowl. Sprinkle topping over apples. Cook on low for 3 or 4 hours or on high for 1½ to 2 hours or until apples are soft. Serve hot or warm, topped with ice cream or whipped cream (if using).

Variation: You can personalize this recipe in so many ways. Add toasted walnuts or pecans to the topping, or include raisins or dried cranberries with the apples. You can also exchange ground ginger for the cinnamon.

Cooker Caveats

It's important to use fresh rather than bottled lemon juice to prevent fruits from turning brown—called oxidation. Most bottled lemon juices aren't strong enough, but you can always use lime juice if you're out of lemon.

Baked Apples

Here's an easy recipe that appeals to all members of the family. The chopped nuts in the middle are a little surprise.

Serves: 4
Prep time: 15 minutes
Minimum cook time: 2 hours in a medium slow cooker

4 baking apples, such as Jonathan or Northern Spy

2 TB. pure maple syrup

2 TB. unsalted butter, melted

¼ tsp. ground cinnamon

¼ cup chopped walnuts

¼ cup rum

1. Core apples and peel the top half only. Place apples in the slow cooker.

2. Combine maple syrup, melted butter, cinnamon, and walnuts in a small bowl. Spoon equal portions of syrup mixture into apple cores. Spoon rum over apples. Cook on low for 4 to 6 hours or on high for 2 to 3 hours or until apples are tender when pierced with the tip of a knife.

Variation: You can vary the seasoning and liquor in this recipe and come out with a very different dish. Try crème de cassis instead of rum, and exchange granulated sugar for the maple syrup.

 Cooker Caveats

It's important to peel the top half of the apples. If you don't, the steam builds up inside the skin and the apples tend to fall apart.

Apple Pudding

This hearty dessert is a cross between a pudding and a cobbler, with raisin bread as the binder.

¾ lb. loaf cinnamon raisin bread, broken into 1-inch pieces

1½ lb. apples, peeled, cored, and chopped

4 large eggs, lightly beaten

1 (14-oz.) can sweetened condensed milk

4 TB. unsalted butter, melted

½ tsp. apple pie spice or ground cinnamon

½ tsp. pure vanilla extract

Vanilla ice cream or sweetened whipped cream (optional)

Serves: 6 to 8
Prep time: 20 minutes
Minimum cook time: 2½ hours in a medium slow cooker

1. Grease the inside of the slow cooker liberally with vegetable oil spray.

2. Combine bread cubes and apples in the slow cooker.

3. Combine eggs, condensed milk, melted butter, apple pie spice, and vanilla extract in a mixing bowl. Beat well, pour mixture over bread and apples, and stir well. Cook on low for 5 or 6 hours or on high for 2½ to 3 hours or until pudding is set and puffed. Serve pudding hot or warm, topped with vanilla ice cream or whipped cream (if using).

Variation: Ripe pears or apricots both work beautifully in this pudding instead of apples.

Slow Savvy

If you want to make this pudding with plain white bread, add ½ cup raisins to the slow cooker along with the bread cubes and add an additional ½ teaspoon cinnamon to the egg mixture.

Rhubarb Cobbler

Rhubarb is officially a vegetable, but when it's sweetened and cooked this blushingly pink, it's called dessert!

Serves: 4 to 6
Prep time: 15 minutes
Minimum cook time: 2½ hours in a medium slow cooker

1½ lb. *rhubarb*, rinsed, trimmed, and cut into ½-inch slices

¾ cup granulated sugar

½ cup strawberry jam

1 cup all-purpose flour

1½ tsp. baking powder

Pinch salt

½ cup whole milk

3 TB. unsalted butter, melted

¼ tsp. pure vanilla extract

1. Combine rhubarb, ½ cup sugar, and strawberry jam in a slow cooker. Cook on low for 4 or 5 hours or on high for 2 to 2½ hours or until rhubarb is almost tender.

2. Combine flour, remaining ¼ cup sugar, baking powder, and salt in a mixing bowl. Stir in milk, melted butter, and vanilla extract. Stir until thick dough forms.

3. If cooking on low, raise the heat to high. Drop cobbler batter by tablespoons onto the top of simmering rhubarb. Cook on high for 30 to 40 minutes or until a toothpick inserted into the center of dumpling comes out clean.

Slow Speak _____

Rhubarb is one of the least understood foods. It's actually a vegetable although we eat it along with fruit and most frequently serve it for dessert. If you buy rhubarb at a farm stand, some of the leaves might still be attached. Discard them immediately because the leaves are poisonous.

Spiced Berry Grunt

In this dish, blueberries flavored with lemon, molasses, and spices are topped with light and fluffy dumplings.

5 cups fresh blueberries, rinsed

½ cup firmly packed light brown sugar

½ cup light molasses

½ cup water

3 TB. freshly squeezed lemon juice

1 TB. grated lemon zest

½ tsp. freshly grated nutmeg

¼ tsp. ground cloves

1½ cups all-purpose flour

2 TB. granulated sugar

2 tsp. baking powder

½ tsp. salt

3 TB. unsalted butter, cut into small bits

¾ cup whole milk

Vanilla ice cream or sweetened whipped cream (optional)

Serves: 4 to 6
Prep time: 15 minutes
Minimum cook time: 2½ hours in a medium slow cooker

1. Combine blueberries, brown sugar, molasses, water, lemon juice, lemon zest, nutmeg, and cloves in the slow cooker. Cook on low for 4 to 6 hours or on high for 2 or 3 hours or until mixture is boiling.

2. Combine flour, sugar, baking powder, and salt in a mixing bowl. Cut in butter using a pastry blender, two knives, or your fingertips until mixture resembles coarse meal. Add milk and stir to moisten dough.

3. If cooking on low, raise the heat to high. Drop batter by tablespoons onto hot blueberries. Cook on high for 20 to 30 minutes or until a toothpick inserted into center of dumpling comes out clean. Serve hot or warm, topped with ice cream or whipped cream (if using).

Variation: Apples are also delicious when cooked this way; you'll need about 8, and they should be peeled, cored, and chopped. Or cut back on the amount of blueberries and add some chopped apple.

Crock Tales

Grunts are another early American dessert. They got their name from the sound the lid of the pan made as the dumplings steamed on top of cooked fruit.

Gingered Peach Crisp

Crystallized ginger is the "secret ingredient" here, adding zesty flavor to the succulent ripe peaches in this cobbler variation.

Serves: 6 to 8
Prep time: 20 minutes
Minimum cook time: 2 hours in a medium slow cooker

6 ripe peaches (about 2 lb.), peeled, pitted, and thinly sliced

1 TB. freshly squeezed lemon juice

3 TB. finely chopped crystallized ginger

2 TB. peach preserves

2 TB. granulated sugar

2 TB. instant *tapioca*

1 TB. Grand Marnier or other orange-flavored liqueur

1½ cups granola

¾ cup all-purpose flour

½ cup firmly packed light brown sugar

½ tsp. ground ginger

6 TB. unsalted butter, cut into small bits

Vanilla ice cream or sweetened whipped cream (optional)

Slow Speak

Tapioca (*tap-ee-OH-kah*) is a starch that comes from the roots of the cassava plant. It's used like cornstarch as a thickening agent.

1. Toss peaches with lemon juice in the slow cooker. Add crystallized ginger, peach preserves, sugar, tapioca, and Grand Marnier. Toss to combine.

2. Combine granola, flour, brown sugar, and ground ginger in a mixing bowl. Cut in butter using a pastry blender, two knives, or your fingertips until mixture resembles coarse meal. Sprinkle topping over peaches. Cook on low for 4 or 5 hours or on high for 2 to 2½ hours or until peaches are tender and mixture is bubbly. Serve hot or warm topped with ice cream or whipped cream (if using).

Pineapple and Mango Granola Betty

Using premixed granola cereal means this dessert made with aromatic tropical fruits is fast and easy to get ready!

2 cups granola (your favorite mixture)

6 TB. unsalted butter, melted

½ fresh ripe pineapple, peeled and cut into ½-inch dice

2 ripe mangoes, peeled, pitted, and cut into ½-inch dice

½ cup firmly packed dark brown sugar

¼ cup freshly squeezed orange juice

1 tsp. grated orange zest

¾ tsp. ground ginger

Vanilla ice cream or sweetened whipped cream (optional)

Serves: 6 to 8
Prep time: 20 minutes
Minimum cook time: 2 hours in a medium slow cooker

1. Combine granola and melted butter in a mixing bowl and set aside.

2. Combine pineapple, mangoes, brown sugar, orange juice, orange zest, and ginger in another bowl. Mix well.

3. Pat ⅓ of granola in the bottom of the slow cooker. Top with ½ of fruit. Repeat layering, ending with granola. Cook on low for 4 to 6 hours or on high for 2 or 3 hours or until fruit is tender. Serve hot or warm, topped with ice cream or whipped cream (if using).

Variation: To keep the tropical theme, you can always use papaya in place of either the pineapple or mangoes. Or for a totally different taste, try a combination of peaches and plums.

 Slow Savvy

Mangoes are difficult to peel because the seed is elliptical. Once the mango is peeled, make two parallel cuts on either side of the seed, and slice the remainder of the fruit off the seed.

Pear Brown Betty

Sweet pears are surrounded by pieces of toast in this easy-to-make dessert.

Serves: 4 to 6

Prep time: 20 minutes

Minimum cook time: 2 hours in a medium slow cooker

---

8 slices white bread

4 TB. unsalted butter, softened

¾ cup firmly packed dark brown sugar

½ tsp. ground cinnamon

4 ripe pears, peeled, cored, and cut into 1-inch cubes

Vanilla ice cream or sweetened whipped cream (optional)

1. Preheat the oven to 400°F.

2. Arrange bread slices on a baking sheet.

3. Mix softened butter with brown sugar and cinnamon. Spread mixture on bread slices. Bake bread for 5 to 7 minutes or until butter melts. Remove the pan from the oven, and break bread into 1-inch squares.

4. Arrange ½ of bread in the slow cooker, and top with pears. Cover pears with remaining bread pieces, and pack mixture down firmly. Cook on low for 4 to 6 hours or on high for 2 or 3 hours or until pears are tender. Serve hot or warm with vanilla ice cream or sweetened whipped cream (if using).

Variation: This dessert is great with apples, too, but they should be cut into ½-inch dice. You'll use the same 4.

Crock Tales

Early American desserts are still part of our repertoire, and the brown Betty is one of them, along with cobblers, crumbles, and dumplings. A brown Betty is any fruit dessert that's made of bread and fruit layers.

Poached Pears

You can also use the poached pears as a topping for pound cake, or coat them in sweetened meringue and brown them under the broiler.

4 to 6 ripe pears, peeled, halved, and cored

1 cup red wine

¼ cup crème de cassis

½ cup granulated sugar

1 cinnamon stick or ½ tsp. ground cinnamon

Serves: 4 to 6
Prep time: 15 minutes
Minimum cook time: 2 hours in a medium slow cooker

1. Arrange pears in the slow cooker; cut them into quarters, if necessary, to make them fit.

2. Combine wine, crème de cassis, and sugar in a mixing bowl. Stir well to dissolve sugar, and pour mixture over pears. Add cinnamon stick to the slow cooker or stir in ground cinnamon. Cook on low for 4 or 5 hours or on high for 2 to 2½ hours or until pears are tender when pierced with the point of a knife. Remove cinnamon stick if using. Serve warm or chilled.

Slow Savvy _____

An easy way to core halved pears and apples is with a melon baller. The shape is efficient, and it leaves a neatly formed round hole.

Winter Fruit Compote

This is such a hearty, warming dessert for a cold winter's night, and it's easy to keep the ingredients on hand.

Serves: 6 to 8
Prep time: 15 minutes
Minimum cook time: 2 hours in a medium slow cooker

1 cup cranberry juice

½ cup granulated sugar

½ cup crème de cassis

1 TB. grated orange zest

2 tsp. grated lemon zest

1 cinnamon stick

2 TB. unsalted butter

3 ripe large pears, peeled and cut into 1½-inch dice

½ cup dried apricots, halved

½ cup dried cranberries

Vanilla ice cream

1. Combine cranberry juice, sugar, crème de cassis, orange zest, lemon zest, and cinnamon stick in a saucepan. Bring to a boil over medium-high heat, stirring to dissolve sugar. Pour mixture into the slow cooker.

2. Stir in butter, pears, apricots, and cranberries. Cook on low for 4 to 6 hours or on high for 2 or 3 hours or until pears are tender. Remove and discard cinnamon stick. Serve compote hot or warm over vanilla ice cream.

Crock Tales

Hot fruit dishes such as this one are part of Colonial heritage, especially in the South. In communities such as Williamsburg, Virginia, the pineapple was a symbol of welcome and hospitality, and a cauldron of fruit was included at many meals or as a welcome snack when guests arrived.

Appendix A

Glossary

al dente Italian for "against the teeth." Refers to pasta or rice that's neither soft nor hard, but just slightly firm against the teeth.

allspice Named for its flavor echoes of several spices (cinnamon, cloves, nutmeg), allspice is used in many desserts and in rich marinades and stews.

almonds Mild, sweet, and crunchy nuts that combine nicely with creamy and sweet food items.

amaretto An almond liqueur.

anchovies (also **sardines**) Tiny, flavorful preserved fish that typically come in cans. Anchovies are a traditional garnish for Caesar salad, the dressing of which contains anchovy paste.

andouille sausage A sausage made with highly seasoned pork chitterlings and tripe and a standard component of many Cajun dishes.

apple pie spice A combination of fragrant spices including cinnamon, nutmeg, allspice, cardamom, and ground cloves.

arborio rice A plump Italian rice used, among other purposes, for risotto.

artichoke hearts The center part of the artichoke flower, often found canned in grocery stores.

balsamic vinegar Vinegar produced primarily in Italy from a specific type of grape and aged in wood barrels. It is heavier, darker, and sweeter than most vinegars.

basil A flavorful, almost sweet, resinous herb delicious with tomatoes and used in all kinds of Italian or Mediterranean-style dishes.

black tree fungus A dried Chinese mushroom traditionally used in hot and sour soup.

blanch To place a food in boiling water for about 1 minute (or less) to partially cook the exterior and then submerge in or rinse with cool water to halt the cooking.

blend To completely mix something, usually with a blender or food processor, more slowly than beating.

blue cheese A blue-veined cheese that crumbles easily and has a somewhat soft texture, usually sold in a block. The color is from a flavorful, edible mold that is often added or injected into the cheese.

bok choy (also **Chinese cabbage**) A member of the cabbage family with thick stems, crisp texture, and fresh flavor. It's perfect for stir-frying.

braise To cook with the introduction of some liquid, usually over an extended period of time.

breadcrumbs Tiny pieces of crumbled dry bread, often used for topping or coating.

broil To cook in a dry oven under the overhead high-heat element.

brown To cook in a skillet, turning, until the food's surface is seared and brown in color, to lock in the juices.

brown rice Whole-grain rice including the germ with a characteristic pale brown or tan color; more nutritious and flavorful than white rice.

bulgur A wheat kernel that's been steamed, dried, and crushed and is sold in fine and coarse textures.

Calvados An apple brandy from Normandy.

capers Flavorful buds of a Mediterranean plant, ranging in size from *nonpareil* (about the size of a small pea) to larger, grape-size caper berries produced in Spain.

caramelize To cook sugar over low heat until it develops a sweet caramel flavor. The term is increasingly gaining use to describe cooking vegetables (especially onions) or meat in butter or oil over low heat until they soften, sweeten, and develop a caramel color.

cayenne A fiery spice made from (hot) chile peppers, especially the cayenne chile, a slender, red, and very hot pepper.

cheddar   The ubiquitous hard cow's milk cheese with a rich, buttery flavor that ranges from mellow to sharp. Originally produced in England, cheddar is now produced worldwide.

chevre   French for "goat milk cheese," chevre is a typically creamy-salty soft cheese delicious by itself or paired with fruits or chutney. Chevres vary in style from mild and creamy to aged, firm, and flavorful.

chile   Any one of many different "hot" peppers, ranging in intensity from the relatively mild ancho pepper to the blisteringly hot habanero.

chili powder   A seasoning blend that includes chile pepper, cumin, garlic, and oregano. Proportions vary among different versions, but they all offer a warm, rich flavor.

Chinese chili paste with garlic   A fiery paste made from fermented fava beans, chiles, and garlic.

Chinese five-spice powder   A seasoning blend of cinnamon, anise, ginger, fennel, and pepper.

chipotle   Smoked dried jalapeño chiles frequently packed in adobo sauce, a spicy sauce made from chiles, vinegar, and salt.

chop   To cut into pieces, usually qualified by an adverb such as "*coarsely* chopped," or by a size measurement such as "chopped into ½-inch pieces." "Finely chopped" is much closer to mince.

chorizo   A spiced pork sausage eaten alone and as a component in many recipes.

chutney   A thick condiment often served with Indian curries made with fruits and/or vegetables with vinegar, sugar, and spices.

cilantro   A member of the parsley family and used in Mexican cooking (especially salsa) and some Asian dishes. Use in moderation, as the flavor can overwhelm. The seed of the cilantro is the spice coriander.

cinnamon   A sweet, rich, aromatic spice commonly used in baking or desserts. Cinnamon can also be used for delicious and interesting entrées.

conserve   A type of preserves made with at least two types of fruit.

coriander   A rich, warm, spicy seed used in all types of recipes, from African to South American, from entrées to desserts.

couscous   Granular semolina (durum wheat) that's cooked and used in many Mediterranean and North African dishes.

crimini mushrooms   A relative of the white button mushroom but brown in color and with a richer flavor. The larger, fully grown version is the portobello. *See also* portobello mushrooms.

cumin   A fiery, smoky-tasting spice popular in Middle Eastern and Indian dishes. Cumin is a seed; ground cumin seed is the most common form used in cooking.

curry powder   A ground blend of rich and flavorful spices used as a basis for curry and many other Indian-influenced dishes. Common ingredients include hot pepper, nutmeg, cumin, cinnamon, pepper, and turmeric. Some curry can also be found in paste form.

devein   To remove the dark vein from the back of a large shrimp with a sharp knife.

dice   To cut into small cubes about ¼-inch square.

Dijon mustard   Hearty, spicy mustard made in the style of the Dijon region of France.

dill   An herb perfect for eggs, salmon, cheese dishes, and, of course, vegetables (pickles!).

dredge   To cover a piece of food with a dry substance such as flour or cornmeal.

drizzle   To lightly sprinkle drops of a liquid over food, often as the finishing touch to a dish.

farro   An ancient grain native to southern Europe also called spelt.

fennel   In seed form, a fragrant, licorice-tasting herb. The bulbs have a much milder flavor and a celerylike crunch and are used as a vegetable in salads or cooked recipes.

fermented black beans   Small black soybeans with a pungent flavor that have been preserved in salt.

feta   A white, crumbly, sharp, and salty cheese popular in Greek cooking and on salads. Traditional feta is usually made with sheep milk, but feta-style cheese can be made from sheep, cow, or goat milk.

floret   The flower or bud end of broccoli or cauliflower.

flour   Grains ground into a meal. Wheat is perhaps the most common flour. Flour is also made from oats, rye, buckwheat, soybeans, and so on.

fold   To combine dense and light ingredients in a mixture using a circular action from the middle of the bowl.

fricassee   A dish, usually chicken, cut into pieces and cooked in a liquid or sauce.

frittata   A skillet-cooked mixture of eggs and other ingredients that's not stirred but is cooked slowly and then either flipped or finished under the broiler.

garbanzo beans (or **chickpeas**)   A yellow-gold, roundish bean used as the base ingredient in hummus. Chickpeas are high in fiber and low in fat.

garlic   A member of the onion family, a pungent and flavorful element in many savory dishes. A garlic bulb contains multiple cloves. Each clove, when chopped, provides about 1 teaspoon garlic. Most recipes call for cloves or chopped garlic by the teaspoon.

ginger   Available in fresh root or dried, ground form, ginger adds a pungent, sweet, and spicy quality to a dish.

grate   To shave into tiny pieces using a sharp rasp or grater.

grind   To reduce a large, hard substance, often a seasoning such as peppercorns, to the consistency of sand.

grits   Coarsely ground grains, usually corn.

Gruyère   A rich, sharp cow milk cheese made in Switzerland that has a nutty flavor.

hazelnuts (also **filberts**)   A sweet nut popular in desserts and, to a lesser degree, in savory dishes.

herbes de Provence   A seasoning mix including basil, fennel, marjoram, rosemary, sage, and thyme, common in the south of France.

hoisin sauce   A sweet Asian condiment similar to ketchup made with soybeans, sesame, chile peppers, and sugar.

hummus   A thick, Middle Eastern spread made of puréed garbanzo beans, lemon juice, olive oil, garlic, and often tahini (sesame seed paste).

infusion   A liquid in which flavorful ingredients such as herbs have been soaked or steeped to extract that flavor into the liquid.

Italian breadcrumbs   Breadcrumbs flavored with herbs and Parmesan cheese.

Italian seasoning   A blend of dried herbs, including basil, oregano, rosemary, and thyme.

julienne   A French word meaning "to slice into very thin pieces."

kalamata olives   Traditionally from Greece, these medium-small long black olives have a rich, smoky flavor.

kale   A member of the cabbage family with frilly deep green leaves and a mild flavor.

kirsch, kirschwasser   A clear, tart cherry brandy distilled from cherry juice and cherry pits.

kosher salt   A coarse-grained salt made without any additives or iodine.

lentils   Tiny lens-shape pulses used in European, Middle Eastern, and Indian cuisines.

linguiça   A Portuguese pork sausage made with garlic, cumin, and cinnamon.

marbling   The shape of fat patterns in raw red meats.

marinate   To soak meat, seafood, or other food in a seasoned sauce, called a marinade, which is high in acid content. The acids break down the muscle of the meat, making it tender and adding flavor.

marjoram   A sweet herb, a cousin of and similar to oregano, popular in Greek, Spanish, and Italian dishes.

mascarpone   A thick, creamy, spreadable cheese, traditionally from Italy.

mince   To cut into very small pieces, smaller than diced pieces, about ⅛ inch or smaller.

nam pla   A salty sauce with a pungent odor made from fermented fish and used in Thai and Vietnamese cooking.

nutmeg   A sweet, fragrant, musky spice used primarily in baking.

Old Bay   A seasoning mix containing celery salt, mustard, cayenne, bay leaves, cloves, allspice, ginger, and paprika.

olive oil   A fragrant liquid produced by crushing or pressing olives. Extra-virgin olive oil—the most flavorful and highest quality—is produced from the first pressing of a batch of olives; oil is also produced from later pressings.

olives   The fruit of the olive tree commonly grown on all sides of the Mediterranean. Black olives are also called ripe olives. Green olives are immature, although they are also widely eaten. *See also* kalamata olives.

oregano   A fragrant, slightly astringent herb used in Greek, Spanish, and Italian dishes.

oyster sauce   A thick Chinese condiment made from oysters that gives dishes a rich flavor.

orzo   A rice-shape pasta used in Greek cooking.

paella   A grand Spanish dish of rice, shellfish, onion, meats, rich broth, and herbs.

paprika   A rich, red, warm, earthy spice that also lends a rich red color to many dishes.

Parmesan   A hard, dry, flavorful cheese primarily used grated or shredded as a seasoning for Italian-style dishes.

parsley   A fresh-tasting green leafy herb, often used as a garnish.

pecans   Rich, buttery nuts, native to North America, that have a high unsaturated fat content.

peppercorns   Large, round, dried berries ground to produce pepper.

pilaf   A grain dish in which the grain is browned in butter or oil and then cooked in a flavorful liquid such as a broth, often with the addition of meats or vegetables.

pinch   An unscientific measurement term, the amount of an ingredient—typically a dry, granular substance such as an herb or seasoning—you can hold between your finger and thumb.

pine nuts (also **pignoli** or **piñon**)   Nuts grown on pine trees, that are rich (read: high fat), flavorful, and a bit pine-y. Pine nuts are a traditional component of pesto and add a wonderful hearty crunch to many other recipes.

porcini mushrooms   Rich and flavorful mushrooms used in rice and Italian-style dishes.

portobello mushrooms   A mature and larger form of the smaller crimini mushroom, portobellos are brownish, chewy, and flavorful. Often served as whole caps, grilled, and as thin sautéed slices. *See also* crimini mushrooms.

preheat   To turn on an oven, broiler, or other cooking appliance in advance of cooking so the temperature will be at the desired level when the assembled dish is ready for cooking.

prosciutto   Dry, salt-cured ham, that originated in Italy.

purée   To reduce a food to a thick, creamy texture, usually using a blender or food processor.

radicchio   A bright burgundy-colored member of the chicory family that originated in Italy.

reduce   To boil or simmer a broth or sauce to remove some of the water content, resulting in more concentrated flavor and color.

reserve   To hold a specified ingredient for another use later in the recipe.

rhubarb   An acidic vegetable frequently sweetened and cooked with strawberries and other fruits.

rice vinegar   Vinegar produced from fermented rice or rice wine, popular in Asian-style dishes.

ricotta   A fresh Italian cheese smoother than cottage cheese with a slightly sweet flavor.

risotto   A popular Italian rice dish made by browning arborio rice in butter or oil and then slowly adding liquid to cook the rice, resulting in a creamy texture.

Rock Cornish hens   A small chicken under 2 pounds.

Roquefort   A world-famous (French) creamy but sharp sheep's milk cheese containing blue lines of mold.

rosemary   A pungent, sweet herb used with chicken, pork, fish, and especially lamb. A little of it goes a long way.

roux   A mixture of butter or another fat and flour, used to thicken sauces and soups.

saffron   A spice made from the stamens of crocus flowers, saffron lends a dramatic yellow color and distinctive flavor to a dish. Use only tiny amounts of this expensive herb.

sage   An herb with a musty yet fruity, lemon-rind scent and "sunny" flavor.

sauté   To pan-cook over lower heat than used for frying.

sear   To quickly brown the exterior of a food, especially meat, over high heat to preserve interior moisture.

sesame oil   An oil, made from pressing sesame seeds, that's tasteless if clear and aromatic and flavorful if brown.

shallot   A member of the onion family that grows in a bulb somewhat like garlic and has a milder onion flavor. When a recipe calls for shallot, use the entire bulb.

shiitake mushrooms   Large, dark brown mushrooms with a hearty, meaty flavor. Can be used either fresh or dried, grilled or as a component in other recipes, and as a flavoring source for broth.

shred   To cut into many long, thin slices.

simmer   To boil gently so the liquid barely bubbles.

skillet (also **frying pan**)   A generally heavy, flat-bottomed metal pan with a handle designed to cook food over heat on a stovetop or campfire.

skim   To remove fat or other material from the top of liquid.

smoking   A technique for flavoring and preserving food by allowing the chemicals from wood smoke to penetrate.

steam   To suspend a food over boiling water and allow the heat of the steam (water vapor) to cook the food. A quick cooking method, steaming preserves the flavor and texture of a food.

steep   To let sit in hot water, as in steeping tea in hot water for 10 minutes.

stew   To slowly cook pieces of food submerged in a liquid. Also, a dish that has been prepared by this method.

Stilton   The famous English blue-veined cheese, delicious with toasted nuts and renowned for its pairing with Port wine.

stock   A flavorful broth made by cooking meats and/or vegetables with seasonings until the liquid absorbs these flavors. This liquid is then strained and the solids discarded. Stock can be eaten alone or used as a base for soups, stews, and so on.

strata   A savory bread pudding made with eggs and cheese.

tahini   A paste made from sesame seeds used to flavor many Middle Eastern recipes.

tamari   A dark sauce made from soy beans with a more mellow flavor than soy sauce.

tapioca   A starch that comes from the root of a cassava plant; used as thickening.

tarragon   A sweet, rich-smelling herb perfect with seafood, vegetables (especially asparagus), chicken, and pork.

thyme   A minty, zesty herb.

toffee   A candy similar to caramel made by cooking sugar with water and butter.

tofu   A cheeselike substance made from soybeans and soy milk.

turmeric   A spicy, pungent yellow root used in many dishes, especially Indian cuisine, for color and flavor. Turmeric is the source of the yellow color in many prepared mustards.

unsweetened cocoa powder   Powdered chocolate with some of the cocoa butter removed.

veal   Meat from a calf, generally characterized by mild flavor and tenderness.

vegetable steamer   An insert for a large saucepan or a special pot with tiny holes in the bottom designed to fit on another pot to hold food to be steamed above boiling water. *See also* steam.

vinegar   An acidic liquid widely used as dressing and seasoning, often made from fermented grapes, apples, or rice. *See also* balsamic vinegar; cider vinegar; rice vinegar; white vinegar; wine vinegar.

walnuts   A rich, slightly woody-flavored nut.

water chestnuts   A tuber, popular in many types of Asian-style cooking. The flesh is white, crunchy, and juicy, and the vegetable holds its texture whether cool or hot.

whisk   To rapidly mix, introducing air to the mixture.

white mushrooms   Button mushrooms. When fresh, they have an earthy smell and an appealing soft crunch.

white vinegar   The most common type of vinegar, produced from grain.

whole-wheat flour   Wheat flour that contains the entire grain.

wild rice   Actually a grass with a rich, nutty flavor, popular as an unusual and nutritious side dish.

wine vinegar   Vinegar produced from red or white wine.

Worcestershire sauce   Originally developed in India and containing tamarind, this spicy sauce is used as a seasoning for many meats and other dishes.

zest   Small slivers of peel, usually from a citrus fruit such as lemon, lime, or orange.

B

Metric Conversion Tables

When baking, scientifically precise calculations are needed, but that's not necessarily the case when cooking conventionally. The tables in this appendix are designed for general cooking. If you're making conversions for baking, grab your calculator and compute the exact figure.

Converting Ounces to Grams

The numbers in the following table are approximate. To reach the exact amount of grams, multiply the number of ounces by 28.35.

Ounces	Grams
1 oz.	30 g
2 oz.	60 g
3 oz.	85 g
4 oz.	115 g
5 oz.	140 g
6 oz.	180 g
7 oz.	200 g
8 oz.	225 g
9 oz.	250 g

continued

continued

Ounces	Grams
10 oz.	285 g
11 oz.	300 g
12 oz.	340 g
13 oz.	370 g
14 oz.	400 g
15 oz.	425 g
16 oz.	450 g

Converting Quarts to Liters

The numbers in the following table are approximate. To reach the exact amount of liters, multiply the number of quarts by 0.95.

Quarts	Liters
¼ qt. (1 cup)	¼ L
½ qt. (1 pt.)	½ L
1 qt.	1 L
2 qt.	2 L
2½ qt.	2½ L
3 qt.	2¾ L
4 qt.	3¾ L
5 qt.	4¾ L
6 qt.	5½ L
7 qt.	6½ L
8 qt.	7½ L

Converting Pounds to Grams and Kilograms

The numbers in the following table are approximate. To reach the exact amount of grams, multiply the number of pounds by 453.6.

Pounds	Grams; Kilograms
1 lb.	450 g
1½ lb.	675 g
2 lb.	900 g
2½ lb.	1,125 g; 1¼ kg
3 lb.	1,350 g
3½ lb.	1,500 g; 1½ kg
4 lb.	1,800 g
4½ lb.	2 kg
5 lb.	2¼ kg
5½ lb.	2½ kg
6 lb.	2¾ kg
6½ lb.	3 kg
7 lb.	3¼ kg
7½ lb.	3½ kg
8 lb.	3¾ kg

Converting Fahrenheit to Celsius

The numbers in the following table are approximate. To reach the exact temperature, subtract 32 from the Fahrenheit reading, multiply the number by 5, and divide by 9.

Degrees Fahrenheit	Degrees Celsius
170°F	77°C
180°F	82°C
190°F	88°C
200°F	95°C

continues

continued

Degrees Fahrenheit	Degrees Celsius
225°F	110°C
250°F	120°C
300°F	150°C
325°F	165°C
350°F	180°C
375°F	190°C
400°F	205°C
425°F	220°C
450°F	230°C
475°F	245°C
500°F	260°C

Converting Inches to Centimeters

The numbers in the following table are approximate. To reach the exact number of centimeters, multiply the number of inches by 2.54.

Inches	Centimeters
½ in.	1.5 cm
1 in.	2.5 cm
2 in.	5 cm
3 in.	8 cm
4 in.	10 cm
5 in.	13 cm
6 in.	15 cm
7 in.	18 cm
8 in.	20 cm
9 in.	23 cm
10 in.	25 cm
11 in.	28 cm
12 in.	30 cm

Index

Tuscan White Bean Dip, 27
Twain, Mark, 176

U–V

unsweetened cocoa powder,
315

veal
Milanese-Style Veal Shanks
(*Osso Buco alla Milanese*),
235-236
Swedish Meatballs, 231
Veal Marsala, 154
Vegetable Frittata with Pasta,
173
vegetables
appetizers
Artichoke and Parmesan
Dip, 29
Asian Beef and Barley
Lettuce Cups, 46
Chinese Chicken in
Lettuce Cups, 43
French Onion Pizza
(*Pissaladière*), 39
Spinach Dip with Feta
and Dill, 30
artichokes, 29
buying, 239
cabbage
bok choy, 137
Corned Beef and
Cabbage, 220
Monkfish with Cabbage
and Bacon, 184-185
Sweet-and-Sour Red
Cabbage Soup, 54
Sweet and Sour Beef and
Cabbage Soup, 91
Sweet and Sour Red
Cabbage, 242
Sweet and Sour Stuffed
Cabbage, 216-217

carrots
Carrot Cake with Cream
Cheese Topping,
319-320
Chinese Beef Stew,
149-150
Curried Carrot Soup, 58
Eastern European Beef
and Carrots with Dried
Fruits (*Tsimmis*), 219
Ginger-Glazed Carrots,
244
peeling, 244, 320
Red Lentil and Carrot
Soup, 61
celery
Italian Eggplant Relish
(*Caponata*), 250
Short Ribs of Beef with
Rosemary and Celery,
210
Chinese-Style Sea Bass
with Mixed Vegetables,
180
corn
Bacon, Corn, and
Jalapeño Jack Strata,
171
Creole Crab and Corn
Chowder, 68-69
Mexican Pinto Bean
Salad, 264
Southwest Corn and
Sweet Potato Chowder,
59
eggplant
Greek Lamb and
Eggplant with Custard
Topping (*Moussaka*),
224-225
Italian Eggplant Relish
(*Caponata*), 250

greens, 79
Chicken Soup with
Fennel and Escarole,
84
cooking, 79
kale, 113
Spanish Fish Soup with
Potatoes, Greens, and
Aioli (*Caldo de Perro*),
74
Stewed Collard Greens,
247
lettuce
Asian Beef and Barley
Lettuce Cups, 46
Braised Radicchio, 245
Chinese Chicken in
Lettuce Cups, 43
mushrooms
Beef, Mushroom, and
Barley Soup, 94
Beef Stew in Red Wine
with Mushrooms (*Boeuf
Bourguignon*), 145
Chicken Fricassee with
Wild Mushrooms, 194
Chicken in Red Wine,
193
Chicken Marengo, 132
Chicken Stew with Wild
Mushrooms, 133
Chinese Beef Stew,
149-150
Chinese Hot and Sour
Soup with Duck, 86-87
Polish, 94
porcini, 94
Pork Loin with
Mushroom Stuffing,
227
Shrimp and Shiitake
Bread Pudding,
188-189

W

Beef Stew in Red Wine
with Mushrooms (*Boeuf
Bourguignon*), 145
Braised Lamb Shanks with
Winter Vegetables, 223
Chicken in Red Wine, 193
Chicken Marengo, 132
Classic French Lamb Stew
(*Navarin d'Agneau*),
156-157
combining with artichokes,
29
cooking with, 193
Halibut in White Wine
with Pearl Onions and
Oranges, 181
Winter Fruit Compote, 336

X–Y–Z

zest, 61
zucchini
Spicy Curried Lentil Stew
with Cashew Nuts, 115
Vegetable Frittata with
Pasta, 173
Zucchini Chili, 110